Culture, Politics and Sport

'Whannel is a foundational figure in the study of sports and the media. ... For 20 years his writing has set a high standard ... and it remains an inspiration to many.'
Toby Miller, Professor of Cultural Studies, University of California Riverside

Garry Whannel's text *Blowing the Whistle: The Politics of Sport* broke new ground when it was first published in 1983. Its polemical discussion brought sports as cultural politics into the academic arena and set the agenda for a new wave of researchers.

Since the 1980s sport studies has matured both as an academic discipline and as a focus for mainstream political and public policy debate. In *Culture, Politics and Sport:* Blowing the Whistle, *Revisited.* Garry Whannel revisits the themes that led his first edition, assessing their 1980s context from our new millennium perspective, and exploring their continued relevance for contemporary sports academics.

This revisited volume will appeal to undergraduate students and researchers in sports and cultural studies.

Garry Whannel is Professor of Media Cultures and Director of the Centre for International Media Analysis at the University of Bedfordshire. His previous books include *Media Sports Stars: Masculinities and Moralities, Fields in Vision: Television Sport and Cultural Transformation, Understanding Sport* (co-authored with John Horne and Alan Tomlinson) and *Understanding Television* (co-edited with Andrew Goodwin), all published by Routledge.

Routledge Critical Studies in Sport
Series Editors
Jennifer Hargreaves and Ian McDonald
University of Brighton

The Routledge Critical Studies in Sport series aims to lead the way in developing the multi-disciplinary field of Sport Studies by producing books that are interrogative, interventionist and innovative. By providing theoretically sophisticated and empirically grounded texts, the series will make sense of the changes and challenges facing sport globally. The series aspires to maintain the commitment and promise of the critical paradigm by contributing to a more inclusive and less exploitative culture of sport.

Also available in this series:

Understanding Lifestyle Sports
Consumption, identity and difference
Edited by Belinda Wheaton

Why Sports Morally Matter
William J. Morgan

Fastest, Highest, Strongest
A critique of high-performance sport
Rob Beamish and Ian Ritchie

Sport, Sexualities and Queer Theory
Edited by Jayne Caudwell

**Physical Culture, Power,
and the Body**
*Edited by Jennifer Hargreaves
and Patricia Vertinsky*

British Asians and Football
Culture, identity, exclusion
Daniel Burdsey

Olympic Media
Inside the biggest show on television
Andrew C. Billings

**The Cultural Politics of the
Paralympic Movement**
Through an anthropological lens
P. David Howe

Culture, Politics and Sport
Blowing the Whistle, Revisited

Garry Whannel

Routledge
Taylor & Francis Group

LONDON AND NEW YORK

First published 2008
by Routledge
2 Park Square, Milton Park, Abingdon, Oxon, OX14 4RN

Simultaneously published in the USA and Canada
by Routledge
270 Madison Avenue, New York, NY 10016

Routledge is an imprint of the Taylor & Francis Group, an informa business

Typeset in Goudy and Perpetua by
GreenGate Publishing Services, Tonbridge, Kent
Printed and bound in Great Britain by
Antony Rowe Ltd, Chippenham, Wiltshire

British Library Cataloguing in Publication Data
A catalogue record for this book is available from the British Library

Library of Congress Cataloging in Publication Data
A catalog record for this book has been requested

ISBN10 0–415–41706–6 (hbk)
ISBN10 0–415–41707–4 (pbk)
ISBN10 0–203–93377–X (ebk)

ISBN13 978–0–415–41706–8 (hbk)
ISBN13 978–0–415–41707–5 (pbk)
ISBN13 978–0–203–93377–0 (ebk)

To Tommie Smith and John Carlos, to the supporters of AFC Wimbledon, and to all other people involved in sport who had had enough, *and* decided to do something about it, thus fulfilling the first criterion of meaningful political action.

Contents

PART 2
Sport, cultural politics and political culture since 1983   **141**

Figures

Series editor's foreword

I still remember the pleasant surprise of coming across a well fingered copy of Garry Whannel's *Blowing the Whistle* (Routledge 1983) in a second hand bookshop that specialised in radical literature. It was the late 1980s, I was in the final year of my politics degree at Liverpool University and my tutor had already advised that I couldn't possibly do a final year dissertation on a socialist analysis of sport and society. His rationale was that sport was outside of real politics and anyway there was not a sufficient literature to support such a study. While we agreed to disagree on what constituted 'real politics', I had to concede the point about the lack of literature (incorrectly it seems, for I was as unaware as were my tutors that there was already a significant literature on sport and society – enough anyway to support an undergraduate dissertation!).

In any case, it was a real joy and a revelation to read *Blowing the Whistle*. I had never come across a book like this: an incisive analysis of sport from a contemporary British socialist perspective; a perspective that revealed the links between capitalism, class, gender, the body and sport. While it came too late for me to convince my tutor that he had been wrong, *Blowing the Whistle* proved to be hugely influential in pointing me in a new direction that took me to Leicester University to study an MA on the Sociology of Sport under the combative guidance of Eric Dunning. Then a couple of years later I was in the fortunate position of being offered posts at three higher education institutions. The choice was not difficult to make – in 1993 I started work at Roehampton Institute, London (now Roehampton University), with two colleagues whose work best represented my idea of a socialist-inspired critique of sport – Jennifer Hargreaves (co-editor of this series) and Garry Whannel. We worked collaboratively to produce study programmes at undergraduate and Masters levels that were interrogative, challenging common-sense ideas and exposing relations of power in the world of sport; interventionist, highlighting the relationship between theory and practice and providing arguments and analyses of topical and polemical issues; and innovative, seeking to develop new areas of research, and stimulating new ways of thinking about and studying sport. Our aim was similar to the aim of this *Routledge Critical Studies in Sport* series – to lead the way in developing the multidisciplinary field of sport studies for university students and to maintain a critical approach to the excessively commercialised, damaging and exploitative culture of top-level competitive sport. We are delighted to be collaborating again knowing that Garry's *Culture, Politics and Sport*: Blowing the Whistle, *Revisited* fits perfectly into our series.

I have regularly used the original *Blowing the Whistle* as a key text to introduce students to the politics of sport. It is well researched, accessibly written, politically astute and highly engaging. Indeed, an excerpt from the text is on the front of my module handbook for a first year 'Introduction to the Politics of Sport' module I teach. Yet, the text is very difficult for students to get hold of as it has been out of print for many years. Hampered by strict copyright laws that prevented the illegal photocopying of large chunks, it has been increasingly difficult over the years for students to be able to read more than a few pages.

But *Blowing the Whistle* was too much of its time to lend itself to mere updating. In its original form it offers an insight into a historical moment when socialism was part of the language of political opposition to Thatcherism. Yet it did not feel right for the text to be simply reprinted. There is a lot more to be said, gaps to be filled, and analyses to be developed. Through dialogue with the author, a solution emerged: *Blowing the Whistle* is reproduced in its entirety, but Garry places it alongside selected previously published articles. In addition, Garry provides an original and substantial autobiographical and political commentary on his writings in which the central thesis of the socialist case for sport is revisited. Two decades on, the language of resistance to neoliberalism in the anti-globalisation movements may not be articulated in traditional socialist terms, but the ideas expressed by Garry in the early 1980s – of equality, fairness, democracy, accountability – express the same aspiration for a more just society. We live in a period of radicalisation once again. *Culture, Politics and Sport*: Blowing the Whistle, *Revisited* signals that the time has come to introduce the post-Thatcher generation of sport studies students to the political ideology that underpins such radical values – namely socialism. And to insist that sport needs more than ever to be part of the debates about resistance and social change.

Ian McDonald
Co-editor with Jennifer Hargreaves

Preface and acknowledgements

The original idea of this project was simply to reprint *Blowing the Whistle* with a short introduction from me, and a similarly short post-mortem. I was adamant that I did not wish to rewrite the original, nor write a new book, in a new millennium, on the politics of sport. I appear to have succeeded in only the first of these two intentions. The new material is now around 50 per cent longer than the original book. I just hope you enjoy it, and if I am still around in 2025 ... get someone else to write on the topic. In addition to the reprint of *Blowing the Whistle*, I have also included, in Part 1 of this book, two articles written at the start of the 1990s, 'Profiting by the Presence of Ideals: Sponsorship and Olympism', and 'Sport and Popular Culture: The Temporary Triumph of Process over Product'. These attracted less attention at the time than they might, and together represent a development of my work after the completion of *Blowing the Whistle*. They were written roughly halfway between 1980 and 2008 and serve as a bridge to the second half of the book, comprising original work written between 2005 and 2007 specifically for this volume.

I am greatly indebted to the work of other writers in this field, many of whom have become personal friends during the last 25 years, but especially to Alan Tomlinson and John Horne for supportive and informed interest and friendship for a quarter of a century – both are everything a critical friend should be. Thanks to Ian McDonald for encouraging me to write this book and for helping to steer it with tact, patience and insight, and to Jennifer Hargreaves whose work has exemplified the importance of political engagement. Thanks to Belinda Wheaton whose work has reminded me that there is sport beyond television, although this insight has yet to lure me to the beach, to Neil Blain, Toby Miller and David Rowe for supportive and ego-boosting comments on occasion and to Raymond Boyle and Hugh O'Donnell for many insights and for pretexts to visit Scotland from time to time. Most of those listed above owe a debt, as do I, to Alina Bernstein and her tireless work to develop the Media and Sport Section of the International Association for Media and Communication Research (IAMCR), and thus enable us to interact more often. Thanks to Ben Carrington for co-organising (with Ian McDonald) a memorable seminar at the University of Texas at Austin, and for periodic critical and thought-provoking comments over the last decade. Thanks to Carlton Brick, Adam Brown and Shaun

Schofield with whom I have talked football and politics on occasion. Thanks to David Andrews for our very grounded exchange on popular memory, alluded to in Chapter 5.

Thanks to my colleagues in the School of Media, Art and Design at the University of Bedfordshire, for helping to make the School a congenial and stimulating place to work, and especially to Richard Wise and Dave Green for football banter, Adam Proctor for explaining how I could access podcasts of Radio 5's *Fighting Talk*, and to both Adam and Paul Hannington for keeping my computers on the road. Thanks to Sean Hamill for the stimulating series of sport management seminars at Birkbeck College. Thanks to Jim Parry for supplying performance-enhancing notes on drugs and sport. Thanks to Samantha Grant, Kate Manson, Ygraine Cadlock and the rest at Routledge. I am grateful to Pluto Press, and to the journal *Innovations*, for permission to reprint material. I am particularly grateful to the International Association for Media and Communication Research and the Leisure Studies Association whose events have been a seedbed for some of the ideas and research drawn on in this book.

There are also people whose chance and casual remarks have prompted reflection, when probably they did not even realise it, and other people with whom I have discussed and argued politics over the years, especially Ian Haywood, Deborah Philips, John Keidon, Kate Whannel and Sam Whannel. Thanks to Stephen McCubbin, who had nothing to do with the book, has little interest in sport and with whom I have never discussed the project; but he could always make me laugh when I needed a good laugh. And finally, thanks beyond elaboration to Deborah Philips, who, incongruously, has no interest at all in sport, but now counts many of the key scholars in the field as friends, and has been an unfailing source of support during the writing of this book.

Abbreviations

AAA	Amateur Athletics Association
ANL	Anti-Nazi League
BOA	British Olympic Association
CCCS	Centre for Contemporary Cultural Studies
CCPR	Central Council for Physical Recreation
EFA	Education for All
ENGSO	The European Non-Governmental Sports Organisation
ERICCA	*Equal Rights in Clubs Campaign for Action*
FA	Football Association
FARE	Football Against Racism in Europe
FIFA	Fédération Internationale de Football Association
FSA	Football Supporters' Association
FSF	Football Supporters' Federation
IAAF	International Association of Athletic Federations
IAMCR	International Association for Media and Communication Research
ICSSPE	International Council of Sport Science and Physical Education
ILTF	International Lawn Tennis Federation
IOC	International Olympic Committee
MINEPS	Ministers for Physical Education and Sport
MCC	Marylebone Cricket Club
MLB	Major League Baseball
NBA	National Basketball Association
NFL	National Football League
NFSC	National Federation of Supporters' Clubs
OTAB	Olympic Television Archive Bureau
PFA	Professional Footballers' Association
PFI	private finance initiative
PPP	public–private partnership
RSI	Red Sports International
SANROC	South African Non-Racial Olympic Committee
SASA	South African Sports Association
SEFT	Society for Education in Film and Television

UEFA	Union of European Football Associations
UNESCO	United Nations Education, Scientific and Cultural Organisation
WADA	World Anti Drug Agency
WHO	World Health Organisation
WISA	Wimbledon Independent Supporters' Association

Part 1

The politics of sport

1 Introduction

July 2005 was an extraordinary month for news events, especially for a Londoner. The Live 8 concerts, the announcement of London's Olympic bid, the London tube and bus bombings, and the opening of the G8 talks all happened in less than a week. The following week I travelled to China, attending a conference and the closing ceremony of a cultural festival organised by the Beijing Olympic Committee, and I observed coverage of the second wave of attempted bombings in London, and subsequent events, on CNN. Real Madrid were staying in the same Beijing hotel that we were based in, placing us briefly in the eye of a celebrity storm. The events of July 2005, my own relationship to them and tra-jectory through them, and the various interconnections between them prompted me to wonder what I was actually doing in writing a book on sport and politics. The politics of sport suddenly seemed somewhat parochial.

The Live 8 concerts on 2 July appeared to be a spectacular success, and a demonstration of the spectacular power of global television spectacle, but of course the television image doesn't tell you much about the experience of being there. The privileged golden circle, the area at the front reserved for privileged guests and corporate clients, was clearly visible and the segregation of a rich elite seemed to echo and symbolise the very disparity of resources the concerts were supposedly addressing. The relative absence of black acts, at least in London, was a mistake, and the organisers really should have known better than to compound the error with the crass concept of a separate concert, with predominantly black musicians, way down in the west country. None of this detracted from the huge success of the central mission to push demands for action on poverty and debt relief to the top of the news agenda. For much of the twentieth century, one of the biggest problems confronting the left has been how to mount political cam-paigns that have effectivity. On this count, the concerts and the associated campaign were exemplary.

By any standards, the 6 July announcement by the International Olympic Committee, in Singapore, of the result of the Olympic bidding race, was a major news moment. It had the suddenness and immediacy of a revelation of the unknown, it involved major nations and star individuals, it had drama, and the sensation of an unexpected and un-predicted outcome. The success of London's bid to stage the 2012 Games took almost everyone by surprise. Paris had been hot favourites since the start of the race over two years earlier. Most experts agreed that London had gained a lot of ground and that the vote would now be close, but that Paris would still win. Even the bid team, despite their immaculately crafted public relations optimism, did not, I believe, really expect to win. So the announcement came as a huge shock in Paris, and as a major sensation in London.

The most striking feature of the London bid was its superb media management. The British media, especially in its tabloid variants, can be very quick to circulate negative and critical stories, especially, in the sporting context, where there is the slightest hint of indecisiveness, amateurism or ineptitude. The precedents of major project mismanagement (the Millennium Dome, the Pickett's Lock Athletics Stadium fiasco, the new Wembley Stadium) were readily available. Yet for the last year, the media coverage of the bid was overwhelmingly positive. Clearly the bid was well run, and, as we now know, achieved success against the odds, but its handling of the press was adroit. One suspects discreet political pressure was also brought to bear upon sports editors. In normal circumstances, following the triumphant moment, there would have been two or three days of front page coverage, featuring celebrations in London, the return of the conquering heroes of the bid team, analyses of 'how we won it', and projections of the work to be done before 2012. However, less than 24 hours later came the barbarity of the tube bombings.

Just before 9.00am on Thursday 7 July, three bombs went off on tube trains in central London, followed around 45 minutes later by a bomb on a bus. A total of 54 people were killed and hundreds injured. The emergency services, benefiting from major incident planning and rehearsal, appeared to cope very well. Nonetheless, London was plunged into a period of fear, confusion and uncertainty. The entire tube system was shut down for most of the day, many buses re-routed or suspended, and the mobile phone system collapsed under the volume of calls.[1] News of the events was followed around the world on rolling news channels. As with the inhabitants of any city, Londoners had an intense awareness of the closeness of the trauma. Most will have travelled through the affected stations at some point, many of them every day. It was all too easy to imagine 'what if'.

I live about 600 metres from the bus explosion, which took place on my normal route to work. The tube explosions were all within a mile of my home. An old friend, staying with me, had set off to travel on a route that would have taken him through one of the affected stations. A fellow academic, in my own field of study, was amongst the injured. Another colleague, from my own university, missed boarding one of the target trains by less than a second. I spent the morning staring out of the window, hearing sirens and watching aimless and stunned crowds milling around whilst, like most of my fellow Londoners, trying to phone relatives and friends, and, of course, staring at the extraordinary scenes on the television.

Indeed, it was striking how the television was the major source, even for someone living within a couple of blocks of the explosions. Despite my own relative proximity, basically I experienced the events in very similar form to people around the world – watching images of police, ambulances and cordons, staring at the stream of updated information scrolling across the screen and tensing every time a new 'Breaking News' banner appeared. On my one descent to street level, it became clear that no one milling around had any clearer sense of what was going on, indeed the absence of media access left them largely uninformed. I returned to the television.

The London bombings stole the news agenda away from G8, which was, conceivably, part of the intention. The G8 summit was, of course, another global spectacle, staged for the cameras, in which the issues supposedly up for debate had largely been sorted out by officials and politicians days or weeks before. Rather as with the Live 8 concerts, African figures became marginal, as the politician stars of the most powerful nations assumed centre stage. The Make Poverty History demonstration offered its own spectacle with the attractive Edinburgh backdrop. Overshadowed by the Live 8 concert it also illustrated, once again, a sad facet of dominant news values – a dozen people in a violent confrontation will get more media coverage than 100,000 who demonstrate peacefully. Meanwhile, the project of easing Africa into modernity through the imposition of Western capitalist neoliberal economic policies being nurtured by the G8 countries offers a frame for understanding the ways in which the Olympic Games and the World Cup have become icons of enterprise that serve as gateways to modernity. Indeed the World Cup, and probably the Olympic Games too, will be staged in Africa early this century.

Less than a fortnight after these dramatic and traumatic events in the UK, I was in Beijing for a conference. I was also able to attend the Closing Ceremony of a cultural festival staged by the Beijing Olympic Organising Committee. This concert of popular music took place in a medium-size auditorium and was also broadcast by television. Like many events of its kind, the event was stage managed for television cameras, with the audience occasionally present, visually, as a cheering mass. Indeed we were carefully rehearsed in our role, given luminous wands, drilled in the manner in which we should wave them and trained to produce wild enthusiasm on cue. As so often on such occasions, the slightly tawdry feel of the dry ice, lighting effects and tinsel, when witnessed directly, is transformed by the magic of television into a spectacular and glamorous sparkle. While the evening was a fascinating and enjoyable experience, it was clear that the impression produced for the television cameras was the primary objective of the occasion.

The conference I attended was a largely Asian event, in which the few Western delegates, for the most part, were doing more listening and less talking, as issues such as media access, censorship and the digital divide were discussed. The conference banquet took place in the Great Hall of the People, and the whole experience of being in Beijing prompted reflection on the strange paradox of China's dynamic economic development, within the framework of an authoritarian communist state. They call it market socialism, but to an outsider it does not appear so very different from consumer capitalism. In China, in Latin America, in Europe and even in the USA, the big cultural differences now seem to be between urban and rural communities rather than between economic systems.

We were staying in the same hotel as Real Madrid, whose imminent arrival prompted a frenzy of activity by builders and decorators attempting to finish the new marble and glass lobby area. The outside of the hotel and the reception area were under siege from teenage Chinese girls with posters, banners and albums of players, and photographers held back by a cordon of security guards. Nor were the conference delegates immune from the siren call of celebrity. Several of us could be seen lurking around the reception area with a studied nonchalance intended to suggest we were merely waiting for the business centre to open. The level of excitement rose as their coach arrived and the players filed through the lobby. Beckham and Raul strode to the lifts amidst screams, whilst Luis Figo paused to greet a rotund male Chinese friend, to the distress of his admirers, who felt they were far more worthy of the great man's attention. Only Real Madrid's manager came over, with a big beam, to shake hands and sign autographs for people, many of whom may have been unsure precisely who he was. Real Madrid were on the Chinese leg of a pre-season tour that took them to the USA, China, Japan and Thailand capitalising on their worldwide fame, and boosting the merchandising of their team brand.[2] Indeed their purchase of David Beckham was driven partly by his prominence in the Asian market in the wake of the 2002 World Cup. This demanding itinerary is not ideal pre-season training and the players appeared exhausted and drained of energy. Their lacklustre mode of self-presentation continued on the pitch – a match played in atrocious conditions after heavy rain all day turned the playing surface into a quagmire, and the team gained negative publicity in the press. After they left Manchester United arrived, on a similar merchandise-inspired tour, and looking similarly drained and jet-lagged. I was not surprised that neither side fared well in the Champions League in the 2005–6 season.

On Thursday 21 July came news of a new wave of bombings on London trains and buses. This time, fortunately, the devices failed to explode. I spent much of the day in my Beijing hotel room watching news of the attempted bombings on CNN. A car filled with bombs had already been found a few days earlier, at Luton Station, near where I work. Indeed, I had walked past the car just a few hours before the police found it, and cordoned off the station, causing me to return home by coach instead of train. Now I was confronted with images very familiar to me – of Warren Street Station, our nearest tube station, of University College Hospital, at the end of our street, and of Stockwell Station, near where we lived for three years. British people of my generation grew up in what was, by world standards, a safe and affluent environment. A prevalent sensibility, a residue of Empire days but still retaining a certain force, was that 'danger' happened overseas. The rest of the world was exotic, other, different, strange and dangerous, whilst home was safe. So, strange it was to be in that most exotic of places for an Englishman, Beijing, deep in the heart of the 'orient' of the colonial imagination, but in that most safe of environments, a five star hotel, staring at images of home, in which home had suddenly become associated with risk, fear, danger and paranoia. One of the striking characteristics of the post-colonial world is that the polarities are reversed: core becomes peripheral, peripheral becomes core, home becomes strange whilst the other becomes familiar. All that is solid melts into air, and as black British academic Stuart Hall succinctly put it to a largely white audience, 'now that you are all de-centred, I feel centred'.

These experiences also prompted reflection on the problem of separating image and experience. In early writing on the media, analysts confidently counterposed a concrete embedded and grounded world of situated experiences with the less tangible but more universalised domain of images, symbols and representations. This distinction is now much harder to sustain. Experience and image entangle each other in ways that are both concrete and disembodied, both global and local, both personal and general, both safe and threatening. Indeed in many social contexts, image seems solid, and experience tentative. In major sporting events, at moments of dramatic action, all eyes turn to the giant screens for insight and clarity.

July 2005 was dramatic and traumatic, for Londoners in particular, although it is always salutary to remember that such carnage is merely a feature of daily life in places such as Baghdad. My own reflections on these events prompted three thoughts. First, impression management has become a central practice of our times. The world is experienced, perceived and consumed largely through the media; so the impression conveyed in media representation becomes crucial. In different ways, the organisers of Live 8, G8, Olympic bidding committees, and even those who plant bombs, understand this and, in radically different ways, attempt to exploit it to their advantage. Second, major events are consumed around the world, and public reaction can be fed into the process with great speed, producing an intensity of focus, which, in *Media Sport Stars*, I termed vortextuality. Third, the events underlay the extent to which risk, fear, suspicion and paranoia have become central organising principles of Western politics. It was with these disconcerting thoughts to the fore that I turned, in the summer of 2005, to writing the final draft of this book.

The most immediately striking sporting question in July 2005 was, how did London get awarded the 2012 Olympic Games? London had momentum, in the sense of a late-running horse coming from behind in the final furlong. In the race to be awarded the Games, Paris was the front-runner from a very early stage, which produces its own problems. There is a tendency to feel that you should not do too much, as there is always a danger of making a mistake that will weaken your bid. So early front-runners have a tendency to lose momentum. By contrast, London, after a late start and a poor start, slowly gained credibility and then began to address its own weaknesses, making a good impression, winning support, and crucially, gaining momentum. It gradually began to impress people as a coherent bid from a well-organised team.

President Chirac is an adept and experienced front person for a bid. He had presented Paris's bid, to good effect, in 1986.[3] But this time, the British Prime Minister, Tony Blair, devoted two days to attending the IOC Session in Singapore in July 2005, when, manifestly, he had other tasks, not least the imminent G8 summit, on his plate. The IOC members are important and powerful people who are used to being courted, and who are not easily flattered. But a head of state or prime minister devoting significant time to them will have made a favourable impression. Juan Antonio Samaranch, Ex-President of the International Olympic Committee (IOC), remains a powerful figure in the IOC. He is very fond of the British bid leader Seb Coe, and encouraged Coe to get fully involved in the IOC as Coe's running career came to an end during the late 1980s. Samaranch appears to regard him almost as a favoured son. When Madrid was eliminated, London benefited. Samaranch knows the strengths and weaknesses of his fellow members very well and doubtless knows how to use his influence. But the lobbying process remains shrouded in a degree of secrecy and we rarely learn the full story about the deals and promises that may be negotiated away from the glare of the media (see Simson and Jennings 1992; Jennings 1996; Lenskyj 2000). When Moscow was eliminated, it seems that many of their supporters threw their weight behind London. Six months later, the Mayors of London and Moscow clasped hands in a New Year celebration in Trafalgar Square, apparently part of a springboard promoting Russian goods in the British market. No one nowadays could claim, with a straight face, that sport is nothing to do with politics.

The year 2012 is still some way off – there will be a period when all goes quiet on the Olympic front, although already there have been headline stories about the problems of acquiring all the necessary land, the issues of legacy, cost-control and security implications. The Beijing Olympics of 2008 will focus London minds around the realisation that the Olympic caravan is heading their way, and there will then be a great deal of mounting excitement over the next four years. London faces some huge construction projects; a nervous fear, in some quarters, of failure; and probably a greater than predicted bill for the taxpayers of London. Two concerns will loom large. Any project involving expensive construction and an immovable deadline is a potential hostage to fortune. Security will be a greater headache than ever, especially in the wake of the London bombings. Security costs for the Athens Olympics effectively doubled the total cost of staging the Games. Security should not be quite as large a percentage cost for London, which already has an extensive infrastructure of security measures, but will undoubtedly be very expensive.

What is sport anyway?

> The cleft sticks alone passed without question, with sympathy.
> 'Ils sont pour porter les dépeches.'
> 'C'est un sport?'
> 'Oui, oui, certainement – le sport.'
>   William Boot goes through French customs, in *Scoop*, by Evelyn Waugh (1938)

English eccentricity, in this case Boot's carrying of cleft sticks, can easily be explained away as a form of sport. In fact, there is no such thing as sport. It defies definition in part because it is not, in the end, a coherent category. It changes

Figure 1.1 The author, by the monument to Pierre de Coubertin, founder of the modern Olympic Games, at Baden-Baden, Germany, no doubt pondering the strange contradictions that the Olympic Movement encompasses, as a global spectacle with immense commercial value, controlled by an organisation with the form of an aristocratic gentlemen's club, and retaining idealist themes about uniting the youth of the world in peace and harmony.

over time, as some sporting practices, such as animal baiting, become residual and then archaic; whilst other emergent practices, lifestyle and extreme sports, for example, become mainstream and challenge the established dominant cultures of sport. Attempts to define sport as competitive physical activity would have to include dance, whilst the restriction of 'sport' to those activities involving physical exertion excludes darts, and, arguably, bowls. Definitions here are contingent on the social practices that produce them, whether in the production of dictionaries or in the categorisations produced in and through the practices of the media. Generalisation becomes a dangerous activity when dealing with a term that embraces modes of competition as distinct and different as wrestling, volleyball and the high jump. However, because generalisation cannot be avoided, let me assert that sport is media sport. The world of grassroots, minority and participatory sport has almost become a different domain – an entirely different mode of cultural practice.[4]

Only a minority of people regularly participate in any active physical activity apart from walking, running and swimming. Far more watch popular television sports. For many people physical exercise is in non-competitive forms, such as keep fit, yoga, working out, or recreational running. For most people competitive sport is what happens in the media. In the media the place of sport remains ubiquitous but still ghettoised. Sport is everywhere, yet is contained within the walls of category – sports news, sports pages, sports sections, sports supplements. It still has a low cultural status – even now, after three decades of expanding scholarship on sport, there are relatively few scholars with a sustained research record in the field, and their work, often interdisciplinary in character and radical in tone, remains relatively unknown or underutilised in its broader parent disciplines of sociology, history, politics, anthropology and literature. Typically, when it comes to issues of politics, many regard sport as epiphenomenal, a marginal and irrelevant activity.

So what are the broader politics that constitute a pressing agenda, in the wake of the cold war? An agenda might include the rise of religious fundamentalisms in the USA and the Middle East; Africa, poverty and governance; the energy crisis and the desperate search for more oil; global warming and climate change; the rise of China; the persistence of racism and ethnic-based antagonisms; discrimination against women; economic exploitation. All of these do and will impact upon and within sporting practices, and analysis of sporting practices and cultures should, in part, examine the complex and contradictory ways in which these processes occur. At the same time, of course, it is also necessary to acknowledge the very real (semi) autonomy of sport, and the extent to which it is, consciously, bracketed off from the 'real' world. It is important to beware of exaggerating the significance of sport, while refusing to consign it to a mere effect of processes that occur elsewhere and only elsewhere. It has fewer global stars than cinema or music. It is, arguably, less economically important than cinema or music, but it has more massive merchandising opportunities. The major brands, such as the Brazil football shirt, are global – on the streets of any major city in North America, Europe or Asia you will not have to wait long before seeing one.

The symbols, icons and brands of sport are great marketing vehicles, associated as they are with youth, fitness, fame and success.

There has, of course, been extensive discussion of sport in relation to ideology; whether posed in terms of the service sport does to a more generalised dominant ideology, or the specific ways in which an ideology of sport is articulated. I just want to draw attention here to one rather dramatic aspect of the ideology of sport that has not attracted as much comment as one might expect. Sport offers an ideology of success – it is 'all about' winning. After winning the Olympic decathlon in 1984, Daley Thompson crowed to the television cameras, 'I've got the big G boys, the big G.' American sporting discussion frequently quotes the line 'winning isn't everything, it's the only thing', attributed to legendary football coach, Vince Lombardi. The Olympic Games may utilise the quotation that 'it is not the winning but the taking part that counts', but no one really believes it any more. The full glare of the media turns winners into instant celebrities bestowing a huge potential for future earnings. Winning grows out of a combination of talent and hard work, and portrayals of sport frequently mythologise the hard, dedicated work that goes into producing success. To a large degree, losers are absent, etched out of the picture, cropped from the image, outside the frame. They are rendered invisible, they disappear from view. Yet losing is a far more familiar and common sporting experience than winning. At every Olympic Games and World Cup, there are far more losers than winners. In every football season, 19 out of 20 teams will fail to win their leagues, and 95 per cent of supporters will be disappointed.

So there is a huge disjuncture between the celebration of winners, and the far more familiar experience of losing. This in turn mirrors the images of capitalist enterprise with which we are all saturated. The great American dream, the rags to riches, log cabin to White House journey that is believed to be the destiny of those who strive, is totally atypical. Most aspiring capitalists fail, most careers do not reach the top, many lives remain trapped in boring, poorly rewarded, low status, tedious and monotonous occupations, but compared with the unemployed, the homeless and the hungry, they are of course the lucky ones. We are dealing here, then, with a massively visible social practice, extensively relayed worldwide by the media, rooted in an ideology that focuses on an experience of winning that will only ever be the social reality of a small minority. To regard this as a form of epiphenomenal marginality of little interest to analysts and critics would seem, to put it gently, foolhardy.

Discussion of sport and politics does not always interrogate 'politics' as a problematic term, with different conceptions of politics in play. It is clear that, underpinning such discussion, there are implicit models of the political process. For some, politics is the process of social allocation of scarce but available resources. For democrats, it is the process of democratic decision making, with the state functioning as neutral arbiter between competing interest groups. For classic Marxist or conflict theorists, politics is the process of struggle between fundamental classes, in which the state, far from being neutral, functions as the executive committee of the dominant class. For feminists it is the struggle against an entrenched patriarchy and systematic institutional dis-crimination. For anti-imperialist writers it is the struggle of the colonised powerless against the colonising powerful. These positions all share the assumption that the social organisation of society is a political process, and it therefore follows that most if not all aspects of social interchange have, inevitably, a political dimension.

Politics, despite the cult of charisma and personality, is not an individual sport, but a matter of team organisation, raising the question of how social groups become represented in the form of organised political parties. This issue underlies debates within left wing politics about the merits of mass party/elite party, centralism/decentralism, class-based politics/rainbow coalition and pro-grammaticism/spontaneous-ism. Allied to this are debates about the nature of change – revolution or reform, sudden change/gradualism, workers' struggle/the long march through the institutions, emphasis on the Western world vs empha-sis on the developing world. The declining influence of a class-based politics in the Western world has to be set against the rise of new social movements with their own apparent power to prompt social change. Within these debates has been the theme of the relevance of popular culture. Is it epiphenomenal, mar-ginal to struggle, or the very site and stake of struggle? There are, it seems to me, no abstract schematic answers to these questions. Solutions can only be pursued through encounter with the confused and contradictory textures of social rela-tions, lived experiences and representations. A politics has to be constantly discovered through process growing out of social relations, and not imposed upon them.

Blowing the Whistle (1983) was not an academic book. It was written for a broad and general audience and deliberately eschewed the scholarly apparatus of footnotes and references, in order not to send the wrong message to readers. This volume too is supposed to be accessible to general readers. However, there is now a much more developed structure of informed and scholarly interest in the issues associated with sport and politics. There are courses, set texts, cut-ting-edge research and key scholars. It is important to situate this book in that broader context. I would not, for example, want to discuss shinty without refer-ence to Dave Whitson's excellent paper on the subject (Whitson 1983). However, I also want to avoid making the book too dense or inappropriately cumbersome, with excessive use of reference and footnote. This has been a dif-ficult balance to strike; I have oscillated between modes of writing and presentation, and I hope that readers, and those upon whose work I have drawn, will take the style of this project in the spirit in which it is intended. The rest of this chapter outlines my own formation, sporting and political, and introduces *Blowing the Whistle*, reprinted here in entirety, in its original form. Also included are reprinted versions of two essays I wrote in the early 1990s. The second half of the book consists of new material mostly written 2005–7.

Writing *Blowing the Whistle: The Politics of Sport*

'It was loosely based on the Berlin cabaret of the 1930s, which did so much to prevent the rise of Adolf Hitler.'

Peter Cook's sardonic comment on *The Establishment Club*,
his comedy nightclub, in the early 1960s

It is almost 25 years since *Blowing the Whistle: The Politics of Sport* was published. It was one of a batch of four, the second batch, as I recall, in the series *Arguments for Socialism*. The series, established by Pluto Press, was intended to feed into, and reinvigorate, debates about practical politics on the left, following the rise of Thatcherism. The book came out in May 1983, as Labour, under Michael Foot, was heading for its massive election defeat, running on the leftist-oriented manifesto, described by Labour MP Gerald Kaufmann as 'the longest suicide note in history'. It was not the most propitious moment for such a book to hit the market.

However, 25 years on, it is still on reading lists for Sports Studies courses, despite having been out of print since the late 1980s, and in a recent review of my book *Media Sport Stars*, in the *International Review for the Sociology of Sport*, Professor Toby Miller, of University of California Riverside, said: 'Whannel is a foundational figure in the study of sports and the media. He more or less pioneered critical leftist analysis in this field. ... For 20 years his writing has set a high standard ... and it remains an inspiration to many, myself included.' Other writers have a stronger claim on the role of pioneer, but I was certainly following the footprints of early settlers in my own rickety wagon. The book clearly had an influence beyond its mere sales and it seemed appropriate that it be made available again. I have rejected the invitation to rewrite and update it. It was very much a text of its time, written by a young man with a perspective shaped by the moment, and a style shaped by the intentions of the series. I could not revise it – it would need to be a completely different book, written by a completely different person in and for a completely different moment. It did not seem appropriate, though, merely to reprint it, as if it was a stuffed mammoth in a glass case, devoid of life and requiring only casual curiosity. Instead it was clearly necessary to contextualise it, and to draw out aspects that have a continuing relevance. In this introduction, I expand on the circumstances in which it was written, the social and political context of the moment, and the process by which organised analyses of sport began to develop. Brecht counselled us not to begin with the good old days but with the bad new ones, and this reissue of *Blowing the Whistle* is certainly not intended as an exercise in nostalgia or archivism. In the second part of this volume, I discuss culture, politics, sport and the media from the perspective of the new millennium.

I was approached by Pluto to write a book on the politics of sport in May 1982. At the time I had recently finished being a full-time post-graduate student at the University of Birmingham Centre for Contemporary Cultural Studies. My three years of funding had run out, but my PhD thesis, on television sport and cultural transformation, was nowhere near finished. I was making a living doing part-time

teaching, some journalism, and television research. At that time, I had only published a couple of academic articles, and the prospect of writing a whole book,
even one of only 40,000 words, seemed daunting. The brief, to write an accessible
book for the general reader that might inform debate about politics and sport, and
the policies of sport, in British leftist circles, had considerable appeal.

I was enough of an arrogant young whippersnapper to have a fair degree of
confidence in my ability to write in a clear and accessible style. I had also had
some journalistic training as part of the Media Studies degree programme at the
Polytechnic of Central London (now the University of Westminster). In 1975 I
was one of just eighteen students on the first intake of this, the first ever degree
level course in Media Studies, and I have always been very grateful for the quality of the course in general and also for the schooling in basic principles of
journalistic writing. When the book came out, some friends found my style brief
to the point of terse, and when I look at it now, I am astounded by the brevity of
both sentences and paragraphs. With Alan Tomlinson I later edited two books
for Pluto, *Five Ring Circus: Money, Power and Politics at the Olympic Games* (1984)
and *Off the Ball: Football's World Cup* (1986), and one Pluto editor dryly
described the style adopted as neo-moronic. The books were printed on a cheap
grade of paper that Alan and I took to referring to as Bronco Moderne, an allu-
sion to the austere bargain-basement cheap Bronco toilet paper, much used by
public institutions in those days.

Many passages of *Blowing the Whistle* I now find embarrassing, crude and strident. Too many sections were insufficiently nuanced, and little of my own
ambiguous passions for sport found their way into the writing style. Other passages, though, now strike me as succinct or prescient. The chaotic, contingent
and half-formed process of state policy formation seems not to have changed
much, even in the era of PPP and PFI, apart from the neglect of the grassroots in
favour of a focus on the production of an athletic elite in pursuit of high profile
international success. The focus of the book on commercialisation clearly caught,
in a snapshot, a process that has become of central importance to sport today.

I knew a lot about sport and the media, through my PhD research, but was
painfully aware that I knew far less about writing on sport and leisure in general
and that I knew few other academics who were interested in, or informed about,
the subject. Word of my project and my feeling of isolation reached Alan
Tomlinson, at Brighton Polytechnic (now the University of Brighton), through a
mutual friend. I met him for the first time at a conference later in 1982, when the
book was nearly finished. A tall dark stranger approached me, and his first words,
in a Burnley accent, were 'I hear you're lonely'! We became good friends, and
collaborators, and he did much to encourage and facilitate my subsequent
involvement in sport and leisure studies and in the Leisure Studies Association.
At the time I began working on the book, though, I knew the first task was one
of rapid self-education. I became a compulsive browser of library shelves, second-
hand bookshops and charity shops, and by this method, I came across many of
the books mentioned in the guide to further reading, adding to my stock of reading done during my postgraduate studies. It was only some years later that I

realised how fortunate I had been in finding, without any structured guide, much of the key writing then available.

In the 1970s the very notion of writing in a serious, analytic or politically informed manner on the topic of sport was regarded by many as eccentric. Indeed these attitudes have by no means disappeared today, even after thirty years in which a large body of critical work has been produced. Sociology of sport was a small field, largely ignored by mainstream sociologists. Histories of sport, apart from the endless recitations of great stars and great events, were few. Academics and political activists alike typically regarded sport as at best epiphenomenal. Even in the emergent field of cultural studies, few writers regarded sport as having any significant importance in the wider scheme of things. Founding figures of cultural studies, such as Williams, Hoggart and Thompson, had little or nothing to say on the topic. John Clarke, Chas Critcher and Roy Peters were the only CCCS-based figures who had published on the subject.[5] Stuart Hall wrote an essay on the media and football hooliganism, which I discovered just as I was completing my undergraduate dissertation on the same subject.[6] To my chagrin, he seemed to have worked out very quickly, and with, apparently, minimal research, patterns and structural regularities that took me three months of work in the newspaper archives to detect and analyse.

There were opportunities as well as problems in this lack of precedent. I was forced to think through precisely what might be implied by a phrase like 'the politics of sport'. The lack of strongly focused policy debates about sport was more of a freedom than a constraint. I interrogated my own feelings about sport, which, then as now, are deeply ambivalent. There were, and still are, some in all parts of the political spectrum who simply condemn sport as fostering negative characteristics – competitiveness, violence, cheating, and self-obsession. I was determined to avoid this line, which negates analysis in its monolithic conception of 'competition'.

My reflections at the time on the ways in which my own biography, post-war British history, and the institutions of sport were related found no place in *Blowing the Whistle* but help to frame the text, and I reconstruct them here. I was born in 1950. My father, the son of a Scottish postman, was a teacher, my mother, from a respectable middle-class family with roots in the north-east, worked in the book and publishing trade. They met at Foyles bookshop. I suppose it is not so surprising that I should have grown up with a love of books and of writing. They were both Labour party members; indeed, somewhat embarrassing to recall now, for a while they had a large colour picture of Nye Bevan hanging in the bedroom, with a rather unnatural tinted socialist realist appearance. In my early teens I began to register that my father was on the Labour left, and increasingly disaffected with the Wilson government, whereas my mother was in the middle of a slow journey rightwards that resulted, after an aberrant, and for my father and I traumatic, vote for Thatcher in 1979, in a defection to the SDP while I was writing *Blowing the Whistle*. Only in 1979, when my father described my mother as having been 'almost a Stalinist' when he met her, did I fully comprehend the degree of this political drift. Only now, when the pain of her 1979 vote has subsided, do I begin to understand something of the factors that lay behind it. So I grew up in a household in which political discussion and debate were part of the environment. Dick Taverne, then prospective Labour candidate for Putney, visited when I was around 12. I remember thinking then that he seemed a bit of a wally – possibly my first political thought (sorry, Dick). Later my mother became a friend of the MP Hugh Jenkins and his wife Marie. More significantly, after we moved to London in 1958, my parents became friendly with a number of early new left figures who were constantly in the house debating and arguing about politics and culture. It was in this environment that my early conceptions of politics were formed.

Both my parents had always had an interest in sport. I believe they went to the London Olympics together in 1948, and I think my mother was at the famous friendly between Moscow Dynamo and Chelsea in 1945 that attracted a crowd of 82,000.[7] My first awareness of sport stars was probably in her describing the fame of Newcastle stars Jackie Milburn and George Mitchell, 'wor Jackie' and 'wor Geordie'. By the time I was in my teens I had my own idols in the shape of Fulham's Johnny Haynes and Bobby Robson, and athletes Gordon Pirie and Bruce Tulloh. My grandfather and my uncle were both highly proficient at bowls, in the very different class-cultural settings of Pitlochry, and Poole Harbour, and my aunt and uncle were keen tennis players. My father learned to play golf as a boy, on the beautiful course at Pitlochry, and continued to play throughout his life, reaching a handicap of five in his peak between the mid 1950s and mid 1960s. He taught me to swing and hit a ball to quite good effect, but though to this day I occasionally practise driving and putting, I never played a whole round. Despite his constant insistence on the working-class involvement in golf in Scotland, I always saw it as terribly Home Counties. More pertinently though, I also perceived it as a thoroughly frustrating sport. After hitting, when I was fifteen, a near perfect 5 iron shot of an unnaturally utopian beauty (at the ninth hole at Pitlochry), I suspected I might never again hit so elegant a shot, and elected not to take the game up. I acted as a caddy on many rounds including one memorable one at St Andrews, and still retain, along with my inverted snobbish hostility to the institution of golf, a fondness for the actual act of playing. I now recognise this combination of hostility to the institutions of sport and love of the acts of performance as being at the heart of my own ambivalence about sport.

Both my parents liked athletics and I was taken regularly to the White City where I remember particularly Derek Ibbotson, Dorothy Hyman and the great 4 × 400 metres relay team featuring Robbie Brightwell and Adrian Metcalfe. The most extraordinary moment, though, was in 1965, watching Ron Clarke running with a frightening intensity and metronomic consistency as he became the first man to run three miles in less than 13 minutes, beating the previous record by around ten seconds. The White City staged both athletics and greyhound racing, and as the afternoon athletics meetings drew to a conclusion, white-overalled staff would begin raising the strange poles supporting floodlights around the dog track. Under the stands were little clusters of wooden bookie's stands, with worn leather satchels. I was dimly aware that here was another world, disreputable,

Figure 1.2 My grandfather, showing off his exemplary technique on the bowling green next door to his home in Pitlochry, Scotland.

Figure 1.3 One of the pleasures of golf enjoyed by my father (left) and his golfing partner.

working class and vaguely dangerous, that I would not be inducted into. My mother did once take me to Epsom races, but neither of my parents really approved of gambling, although the whole family did win money with a rare bet on the Derby winner St Paddy, Paddy being my father's name.

My mother tried to encourage me to play tennis, which at first I hated, and only learned to play properly in my twenties. We did go to Wimbledon on more than one occasion, but as a sport to play I preferred badminton. My father despised cricket and rugby union, perceiving them as middle class, Home Counties and dull. Despite watching Roslyn Park a few times I inherited his dislike of rugby union. In 1961 I went to Wandsworth School, an ex-grammar school that had become one of the first comprehensives. Retaining its grammar school orientation towards sport, it allowed boys in the 'lower' streams to play soccer, but those of us in the 'top' stream had to play rugby union for the first two years. Being the youngest of the class and slight of build (believe it or not) I got knocked around a fair bit and came to see the sport as little more than licensed bullying, verging on assault and battery. Cricket, though, I gradually came to understand and appreciate, although my general technical ineptitude meant this involved watching rather than playing. My love of the feel of being in that establishment bastion, Lord's, and of the moment of silence that characteristically descends just before a ball is delivered, along with a hostility to the ways in which the sport embodied a culture of class deference, is another instance of my ambivalence towards sport and its institutions.

Figure 1.4 School football: possibly best when it's over. Neither my father, myself, nor my
son, shown here, went on to become professional footballers, and nor do 99%
of the people who dream of it.

When my father went, in 1971, to work at Northwestern University in Chicago (more precisely in Evanston, IL, immediately north of Chicago), his interest in darts heightened to the extent of entering, with his colleague and darts partner, the US Open Doubles Championship. They also wrote a book on darts, in collaboration with a Chicago-based artist of some note, Sig Purwin (Whannel, Hodgdon and Purwin 1976). The inclusion of material about the history, culture and rituals of the game must have heightened my own interest in the social, cultural and historical context in which sports exist.

My major sporting preoccupation, though, in the years between the ages of 8 and 18, was football. Although I was never very good, I played football in the playground and in the local park all the time. For several years, we had a large informal kickabout every Saturday morning, in Bishops Park, by the Thames in Fulham, with a floating population of Fulham and Chelsea supporters. I used to dash home for lunch and then, if Fulham were at home, return across Bishops Park to go to the match. Although I loved to play, I was never good enough to get into organised teams. At school, prevented from playing football for the first two years, and subjected to two years of rugby, the top stream boys were finally allowed football, but regarded as useless duffers to be exiled to the third best pitch. It was the lower stream boys who had been nurtured from year one to be the school team. They got the best pitch, the most enthusiastic teacher, and coaching from the occasional visiting player from Fulham and Chelsea. Bitter with jealousy, I also, in some vague way, perceived that class and school tradition were intertwined here. Outside school hours, at weekends, I became a follower of Roehampton Wanderers, a 14 to 16-year-old age group team, who played in a local league on the cinder pitches. I seldom got offered a chance to play, although I did, bizarrely, receive a league champions medal, when one of the squad failed to turn up for the ceremony, held, incongruously, in the officers club at Brixton prison (the league was organised by prison officers).

From age eight, though, I was a spectator of great commitment, supporting Fulham and going to an average of 30 games a year for the next ten years. What was it that made following a football club so appealing? There was the sense of spectacle, the sheer noise and density of the crowd, the quest for excitement, the experience of being in a world apart, the emotional intensity, and the communality.[8] Like Nick Hornby (Hornby 1992) I was struck by the 'overwhelming maleness' of it all. I was attracted by the low life, forbidden 'rough boys at the back of the bus' feel of it, the threat of violence and the fear. Now of course, for someone like myself, brought up in a middle-class home, socialised into codes in which violence was not ever an acceptable mode of conflict resolution, there is nothing romantic about actual violence. Being punched or kicked or punching and kicking someone else has no appeal. Symbolic violence, which predominated in the terrace cultures of the 1960s, was another matter, involving the adrenaline rush of fear. Merely getting off the station at Old Trafford, part of a small group of away fans, chanting and waving scarves, got the heart pounding; being chased through the streets of Nottingham all the way to the station and onto the train was hair-raising; and this was after the cancellation of the match itself due to a waterlogged pitch! I still recall with a frisson the cry of another fleeing fan behind me, who yelled in fright, 'They're buying platform tickets!' Somehow this combination of thuggery and respect for British Rail Transport Regulations now seems, in retrospect, terribly 'English'.

I enjoyed having mates who were people I only knew by first names and only saw on the terraces. I enjoyed the travel, the swaggering through other people's towns, the sense of invasion of territory, and, for us, an away mob with no reputation for toughness or violence, the sheer nerve of even going to Anfield, Goodison or Old Trafford. I was fascinated to be exposed to a different world, and at an age when few of our classmates had been north of Watford, those of us who were football followers cherished our semi-secret encounters with Birmingham, Liverpool, Leeds, Manchester and Newcastle. Also, the team should not be forgotten. Fulham had a fine defence and midfield with players of the quality of Tony Macedo, George Cohen, Jim Langley, Alan Mullery and Bobby Robson in this period. They also had that majestic passer of a ball, Johnny Haynes, and for a while, the precocious clown prince to be, Rodney Marsh. They were in the top division, so I got to see the top teams, and I remember vividly the very special combination of excitement and apprehension on seeing the Manchester United team including Bobby Charlton, Denis Law and George Best run out onto the pitch to warm up. Recalling those days on the terrace, I am shocked at my lack of awareness of the constant and routinised vicious misogyny and racism. I had an extraordinary ability to compartmentalise, and to excuse football fans for behaviour that would not have been tolerable in other contexts. We were in a world of young male adolescents who, disrupted and disturbed by the onset of sexuality, resorted to misogyny and homophobia as a defence against fear of sexuality. It would be comforting to recall that I felt a sense of distance and disdain, but the sad reality is that, at best, I gravitated to those who were less audibly abusive.

At the end of my teenage years, I was drifting away from being a regular attender at Fulham. I had discovered music, drugs and girls, and Fulham had been relegated after a dozen years of brinkmanship. I entered a phase of being an epicurean dilettante. With my partner for some twenty years, I watched occasional games featuring the superb Leeds United team of 1973–74. We lived near QPR's ground at this time, and for one season watched a few games as their amusingly eccentric collection of erratic geniuses, including the legendary Stan Bowles, came desperately close to winning the league. Our interest in football declined, hers more rapidly than mine, which remained in rather lukewarm fashion, during the 1980s. We began going regularly to athletics, just as Steve Ovett and Seb Coe emerged in the late 70s; the media portrayal of their 'rivalry' provided the first case study of my postgraduate work. We also started going to watch cricket at Lord's and the Oval just as Ian Botham began to emerge as a star. Research and pleasure do not always connect, but in this period, for me, they were certainly converging.

People my age, with leftist inclinations, would, like me, have been excited by the Labour victory in 1964, putting an end to what had been dubbed, by Labour leader Harold Wilson, 13 years of Tory misrule. But such hopes rapidly turned to disillusion, as Wilson flayed the leaders of the Seaman's Union as 'a tightly knit group of politically motivated men' and went on to back the Americans over Vietnam. More recently, Wilson has been compared favourably to Blair, in that while both appeared to lick Uncle Sam's arse, only Blair provided troops. Wilson, it has been suggested, displayed courage in refusing to send British troops to Vietnam. It seems a small enough reason to re-evaluate Wilson, although holding together the frail coalition of the broad church that is the British Labour Party, and winning four elections in the process may, in the end seem a greater success than Blair's eradication of Clause Four socialism, taming of the Parliamentary Party, neutering of the constituency parties, and steering of the party well to the right of the Liberal Democrats.

For many in my generation, the growing campaign against the Vietnam War, the emergence of the underground, alternative society, counter culture, psychedelia and the original summer of love were woven together in a tapestry that, just briefly, in early 1968, seemed to us in our self-regarding euphoria to be about to provide Western nations with an entirely new form of politics. Such hopes were rapidly dashed in the period of backlash and repression that followed. The various social movements and cultural practices that became labelled variously hippie, underground, alternative society, counter culture, psychedelia, were never in themselves cohesive in the moment of 1968. Hard left politics rubbed up against avant-gardist cultural experimentation and an eclectic appropriation of eastern mysticism, and bardic and druidic borrowings that would now be called 'new age'. Yet there were debates, arguments and political strategies – the dialectics of liberation, the Hyde Park Diggers, the Situationists, that promised an emergence of a new politics. Growing up in such a heady atmosphere, it is perhaps no surprise that sport receded in importance for me for a while. I recall no reference to it in underground literature, until the emergence of the anti-competitive sport movement and the proselytising for non-competitive forms of playful physical activity, like Frisbee. I can't avoid a wry smile whenever I encounter mention of events such as the World Ultimate Frisbee Championships.

By 1970 the alternative society was rapidly fragmenting. Some moved to the country, and took to scraping a living through craft skills. Some drifted into hard drugs and a self-indulgent route to despair. Some became entrepreneurs. Fractions of the more politically oriented, despairing of the failure to generate a real movement, went into small, disciplined, cell-based organisations committed to using violent methods – the Weathermen (later Weather-people), the Red Brigades, the Baader Meinhof gang, and the Angry Brigade. Perhaps the most dramatic legacy of the underground was the impetus it gave, by its general sexist and exploitative attitude to women, to the Women's Movement, which emerged with immense force and impact in the 1970s. Like so many men in this period I found myself being forced to confront and change my own sexism and lack of awareness of women's oppression, an experience that, while painful, was enriching, and ultimately transformative in terms of my own political landscape. Meanwhile in mainstream politics the process, described in *Policing the Crisis* (Hall *et al.* 1978) as the exhaustion of consent, was well underway, as neither the Conservatives under Heath, nor Labour under Wilson and then Callaghan, could find a viable mixed economy and expansive state solution to either the long-term structural decline of the British economy, or the impact of changing global economic conditions. The seeds of Thatcherism and Reaganomics were beginning to sprout.

From 1968 onwards I spent seven years of trying hard but failing to win success with a band whose manic commitment to loud, fast avant-garde music with complex time signatures was never likely to be commercially popular, especially given our disdain for the notion of a vocalist front-man and our total lack of understanding of how to get gigs or promote the act. I then became a student, enrolling on the first ever degree in Media Studies, at the Polytechnic of Central London (now the University of Westminster). From a young age I had been fascinated by the media. I can remember, at age nine, trying to produce a newspaper using a John Bull printing set. I wouldn't recommend it as a technique, and I still find it rather extraordinary that modern computer technology enables a competent 12-year-old to make a newspaper, produce music or edit video. Not only do I wish that more of them did, but I think that it is politically important to foster such independent and alternative productivity. I always wanted to be a journalist when I was young, and although my academic trajectory took me in a different direction, one significant portion of my freelance earnings during the 1980s came from journalistic writing and television research. My course was ambitious, well taught and stimulating, and those of us who were on it realise that we were very lucky. We had some great teachers, some challenging material to come to terms with, and we got to play with television, radio, film and photography kit all the time. We even had an Associated Press wire feed.

During the 1970s a range of developments was fostering a new engagement with cultural politics. The women's movement's insistence that the personal is political; the growing influence of semiology, with its focus on the meanings, myths and ideologies embedded in language and representation; Althusser's model of ideology as all pervasive and structured into institutions and practices – all contributed to modes of analysis that aimed to deconstruct culture to unmask its profoundly political nature. When I graduated I was able to go to the Centre for Contemporary Cultural Studies (CCCS) at the University of Birmingham, then well established as a formidable intellectual and political hothouse. The Media Group was making a transition from the analysis of news and current affairs into the heartland of popular television. Already aware that there seemed to be very little if any analysis of media sport, I elected to do a PhD on the subject. It was a good moment to commence research into an aspect of popular culture. After ten years in which the women's movement, History Workshop, SEFT, the journals *Screen* and *Screen Education* and CCCS had all contributed to the emergent relation between cultural analysis and cultural politics, the study of popular culture in terms of politics and ideology was about to commence a period of explosive growth. As I began work on *Blowing the Whistle*, the innovative and influential Open University course U203 on Popular Culture was commencing its first year.

Meanwhile the political landscape was changing dramatically. Thatcher succeeded Heath as leader of the Conservative Party, and the flood of young leftists back into the Labour Party ushered in a period of constitutional change that, briefly as it turned out, strengthened the hand of the left, culminating in the selection of Michael Foot as leader and the near success of Tony Benn in winning the deputy leadership. Municipal socialism emerged as a force – most notably in London, with Ken Livingstone's GLC, and in South Yorkshire. The despair of the left at the Thatcher victory in 1979 was counterbalanced by a degree of enthusiasm at the possibilities it opened up for struggle, particularly in Thatcher's early years, before the Falklands War, the destruction of the National Union of Mineworkers, and the mid 1980s boom made her, for a while, unassailable. Ken Livingstone's own re-emergence as independent elected Mayor of London in 2000, succeeding in part due to the positive popular memories that many Londoners retained for the Livingstone-run GLC in the early 1980s, and in particular its Fares Fair transport polices, now seems the most lasting accomplishment of this period of left labourism and municipal socialism.

My research gave me a way of combining my media interest, my sport enthusiasm and my political perspective. It was at this point that I was approached to write *Blowing the Whistle*. It is worth reiterating the aspirations of the Arguments for Socialism series, of which the book was to be part. On the back cover of *Blowing the Whistle*, Tony Benn is quoted as saying that 'Arguments for Socialism can play a significant part in re-establishing the necessity for a socialism that is democratic, libertarian and humane'. Hilary Wainwright is quoted as saying that 'socialists have been working at redefining the socialist vision' and that the Arguments for Socialism series 'brings the new socialism together into public view'. Ken Livingstone is quoted as saying that 'Arguments for Socialism has a major role to play in building the intellectual framework for the radical socialist struggle of the 1980s'.

In retrospect, the series seems more like part of a high water mark for this radical socialist agenda than a new wave. In the early 1980s, Michael Foot became leader of the Labour Party, Benn came within a whisker of the deputy leadership, Labour fought the 1983 election with their most radical manifesto to date, and Ken Livingstone's GLC was able to implement some radical transformation in the governance of London. After 1983, Foot was replaced by Kinnock, members of the Militant Tendency were expelled, Benn's career began a slow decline from its high point, the GLC was abolished, municipal socialism was undermined and disciplined by the rate capping legislation, the Labour left marginalised, and at the end of the decade, Eastern bloc communism collapsed. The new agenda being formulated from the late 1980s was not that of a radical socialism but that of the Third Way (see Giddens 1988).

Yet, far from being a historical irrelevance, this moment of radical socialist debate remains deeply relevant because it raised themes of direct pertinence to people's lives. The issues of real democracy, accountability, public provision, and the critique of the power of corporate capitalism remain in circulation in various forms in the new social movements – anti-globalisation, anti-capitalism, and eco-warriors. Municipal socialist politics too may be making a come-back – it is noticeable that Paris, Berlin and London all currently have Mayors whose political

Figure 1.5 The Downtown Athletic Club, New York, home of the Heisman Trophy, awarded to the most outstanding college footballer. The Club closed in 2002, after damage sustained in the 9/11 attack on the World Trade Center. Sporting cultures in the 1980s were characterised by values of self-reliance, achievement and meritocratic elitism: the themes that linked Thatcher and Blair, the 1980s and 1990s.

initiatives have drawn on ecological concerns. Socialism may be regarded by many cultural commentators in Europe as 'dead', but it certainly doesn't look that way in South America. In sport too, the concerns aired in the 1980s over the commercial-isation and commodification of sport have re-emerged in the football supporters' movements that demand greater democratic participation in their clubs (see the final chapter on politics).

Up to the start of the 1980s, there was an absence of discussion of sport in mainstream academic writing. For historians it was a minor activity, buried within descriptive passages on 'culture'. Most sport histories up until the 1980s were written by non-historians, whose work tended to offer a plethora of minutely detailed factual information with a paucity of analysis, context, or per-spective. Like historians, mainstream sociologists regarded sport as marginal or epiphenomenal. In traditional political writing, too, sport was seen as epiphe-nomenal or as the opium of the masses. Interestingly, in political manifestos, sport has only ever been a small subsection. The dominant tendency has been to regard sport as, like religion, an opium of the masses. Very few of the cultural crit-ics of the left tradition, from the Frankfurt School to the New Left, have paid more than passing attention to sport.

The influence of debates over Western Marxism, focusing attention on issues of culture and ideology, did, however, lay the ground for the emergence of new political analyses of popular culture. One approach, that emerged from the end of the 1970s, partly from the Centre for Contemporary Cultural Studies at Birmingham University and blossomed in the context of the Open University Popular Culture, argued that popular culture was not simply 'imposed from above' by powerful capitalist corporations; but could not be regarded as 'risen from below' in an authentic expression of 'the people'. Rather it was the site of struggle between contending forces, and in the tensions and contradictions of that struggle could be seen the state of political contestation in its symbolic form. Popular culture, from this Gramscian perspective, becomes the interface between everyday language and common sense, and organised political discourse. One problem with this model is that in analysis it tends to produce a premature politicisation – everything has to have a political effectivity. Sometimes it is necessary to acknowledge that not all aspects of popular culture are equally significant, and that some things really are simply trivial. So it was in this context, then, that as an ex-technician, failed musician, lapsed football fan and media graduate, I sat down in 1982, when I should have been working on my thesis, to write *Blowing the Whistle*.

2 The complete original text of *Blowing the Whistle: The Politics of Sport*

To Paddy

2.1 Politics on the pitch

The 1980 Moscow Olympics were the occasion of an enthralling battle, fought out between the stadium and the television screen. At stake was the interpretation of the games. The Soviet Union controlled the pictures, British television commanded the microphone. The Soviet Union started impressively with a huge mosaic of people holding coloured cards that spelled the message 'Sport, you are peace'. David Coleman, playing for the BBC, countered by referring to the human mosaic, 'so popular in communist countries'. At home we wondered if he had ever watched BBC's *Match of the Day*, which used to kick off with a similar mosaic revealing the inspiring sight of Jimmy Hill. The Soviet Union then undermined its early advantage with the bizarre sight of a phalanx of men goose-stepping along, right arms aloft clutching doves. Few images so perfectly captured the ambiguities of the Olympic movement. The battle raged on through the games. British television constantly reminded us that 'our' team was competing under the Olympic flag, while Russian cameras zoomed in on hordes of 'unofficial' Union Jacks in the crowd. Lord Killanin, head of the International Olympic Committee, made a dramatic late appearance in the closing ceremony to ask sportspeople of the world to unite in peace before a holocaust descended. The great mosaic produced an image of the Moscow mascot crying in sadness at the closing of the games. Coleman countered brilliantly: 'Mika the mascot sheds a cardboard tear – so this is, perhaps, a moment to remember the real grief called for elsewhere which has led to half the world staying away.' It is hard to believe that anyone will ever be able to say again, with a straight face, that sport is nothing to do with politics.

Yet 'Keep politics out of sport' has been the traditional cry of sports leaders, journalists and politicians. Any attempt to raise questions about sport and the society in which it is played is habitually derided. This criticism, levelled with monotonous regularity at the anti-apartheid movement, enables the sport and political establishments to preserve the image of sport as a nice cosy ghetto, insulated from the rest of the social world. So it came as a shock to many when 1980 began with strident calls for a sporting boycott from the establishment. In the closing week of 1979 Soviet troops had poured into Afghanistan to buttress the crumbling government. President Carter and Prime Minister Thatcher responded by calling on Western nations to boycott the forthcoming Olympics. Overnight people who for years had been insisting that politics be kept out of sport began shaking their heads and saying that unfortunately you cannot keep politics out of sport. It was a dramatic U-turn. Six months of drama and farce followed. In January the International Olympic Committee refused to move the games from Moscow and in February the Sports Council and the Central Council for Physical Recreation opposed the boycott. But a United States boycott looked more likely.

In March 78 British athletes said they would go even if the British Olympic Association (BOA) pulled out. But the BOA soon confirmed that it would go to Moscow. The government stepped up its pressure. In a petty and vindictive move it instructed civil service departments not to award special leave to Moscow-bound athletes. In April top British shot-putter Geoff Capes, refused time off for Moscow, resigned from the police force. Pressure seemed to hit the television plans. Cliff Morgan, head of BBC Outside Broadcasts, announced that coverage of the games would be as normal. The following day the board of governors issued a statement saying that there would not be full coverage. Both BBC and ITV slashed planned coverage by 75 per cent. The forty-odd hours screened by each channel were almost entirely outside peak viewing time.

In retrospect the Carter–Thatcher boycott attempt was a dismal failure. It alienated public opinion whilst having no discernible effect on Soviet policy towards Afghanistan. The games were a great triumph despite the absent countries. British athletes were conspicuously successful. The boycott campaign was actually less of an about-face by the establishment than is often supposed. Many people had suggested a boycott of Moscow long before Afghanistan, not least British Foreign Secretary David Owen in 1978. A boycott campaign supported by Tory MPs and members of the National Association for Freedom had been active from the start of 1979. The idea had been floated within the sport world too. Sports Council member Laddie Lucas suggested a Moscow boycott two years before the Olympics, in protest at the treatment of Jewish dissidents. The proposal was discussed by the Sports Council, which decided it was a matter for the British Olympic Association. Government attempts to use sport to further foreign policy are nothing new. From its modern revival in 1896 the Olympic movement has often been the site of international wrangles and power politics.

The Olympic Games

The first modern Olympic Games were held in Athens in 1896. They were a somewhat disorganised affair. But the potential of international competition was evident and the movement was under way. Links with international capitalism were soon apparent in the connections between the 1900 games and the Paris Universal Exhibition, and the 1904 games, held alongside the St Louis World Fair. Business interests were again apparent in the 1908 London Olympics. Britain, who had just signed a trade agreement with the Russians, tried to insist that Finland march behind the Russian flag, a demand the Finns resisted. The American team refused to dip their flag in homage to the British king.

In 1912 in Stockholm competitors could no longer enter as individuals but only as part of a national team, and the Finns had to compete under the Russian flag. After war prevented the 1916 games the defeated nations – Germany, Austria, Hungary, Bulgaria and Turkey – were barred in 1920 and so, in the wake of the communist revolution, was the Soviet Union. The Amsterdam Games of 1928 included women's athletic events for the first time. But the sight of exhausted women in the 80 metres so upset the men of the IOC that they refused to allow women to run the distance again. This absurd ban lasted until 1964. The Berlin Games of 1936 are notorious for their Nazi pageantry. A strong campaign in America to boycott the games in protest at the vicious suppression of the Jews was foiled when the American representative was expelled from the IOC. But Hitler's attempt to use the games to celebrate Aryan superiority was beautifully undermined. Black American athlete Jesse Owens won four gold medals, breaking the Olympic Record each time. Hitler stalked out in disgust.

The first post-war games were held in London in 1948. Once again the defeated nations – Germany, Italy and Japan – were not invited. Up until 1952 military men could enter only if they were commissioned officers, but from this date the privilege was extended to sergeants. Corporals and privates remained barred. In 1956 five nations – Iraq, Netherlands, Lebanon, Egypt and Spain – withdrew in protest at the British and French invasion of Suez. Following the Soviet invasion of Hungary, tension was high and there were violent incidents in a water-polo match between the Soviet Union and Hungary, and in a football match between the Soviet Union and Yugoslavia. In 1964 South Africa was suspended for practising apartheid in sport and persistently selecting all-white teams. It was finally expelled from the Olympic movement in 1970. In 1972 the rebel regime in Rhodesia was barred. In 1976 20 African nations withdrew in protest at New Zealand's tour of South Africa. Taiwan also withdrew after the Canadian government refused to allow it to compete as 'The Republic of China'. Sport has always been an integral part of international diplomacy. When the United States first began to reopen relations with China in the 1970s the first sign of a thaw was the arrangement of a table tennis match. This gambit became known as ping-pong diplomacy. I can never hear the phrase 'shuttle diplomacy' without imagining Kissinger umpiring a nightmare badminton match between Sadat and Begin.

Outside the stadium

Governments use major sporting events to present a national image on the world stage. So those who stage Olympics and World Cups become determined not to allow the appearance of dissent to mar their public relations. When the 1968 Olympics were allocated to Mexico the student movement mounted a campaign to protest at the cost of the games, a huge financial burden on a poor country. Shortly before the games began the army opened fire on a demonstration, killing 260 and injuring 1,000. The allocation of the 1978 World Cup to Argentina strengthened the resolve of the junta to present an acceptable image to the world. During the years leading up to 1978 an estimated 15,000 people disappeared, believed killed by the security forces. In the months leading up to the Moscow Olympics drunks, hooligans and dissidents were rounded up and headed out of Moscow. They were allowed back only after the tourists had departed. In 1982, during the Commonwealth Games in Brisbane, police mounted a major operation to keep aborigines demonstrating for human rights away from the television cameras. Nothing was to divert us from the sight of a giant inflated kangaroo being paraded around to the strains of Rolf Harris singing 'Tie Me Kangaroo Down, Sport'. The next Olympics are to be in Los Angeles in 1984. It will be interesting to see what measures the authorities use to keep black militants, gay rights activists or organised feminist groups out of the stadium and off the screen.

Once sport became a global television spectacle it provided a means for groups normally denied a public voice to make themselves heard. The outcome in 1972 was tragic. During the Munich Olympics eight armed Palestinians occupied the Israeli quarters in the Olympic Village, killing one athlete and holding nine others hostage. They demanded the release of 200 Palestinian prisoners in Israel. After protracted negotiations five Palestinians and all the hostages died in a shoot-out with German security forces. Even this traumatic episode did not disrupt the spectacle for more than a few hours. Amidst controversy, the International Olympic Committee declared a day of mourning but timed it retroactively to start at 4 p.m. the previous day, apparently so the games could start again quickly. In the memorial service IOC president Avery Brundage outraged many by equating the massacre with the successful attempt to force the IOC to exclude Rhodesia that had preceded the games.

The Munich episode and the Moscow boycott had one thing in common: they both exploited the prominence of sport to make a political point. But in neither case did the political struggle specifically relate to sport itself. Unlike the struggle over apartheid, neither the Moscow boycott nor the Munich incident was an attempt to challenge the organisation of sport itself. They were examples of the contact between politics and sport, a contact that is inevitable, as sport is part of society. The choice of sport to make a political point was, however, relatively arbitrary. It was determined by the prominence of sport in the public eye rather than by any intrinsic property of sport.

This book will concentrate, not on politics *and* sport, but upon the politics *of* sport. By this I mean the social organisation of sport, the institutions that govern it and the values invested in it. In particular, I want to look at the social base of these forms of organisation and values and at the extent to which they are contested rather than merely accepted. Sport is difficult to explore precisely because it has so successfully preserved an apolitical appearance. There are no broadly accepted socialist principles, let alone strategies. There have been political struggles over leisure but they have had little in common.

Invading the pitch

One of the better-known incidents of suffragette history is the death of Emily Davison, a member of the Women's Social and Political Union. She died at the 1913 Derby when she threw herself under the king's horse, Anmer, as it rounded Tattenham Corner. Her funeral was attended by 6,000 women. This was only the most publicised of a series of incidents throughout 1913 as the suffragettes adopted a more militant stance. Many involved sport facilities. All over the country suffragettes tore up the turf of cricket and football grounds, bowling greens and golf clubs and burned buildings down. The choice of sport as a target was not coincidental. Sport is a symbol of masculinity and male chauvinism. In attacking sport facilities the suffragettes were attacking a social institution rooted in male power.

Over 50 years later two black American sprinters chose the 1968 Mexico Olympics to make their statement to the world. Tommie Smith and John Carlos finished first and third in the 200 metres. They walked out to the medal ceremony each wearing one black glove. During the playing of the anthem they both looked down and held one fist aloft – the Black Power salute. Both the two Americans and silver medallist Peter Norman wore human rights badges. The gesture was intended to highlight the contrast between the place of black people temporarily in the world spotlight and their place in society as a whole. As Tommie Smith pointed out, all his victory meant was that whereas before he was called a nigger, now he was a fast nigger.

It was particularly appropriate that this protest occurred at a sporting event. Like music, sport has often been represented as an arena in which black people can succeed – it is the mythical escape route from the ghetto. Even if the route were real it would merely divert attention from the oppression of black people in almost all other areas of social life. But black people also encounter prejudice and oppression within sport itself. During the 1970s a number of campaigns developed in this country aimed specifically at the sporting world. The highly successful Anti-Nazi League (ANL) was formed to combat the menace of fascism. Concern grew at the attempts of right-wing groups to recruit support at football grounds and a number of ANL offshoots developed to combat this (e.g. Spurs against the Nazis). In 1977 another football-oriented campaign developed north of the border. The Scottish football team was scheduled to play Chile on a forthcoming South American tour. The venue was the notorious Santiago stadium, used as a concentration camp after the 1973 military coup which overthrew the Allende government. The campaign objected, without success, to both the visit and the venue.

The movement against hunting has a longer history and has continued to make inroads into this disgusting pastime. It has been able to persuade councils and some private landowners to bar hunts from their property. The adoption of sabotage techniques has helped to expose some of the arrogance, hypocrisy and underlying violence of the fox-hunting class. Struggle over leisure is not a recent development. One of the largest campaigns over leisure provision developed in the 1930s. In 1932 500 people took part in a mass trespass on the Kinder Scout grouse moor in the Peak District, demanding public access. They were met by a gang of gamekeepers wielding sticks. Five were arrested. A subsequent ramblers' rally attracted 10,000.

The 1949 National Parks and Access to the Countryside Act was intended to open up the countryside but had little success. Existing public paths are constantly menaced by landowners and if anything the degree of public access to the countryside is declining. A 1974 survey of Oxfordshire found that only 111 of its 27,000 acres of woodland were open to the public. The *Sheffield Campaign for Access to Moorland* celebrated the 50th anniversary of Kinder Scout with more mass trespasses in 1982. What Britain needs is an equivalent to the Swedish 'right to ramble' laws which give everyone the right to walk where no danger of damage or invasion of privacy exists.

Another campaign to emerge from Yorkshire is the *Equal Rights in Clubs Campaign for Action* (ERICCA), which is challenging the discrimination against women in club and institute union clubs. A majority of the 4,000 clubs operate a two-tier membership system. Most women cannot vote, stand for office, nominate others for office or use men-only rooms. The campaign grew out of Sheila Capstick's struggle to be allowed to play snooker at her local club. She and her husband started a snooker for women campaign, with the slogan 'A woman's right to cues', and collected 2,000 signatures on a petition. Supporters of the campaign then set up ERICCA. But a recent private member's bill failed to amend the law to prevent discrimination in private clubs. Vera Selby is the women's world snooker champion and also the first woman snooker television commentator. Yet in her local league 11 of the 13 clubs are men only. So she must withdraw from away matches, allowing her opponents to claim the points by default.

These campaigns show that people are prepared to struggle over sport and leisure. But the support they have won and the success they have achieved have both been limited. One campaign, however, has succeeded both in gaining widespread support and in winning significant victories. In just over a decade the anti-apartheid movement secured a substantial isolation of South Africa in world sport. The fight to prevent these gains being eroded continues. The apartheid system rests on legal apparatus which treats black and coloured people as second-class citizens. This is enforced by draconian police power. South Africa is a racialist police state. In the late 1950s the anti-apartheid movement began to identify sport as an area in which apartheid could be exposed and attacked. Bishop Trevor Huddleston did much to bring the issue into public debate in Britain.

In South Africa the South African Sports Association (SASA) was formed in 1958 to promote black opportunity in sport. In 1962 the South African Non-Racial Olympic Committee (SANROC) was formed. The SASA secretary Denis Brutus was banned from teaching and journalism and from attending social and political gatherings. He could not be quoted in South Africa, was not allowed to leave Johannesburg, could not visit his family and had to report to the police every week. He managed to leave South Africa in 1965 in an attempt to get to Baden-Baden to lobby the International Olympic Committee, but was captured by Portuguese security police and returned to South Africa. He was shot and seriously injured by Johannesburg police while trying to escape. By the mid 1960s repression had forced SASA to suspend its activities, and SANROC, along with Brutus himself, had been forced into exile in London. But SANROC did succeed in getting South Africa suspended from the 1964 Olympics.

Apartheid first became a major issue in Britain during the D'Oliviera affair. Basil D'Oliviera was a highly talented cricketer and a coloured South African who had been forced to leave and settle in England to pursue a cricket career. He was a contender for the MCC team to tour South Africa in 1968 but was not selected. There was widespread suspicion that he had been rejected in accordance with the wish of the South African government. A late injury to another player and pressure on the MCC then led to D'Oliviera's inclusion in the touring party. South Africa announced that he was unacceptable and after great turmoil the MCC called the tour off. With the issue firmly in the public eye, the campaigns against apartheid were stepped up. A South African cricket tour was due to visit England in 1970 and Young Liberals, including Peter Hain, were active in forming the *Stop The Seventy Tour* (STST) campaign. Their first move was to organise a highly successful direct action campaign to disrupt the South African rugby tour of winter 1969–70. The matches were played to an accompaniment of chanted slogans, pitch invasions and struggles between demonstrators and police. The tour staggered through to a conclusion although halfway through the players voted to go home. Although no matches were actually prevented, it was clear that the cricket tour was in grave doubt. (Cricket pitches are considerably more vulnerable than rugby grounds, as the *'George Davis Is Innocent OK'* campaign later proved when it brought a test match to a premature conclusion by digging holes in the wicket.) Public and government pressure on the MCC mounted and even inside cricket there was growing opposition to South Africa. In May STST won their victory – the tour was cancelled.

This cancellation was only part of a major breakthrough in the struggle against apartheid. In 1970 South Africa was expelled from the Olympic movement and from the Davis Cup and was suspended from international athletics and gymnastics. White South Africans, fanatical about sport, found this isolation hard to take. During the 1970s there were attempts to undermine international hostility to apartheid. The adoption of a 'multinational sport policy' allowed whites, Africans, blacks and Asians to compete, but only as four separate 'nations' within the country, and then only in competitions that also involved foreign teams. Mixed sport was still barred. When this had little effect on international hostility, a co-option strategy, which attempted to include some black sport groups within the white sports structure, was developed. Some black sport bodies were absorbed by this. But the real stronghold of the anti-apartheid movement, the non-racial black sport organisations, saw through the policy and rejected co-option.

Apologists for apartheid argue that there is no law specifically prohibiting mixed sport. But there is a mass of legislation controlling the use of sport facilities and the movement of black people in sport. The pass laws can be effectively used to prevent black participation in sport except on terms dictated by the white authorities. Any pretence at 'normal' non-racial sport in such a society can only be a hollow sham. Third world and socialist countries have orchestrated the international pressure on South Africa. The Western nations have dragged their feet. The boycott threats that led to the expulsion of South Africa from the Olympic movement were led largely by African nations. It was not until the boycott of the 1976 Commonwealth Games that Western nations were forced to declare their positions more clearly. Meeting in Britain in 1977, the Commonwealth Ministers drew up the Gleneagles agreement. This declared that it was the urgent duty of each government vigorously to combat the evil of apartheid by withholding any form of support for, and by taking every practical step to discourage, sporting contact with South Africa.

The South African response has been to offer huge sums to tempt sports competitors to tour. South African Breweries spent £1.2 million setting up the 1982 cricket tour that led to Geoffrey Boycott and Graham Gooch being banned from test cricket. Another £1 million was spent on setting up a football tour later the same year. Despite reference to a range of star names, most of the players who actually toured were at the end of their careers. The tour became a farce. The party were met at Soweto airport by several hundred blacks chanting 'Rebels go home', three black teams pulled out of arranged matches and the tour was cut short. The main problem currently facing the anti-apartheid movement in sport is the lack of enthusiasm shown by Western nations, and particularly Britain, for implementing the spirit of the Gleneagles agreement. Neither the government nor the Sports Council has shown a lead.

The government says that it cannot interfere with the rights of independent sports organisations or individuals. Yet in 1980 in efforts to enforce a boycott of the

Moscow Olympics it withheld foreign office co-operation, instructed the civil service and police to refuse to grant leave to Moscow-bound athletes and offered large sums of public money for alternative events. While the Sports Council formally supports the Gleneagles agreement, it has done little to pressure those sports that maintain links with South Africa. The Rugby Football Union defied the government's expressed wish in approving a British Lions tour of South Africa in 1980. Yet the same year the Sports Council presented them with £500,000 towards a £3.4 million rebuilding project for Twickenham. Sports Council chairperson and ex-rugby player Dick Jeeps accepted an invitation to South Africa to be the guest speaker at the 1980 Sports Greats Awards. By contrast, black Sports Council member Paul Stephenson, who is rather more critical of apartheid, was refused admission to South Africa.

In the absence of a clear lead from governments the United Nations Register of Sports Contacts with South Africa has become an important means of maintaining pressure. The register lists organisations and individuals who maintain sporting links with South Africa. The anti-apartheid movement has been of great importance. The sporting isolation of South Africa has been a highly successful political campaign. It has kept apartheid a prominent issue worldwide and has prevented South Africa from masking its oppression with a veneer of normality. It has also been powerful enough to cause changes in South African sporting policy. Even though these changes are little more than cosmetic, they help to maintain the pressure upon the whole apartheid system. South Africa is now caught in a dilemma. It has tried to create the impression of a relaxation of apartheid by producing pseudo multi-racial sport organisation at national level, while continuing the brutal repression unabated in social life. The various struggles outlined here challenge the view that sport is a world of its own. They treat the social organisation of sport as part of that of society as a whole. But they do not amount to a coherent strategy. They are not informed by an overall socialist attitude to sport.

Standing on the sidelines

Most socialists don't take sport very seriously. It is not seen as a site of struggle, nor even as a very significant part of social life. In part this is a product of the labour movement's traditional focus on economic and political struggle. The core of much socialist analysis is the class struggle. For many this struggle takes place at the workplace, in confrontation between worker and boss. Other forms of politics are peripheral. Victory is to be sought in workplace organisation and victory is inevitable because sooner or later workers will realise where their true class interest lies. The failure of socialism to become genuinely popular in the 1950s and 1960s was attributed to rising affluence. Wait until the next crisis, the pundits said, and a more radical mood will develop. For a time in the early 1970s this scenario seemed to be coming true. There were massive mobilisations to fight industrial relations legislation, culminating in the defeat of the Heath government by the 1974 miners' strike.

But recent developments are more disturbing. The adoption of hard-line monetarist economic policy, extensive cuts in public spending and an engineered rise in unemployment to nearly four million have failed to produce an upsurge in socialist consciousness. Despite the very real decline in the living standards and the very bleak prospects facing working people, the Thatcher government appears to be popular, even with people who suffer most from current government policies. The labour movement has to confront the failure of socialism to become a popular force. The question of consciousness – what people think about the world and why – is central. Working-class people do not automatically turn to socialism any more than women automatically turn to feminism.

Socialists have always been aware of this problem. The last 15 years have seen a growth of interest in problems of ideology – of how people in subordinate classes come to consent to, and acquiesce in, class domination. There has been a mounting interest in the media and other cultural institutions and in the part they play in shaping people's understanding of the world. This interest has led to a developed critique of the media and of the dominant culture. Analyses of the media have attempted to investigate the way that consensus is maintained, the way that a particular view of social reality is reproduced, and the way trade unionists, women, blacks and other groups are presented in a stereotypical manner.

New forms of cultural struggle have confronted this pattern of domination. The opening up of a range of alternatives – the radical press, independent cinema and fringe theatre – has attempted to challenge the power of dominant voices. The existing practices of media production have come under greater pressure from antiracist and anti-sexist campaigns. Struggle to make greater space for alternative views has taken place around, for example, the formation of Channel Four. The growth of interest in culture has enlivened socialist debate in a variety of fields – the press, cinema, television and publishing. But sport remains largely neglected.

This neglect is part of a broader pattern. The socialist tradition generally gives physical matters a low status. The body has been seen as a personal, individualised concern, somehow apart from society. Only in debates about the health services does the physical side of life figure and then only in a marginal fashion. The rise of feminism has challenged this blind spot. The insistence that the personal is political, that social practices structure people's physical lives and that sexuality and relations between men and women are political, has begun to transform the place of the physical in socialism. Childcare, nursery provision, women's right to abortion on demand and the nature of health care are all, quite rightly, being pushed to greater prominence on the labour movement's agenda. But even within feminism there has been surprisingly little discussion of sport.

Sport has traditionally been such a bastion of maleness that it offers a perfect site for a critical exposure of the culture of masculinity. But the redefinition of femininity being produced by the strength of the women's movement has also begun to transform sport. Women are increasingly prepared to challenge male definitions of their capabilities. The growth in women's marathon running is only the most publicised example.

There are also deeper reasons for the neglect of sport as an aspect of social life. Just as there is a division between mental and manual labour, so there is a division between mental and physical activity. English cultural life is marked by a very distinct division between two types of person – the sporting philistine and the non-sporting aesthete. These are the two archetypal products of the English public school and university education. One is the hearty muscular sportster, manly, friendly and insensitive, who knows nothing of art, music or literature. The other is the sensitive aesthete who finds energetic physical activity vulgar.

So sporting culture is, compared to that of many other countries, intellectually empty, and our artistic life has no sense of physical dynamism. Sport is marked down as a natural, taken-for-granted activity. You don't need to talk or write about it. You just do it. This division between the mental and physical has its impact on the left. Am I alone, when sitting in damp meeting halls in clouds of cigarette smoke gazing around at the sea of drawn faces, slumped shoulders and pot bellies, in wondering how many of us are going to be alive when the revolution comes? How many will be fit enough to storm the barricades? It is a great irony that we who would fight against capitalist exploitation are so often unable to combat its destruction of our own bodies with products like tobacco. We need to recognise that capitalism has deformed more than just our working relations. The right to a fit, healthy existence should be an integral part of the struggle for socialism. We cannot afford to treat the physical as peripheral. Because physicality is marginalised in this way, socialists tend to comment on sport only when it is overtly political. So socialist writing on sport has a rather one-dimensional character. It has consistently sought to assert that you cannot keep politics out of sport, that sport is not a world of its own but a part of social life. It has been less successful in exploring the complex and contradictory nature of the politics of sport.

I think there are five reasons why socialists should take sport more seriously. First, there is a need to avoid the traps of the past. There are great dangers in focusing too narrowly on industrial struggle. Relations between capitalists and workers in the factory may indeed be crucial, but not to the exclusion of all else. Many of the areas in which socialist organisation has most successfully caught the popular imagination recently have been aspects of cultural struggle – the anti-fascist movement, the fight against sexist representations of women, rock against racism, and so on. We need to take all aspects of social life seriously, especially popular cultural forms like sport.

Second, the way people see the world presents major problems for socialism. To build a genuinely popular movement we need to develop and spread a socialist way of looking at the world, and dislodge the dominance of the bourgeois world-view. Sport as it exists in this country contributes to the way people see the world. We need to work out how to engage with this problem. Is it possible to work for a non-racist, non-sexist, non-nationalistic and more co-operative form of sport? Or should the whole institution of sport merely be exposed and attacked?

Third, physical well-being, health and fitness are important to human development. Socialism should be a way of making a healthier life possible for all. It should make clear that capitalism inhibits the possibility of universal fitness. Some forms of sport could be an important element in the path to greater health and fitness.

Fourth, play and pleasure are also important in human development. The old Salvation Army adage was 'Why should the devil have all the best tunes?' We need to start asking, 'Why should the bosses have all the best games?' There are great dangers in appearing too puritan about fun. Play in some form will be an important element of a more fulfilling society. We need to see what possibilities lie in more playful forms of sport.

Finally, mechanisation, new technology and electronics have already begun to transform the nature of work. Physical labour is on the decline. At present these changes are used primarily to create more profit, with the by-product of large-scale permanent unemployment. The much-touted leisure society is already here for four million on the dole. The only problem is that they've given us the leisure and kept the money. But even if unemployment is tackled, shorter working hours will mean more leisure time. Leisure will become an increasingly politicised issue. Battles will be fought over who has leisure time, how it is spent and how it is provided for. Socialists should intervene in these debates and be active in struggles.

The questions raised here are difficult and there is no merit in quick, glib answers. This book is intended to open a debate – to place sport and physical leisure on the socialist agenda – and not to provide instant solutions. The second chapter surveys some socialist critiques of sport. The institutions of sport have been attacked for being a form of distraction, a tool of the state, a part of capitalist business and a part of bourgeois ideology. These critiques are valuable but only as a starting point. Chapter Three outlines the historical development of the institutions of English sport, showing how the major sporting institutions came to be dominated by a stratum of the male bourgeoisie. Chapter Four examines the development of sport as large-scale entertainment reproduced as spectacle for television, the degree of resistance to this process and the existence of possible alternatives. The last two chapters examine state policy and socialist alternatives. Chapter Five suggests that England has always lacked a coherent direction in sport policy and that the private sector is increasingly likely to fill the vacuum. Chapter Six outlines various options to be considered in any attempt to develop a socialist strategy for sport.

2.2 Arguments about sport

Not many socialists have taken an interest in discussion of sport. But the few who have written on the subject have produced lively and trenchant criticism. Sport has been attacked as a distraction, a way of providing a safety valve and keeping the masses quiet, as an arm of the state and a way of building nationalism, as a part of capitalist business and as a form of bourgeois ideology. This chapter will outline what socialists have said about sport and its forms of organisation. These criticisms are important if we are not simply to take sport for granted as a natural activity. They seek to challenge much of the existing common sense concerning sport, which is a combination of idealism and an apolitical liberalism. To appreciate these criticisms we must first look briefly at these conventional attitudes towards sport.

The idealist view of sport has some of its roots in Greek attitudes. It relates sport to physical perfection and sees athletic endeavour as the body striving for perfection. One variant of this view is the concept of physical and mental harmony. A rather more influential one is the concept of the healthy mind in the healthy body. Consistent improvement in sport performance is seen as an indicator of human progress. The emphasis on records and measurement is even enshrined in the Olympic motto – 'Faster, Higher, Stronger'. A rather different variant stresses the importance of play, which is seen as non-purposive activity important to human development. The ability to have fun is viewed as a fundamental human trait. There are two rather different ways of applying this notion to sport. Some hold that sport is essentially irrational and so a form of play. Others argue that sport represents the more organised, rational, and consequently negative form of play. Most popular sports are played at very informal levels – street football, beach cricket, tennis against a wall, children's races – and may here be closer to play than in their more organised forms. The opponents of professional sport often argue that at the highest level all the fun has gone because here people take sport too seriously.

The classic liberal/apolitical view is that sport is a world of its own, apart from the rest of social life. It is full of fun, excitement, drama and involvement. But it has nothing to do with the real world and should be shielded from it. In other words, keep politics out of sport. This view wrongly assumes that the existing organisation of sport is non-political and opposes any external interference (except government funding, ideally with no strings attached). For 'Keep politics out of sport' read 'Keep the politics of sport the way they are'.

A cultural approach is directly opposed to this apolitical one in that, far from attempting to separate sport from social life, it seeks to emphasise the relation between the two. The significance of particular sports is then located in the way that the culture surrounding a particular sport expresses the social values of those involved. So football is seen as deeply embedded in the social and cultural experience of urban working-class man. The solidarity within the crowd, the local loyalties, the conventions of tough physicality, and the particular forms of humour, all stem from the basic connection between football and its social roots. This last position brings us much closer to a socialist analysis of sport. Clearly, in order to understand sports fully, it is crucial to situate them within their social and historical contexts. Socialist analysis raises a whole set of questions about the nature of this context. How does sport relate to the development of industrial capitalism? What place does sport have within the state apparatus? To what extent is sport part of the dominant ideology – the system of ideas that work to perpetuate class domination? Does socialism need sport? The rest of this chapter will examine four types of socialist critique, in which sport is attacked as a distraction, as an arm of the state, as a part of capitalism and as a form of ideology.

Bread and circuses

There is a long tradition of viewing sport and leisure as distractions, keeping the oppressed masses from more disruptive activity. Leisure time is seen as that time spent outside working hours when people are temporarily free of labour discipline and so relatively unoppressed. The idea that some form of excitement might distract people from their mean conditions is not new. The Roman emperors believed they could keep the masses quiet with bread and circuses. Some recent socialist thought has seen sport as a form of circus, a gaudy spectacle. Just as religion was once the opium of the people, now it is sport that narcotises the working classes. Traditionally, religion provided elaborate venues, separate from the rest of social life, in the form of churches. Inside, idols and mythical figures were worshipped and a series of rituals, spread through the calendar, were performed. Today the stadiums of sport, equally separate from social life, provide the venues for worshipping stars. Sport has its own rituals throughout the calendar – the Cup Final, the Boat Race, the Grand National and so on.

The growth of television on a global scale has accelerated this tendency, creating the society of the spectacle. The world is increasingly dominated by elaborate spectacles which serve to mask the ruthless exploitation of the existing economic order. Life is seen through television. A world of passive spectators rooted to the screen is pacified by ever more elaborate entertainment, spectacular yet devoid of any real substance. All events become reduced to the same level – coronations, moon shots, assassinations, elections, World Cups, papal visits, Olympic Games, wars – all become part of the great global television show. If social reality cannot be absorbed within the spectacle then it must be excluded. The coverage of the World Cup in Argentina managed to avoid comment on the brutal military dictatorship. Television commentators assured us that they had been made very welcome. In the light of the subsequent Falklands war, television's silence on the subject of the fascist junta and the 'disappearance' of thousands of Argentine citizens is deeply ironic.

Presenting sport as a world of its own enables the media neatly to bracket out other events. The killing of 1,000 demonstrators by Mexican authorities just before the 1968 Olympics was quietly forgotten once the games started. Only in 1972, when the Palestinian seizing of Israeli hostages and subsequent deaths disrupted the flow of the games themselves, was the spectacle briefly dislodged. The importance of sport is grotesquely inflated by its place in the global spectacle. During the 1982 World Cup there were strong hints in the media that an England win would provide a third great event, to go along with the birth of the royal baby and the Falklands victory. This bizarre suggestion was most apparent in those papers which insist most strongly that politics must be kept out of sport.

It is not only at the level of television spectacle that sport can be seen as a distraction. Many people in the sports world, battling for years for adequate financing for inner-city projects, have discovered that, since Brixton and Toxteth, the easiest way to get funding has been to mutter grimly about riots. Involvement in sport is seen as a diversion, keeping the working class, and particularly the black working class, from engaging in class struggle. Were they not spending their time on the terraces, watching the box or in sports halls, so the argument goes, they might be out seizing state power. Just as this view alarms the establishment, it attracts the left. It is easy to see why. The spectacle of 20,000 people behind the goal at a football match chanting 'Come on, you reds' is both intriguing and frustrating. All that energy wasted on 22 men and a bag of wind. What might 20,000 Liverpool workers achieve if they travelled up and down the country for socialism instead of football? How might South American dictators tremble if they heard 10,000 Scots heading their way, not for a football match, but to pursue enquiries about missing trade unionists? The fantasy is beguiling. But it is a fantasy. The failure to win people to socialist activity cannot simply be blamed on the other activities that fill their time. Football crowds have slumped drastically with massive unemployment. Yet no whirlwind of socialist struggle has arisen in football towns.

When all is blamed on 'distractions', people are seen simply as mindless dupes and their use of leisure as manipulation by the ruling class. In reality, people make choices in their lives. Of course the fact that we make choices does not mean that we get what we want. We choose from a limited set of options determined largely by forces beyond our control. The pattern of work determines the amount of time and money available to us. The range of options is limited by the operation of the leisure industry and the nature of state provision. But if socialism currently fails to galvanise the working class of Liverpool, it is not because 90 minutes of football are played every week.

Sport and the state

Attempts at social control are not the only close links between sport and the state. Sport is closely associated with the military in many countries. It has been used to boost national fitness in preparation for war. It has close associations with the monarchy and various sports are an important part of the royal family's public image. International sport has always been manipulated according to the needs of diplomacy. The English empire and its attitudes to other races affected the development of international sport. Sport is also important in the self-image of most nations. Sport has traditionally been seen as a way of boosting patriotism. In 1773 Rousseau said that games should be used to create a deep love for the nation. After the Napoleonic wars, Friedrich Jahn, a founding figure of gymnastics, said that a national sporting movement could regenerate the German people. A century later Nazi generals were to see sport as a form of military service. Much of the Soviet Union's sporting success, notably the Moscow Dynamo football team, grew out of the KGB's sport organisation. In pre-revolutionary China games were used to build people's health to fight imperialism.

In Britain sport has been important to the public schools in their role of providing an officer class. The famous poem 'Vita Lampada' ('There's a breathless hush in the close tonight ...') directly links the skills needed to inspire a cricket team with those used to rally an imperialist army. Team sport was held to foster and develop leadership qualities needed by the empire. This system provided officers, but the establishment worried periodically about the state of the potential 'other ranks'. The concept of national fitness has different implications in different contexts. The mass fitness programme of Nazi Germany and the sport-for-all policies of the German Democratic Republic are only superficially similar. In Britain, war usually triggers off a sudden interest in the physical fitness of the proletariat. These worries surfaced after the Crimean war, during the Boer war and before the first and second world wars. But attempts to remedy the problem were seldom successful.

There were a number of reasons. First, the fear that national fitness was inadequate never really gripped the ruling class as a whole. Second, especially before universal secondary education, the state lacked adequate machinery to promote programmes for national fitness. Third, there were differences within physical education over the value of physical training as opposed to games as such. There was also some mutual hostility between military-trained drill teachers and college-trained physical education teachers. Fourth, there has always been a substantial degree of resistance to organised physical activity amongst the people. The system of sport in Britain has a strong *ad hoc* improvised character to it. The attempt to boost national fitness in the late 1930s was widely considered a failure. When the Second World War started, fears over fitness were seen to be largely unfounded. After the Second World War the expansion of the welfare state provided the machinery for boosting national fitness. But the long-term future of the military was now seen in a technological light. National fitness became associated more with the need for a healthy productive workforce, to be reared on free milk, orange juice and organised games.

Sport and the state are also linked through the involvement of the monarchy. The British royal family follows the aristocratic leisure tradition. Its members prefer hunting, racing and equestrian sports. But they have taken care to associate themselves with more popular events by ritual appearances on occasions like the Cup Final. They leave their mark in peculiar ways. The marathon is a foot race lasting 26 miles and 385 yards. This odd distance is generally believed to commemorate the carrying of a message in the Battle of Marathon. In fact the marathon used to be run over 26 miles. The extra 385 yards were added so that the 1908 Olympic marathon, which started at Windsor Castle, could finish opposite the royal box at White City Stadium. Royalty have shaped international sport much more than is generally realised. During the 1960s the self-electing International Olympic Committee, supreme authority over the Olympic Games, had among its members Prince Alexandre of Belgium, Prince Georg of Hanover, Prince Cholum of Iran, Prince Tsuneyoshi Takeda of Japan, Prince Franz Josef II of Lichtenstein, Grand Duke Jean of Luxembourg and King Constantine of Greece.

International sport is often the tool of diplomacy. The Football Association has taken instructions from the Foreign Office as to which countries to visit and which to avoid. In 1938 the England team visited Germany and, despite protests from the players, were instructed by the FA to give the Nazi salute in the pre-match line-up. Sadly, as England were eliminated from the 1982 World Cup, we will never know if the Thatcher government would have taken the politically unpopular move of withdrawing rather than playing Argentina so soon after the Falklands war. The state looms large where national image is concerned. International sport has always been a battle for national self-pride, a war without weapons. Sporting success has been regarded as a matter for national self-congratulation, failure as a matter for state concern. Newly independent nations have devoted great energy and resources to sport as a way of establishing themselves on the international stage. The communist countries of eastern Europe consciously adopted a policy of proving communist superiority by outstripping the Western nations in Olympic performance, a goal which they have achieved remarkably successfully.

Western media lay great emphasis on competition at the national level. The fate of the England football team is taken as a symbol of national well-being. Harold

Wilson, having attempted to identify himself with the England World Cup victory of 1966, hoped to retain office in a quiet election in 1970 timed to coincide with the World Cup. Unfortunately England and Harold were both eliminated. This prominence of sport in the English national identity was heightened by arrogance. For years the English assumed that their football team was the best in the world. They held aloof from the World Cup when it was launched in 1930, preferring to challenge the victors at their leisure. This assumption was not to be rudely shattered until the 1950s; first, when during England's first World Cup in 1950 they were beaten by the USA, a nation with no tradition of playing football, and, second, when Hungary came to Wembley in 1953 and won 6–3. The myth of national superiority was also undermined by increasing American and Russian dominance in the Olympics. The quest for international success became a concern of the state and a rallying call of those within sport pressing for greater funding. But the involvement of the British state in sport has been somewhat half-hearted. The overwhelming proportion of funding is at a municipal level. There has rarely been a coherent national policy or an adequate level of funding.

No business like sport business

A rather different form of critique emphasises the penetration of sport by business. It argues that sport is owned and controlled by the capitalist class and run like a business. Its internal organisation is hierarchical. It has a highly developed division of labour. Its techniques are designed to extract maximum productivity from its performers. It is increasingly dominated by the need to be profitable or at least to avoid losses. Its potential for promotional activity and the growth of sponsorship are increasingly transforming it into a branch of the advertising industry. Organised sport in Britain exists within a capitalist society. So it is constrained by the economic and social relations particular to capitalism.

But it is a simplification to say that sport is run like a business. Take the case of professional football. Probably the sport with most potential for profit, it currently faces severe economic problems. While clubs operate as limited companies, they have not been run predominantly for profit. Indeed Football League restrictions limit the distribution of surplus in the form of dividends. Clubs have been controlled mainly by local businessmen, not for gain so much as for power and influence in the community and as a hobby. Some would suggest that many of football's problems stem precisely from the fact that it is *not* run as a business. The striking thing about the organisation of many British sports is that they have remained cushioned from economic pressures for so long by a combination of insularity, conservatism, exploitation of voluntary labour, amateurism and hostility to commercialism. It is only in the last 20 years that this rather cosy, enclosed world has been penetrated much by harsh economic realities. Pressures towards commerce and profit have largely come from outside the structure of British sport – from television, sponsors, agents and advertising.

The organisation of British sport has been hierarchical. A top layer of elderly, male administrators holds power over most sports. A middle stratum of managers, coaches and trainers also exercises substantial control over players. In football the manager, always called 'the boss', has become, via the media, the pivotal figure of the game. The boss wields complete power over players, yet can be, and frequently is, sacked at a moment's notice by the board of directors. There is a widening gap between the few star players who can receive vast amounts in pay and fringe earnings, and the rest, who are often fairly badly paid. If they fail to make the grade they can find themselves unemployed and unemployable in their late 20s. Below the players and performers come the ranks of unseen workers who help to make sports possible. The recent strikes of stable lads revealed to the public the appalling rates of pay and conditions typical of this level of sport labour. At the top, training methods are geared to obtaining maximum productivity from the human body. Great stress is laid on work rate, commitment and dedication. Top athletes have to cross the pain threshold constantly. This type of training has been compared to the time and motion methods used to obtain maximum productivity in industry.

In many ways sport is a form of business. The crisis facing many traditional amateur organisations has made financial survival a key concern. Many have responded by stepping up sales in club shops, squeezing more from catering concessions, aiming at a family audience (that is, middle-class consumers) and opening potentially lucrative leisure centres. The growth of television, and consequent massive expansion of sponsorship, has led many to see today's sport as a branch of the advertising industry. But, if sports are businesses, they are businesses of a very particular kind. In most British sports the need to make a profit, or at least avoid a loss, is not the main motive. Most of the people involved see it as a regrettable necessity. The tradition of amateur paternalism is still strong in British sport. Many people are more interested in control and power than in money. There is often a tension between the money-making potential at the top and the needs of the grassroots. Many governing bodies are fighting a battle, often a losing one, to redistribute some of the wealth available at sport's highest levels.

A sporting idea

Sport offers a way of seeing the world. It is part of the system of ideas that supports, sustains and reproduces capitalism. It offers a way of seeing the world that makes our very specific form of social organisation seem natural, correct and inevitable. Sport does this in four main ways. It presents a series of ideas about the relation of individuals to spectacle, of active and passive behaviour, of the relation of elite performers to mass audiences. It also presents a way of seeing our nation and the nations of others. The values of the sport world stress individual endeavour and achievement. And sport offers a model of the relation between men and women. Sport provides spectacles. In the twentieth century sport has come to mean spectator sport to most people. The handful of players are greatly outnumbered by the millions who watch. We have become a world of televiewers. We are passive consumers, entertained by a small elite of stars. Our attention is increasingly focused on the highest level. Sports meetings find it more and more important to have stars, made familiar by television, to attract crowds. A major distinction grows up between *us*, the mass of passive consumers, and *them*, the active elite. As in sport, so in politics. *They* are the actors, the people who appear on the screen to make news, control events and so make history. *We* are the people who gaze at them in awe and wonder.

But sport also offers a way out of passive individualism. It offers us a greater collectivity to identify with, a way of feeling less of a lone individual. It offers us the team, the county and above all the nation. National sport is a powerful component of national symbolism. Many people who laugh at the monarchy identify with their national football or cricket team. Terms like English or British derive much of their significance from national sporting traditions. Sport provides us with a sense of belonging to a nation, however irrational that may be.

Sport also reinforces stock stereotypes of other nations. Italians are temperamental. The French are over-excited and a bit incompetent. Russians are dour and unsmiling, South Americans are unpredictable and violent. West Indians are flamboyant and undisciplined. East Germans are over-disciplined and unsmiling. Africans are enthusiastic but lack concentration. Our images of Britishness are reinforced by sporting comparisons with other nations. The force of all this is heightened by the way that Britain for years sustained its notions of natural superiority based on the empire. Everyone else is held to smile too much or not enough when compared to us. Within this comforting feeling of national unity, sport offers a model of the place of individuals. It provides a series of success stories – people who have achieved all the glories and rewards. We ignore failure and focus on winners. And these winners did not get where they are through unfair advantage, through accidents of birth. They got there through unremitting hard work, relentless application and commitment.

This is the message of the constant stress on work-rate and commitment. Anyone can make it but you have to work hard. You don't just work hard, you work harder than anyone else. Then you succeed in competition. You are prepared to go through the pain threshold more often, to give your all. At the same time you follow the commands of your boss, who knows best. This notion of sport success provides a role model for the ideal worker, though an 'efficient' worker wouldn't reap the same rewards. It also offers a model for the struggling small business owner. This view is supplemented with the rather contradictory notion of 'natural talent'. Hard work put sport stars where they are, but they also happen to be naturally gifted. It is all down to fate. Some have talent. Some do not. The rest of us are lucky to be able to watch the action replay on television. Natural talent is never enough of course. George Best and John Conteh are salutary reminders of what happens to those who don't work hard to preserve their talent.

Sport also offers us a way of living by presenting particular notions of maleness and femaleness. In Britain sport culture is deeply embedded in traditional notions of masculinity. The stress on toughness, commitment, competitiveness, aggression and courage in sport all fit neatly into the traditional notion of 'being a man'. Sporting activity is an important part of a boy's schooling. If you take part you are accepted as one of the chaps, a real man. If you reject sport, doubts are raised about your masculinity. Sport both defines and completes the image of maleness. Girls pass through school rather differently. Sport is often as popular with girls as with boys until early in secondary school. From then on notions of femininity intervene. The impact of images of femininity leads many girls to reject sport as inappropriate. Girls who continue with it are often seen as a bit deviant, just like boys who reject sport. So sport is part of the process of defining differences between men and women. Men are supposed to play it, women are not. So men who reject sport and women who pursue it find that their sexuality is questioned.

This fits in with broader definitions of male and female. Boys are active, girls passive. Men do, women watch. The media find it difficult to treat women simply as sports people. They constantly refer back to their prettiness or lack of prettiness, to their husbands and children. Active physical activity is for men. Women who succeed in sport are treated as unusual. Sport both generates and reinforces a very traditional image of the difference between men and women. This helps to sustain male power. The ideologies expressed through sport and the practice of sport reinforce each other in a vicious circle. Sport powerfully suggests itself as a male activity, so few girls persist with it. Few women then reach the public eye. The facts then confirm the image that sport is for men.

This pattern has been undermined in the last decade. Women have always been active in sport, although their involvement has typically been underplayed by the male focus of media coverage. But the success of the women's movement in dislodging traditional attitudes to femininity has changed attitudes to women's involvement in sport. Women's sporting achievements are growing apace. But these successes require struggle against male-defined and -controlled structures, in sport and in society as a whole. This struggle helps to undermine the existing ideology. Ideas about society are not simply transmitted from the dominant class to subordinate ones. There is always struggle over the power to define social reality. Certain ideas are dominant in sport, but they are not the only ones around. Women in sport are increasingly powerfully challenging the ways that men have portrayed them.

Stop the game or change the rules?

One conclusion drawn from these four lines of attack is that sport is not worth reforming. It has no place in a socialist society and should simply be exposed as a male-dominated, capitalist institution. I reject this argument. Before saying why, however, I will outline the bases of an anti-sport position. There are really two rather different positions. Both emphasise the negative character of competition. The first sees competition as inherently capitalist. Competition in sport is treated as an analogy of competition in capitalism. Just as socialism will eliminate the need for competition between capitalist businesses, so it will eliminate any need for competition in sport. So sport will wither and die. The second position sees competition as an inherent feature of masculinity and its prominence in our society as an effect of male dominance. If patriarchy is overthrown, competition will no longer be a socially important activity.

There clearly are close links between the values of sport and the place of the individual in capitalism. The individual is in competition with other individuals to achieve. Success is rated highly and people who achieve become celebrated. World records are a form of fetish-creation, which extracts a product from the labour of athletic endeavour – the record and the statistic. These figures then take on an independent existence as marks against which others must compete. This process has been particularly noticeable in world athletics recently. The boom in middle-distance running inspired by Coe and Ovett has involved highly constructed paced record attempts and a decline in tactical racing. The emphasis in sport on the need for hard work, individual sacrifice and the winning of rewards certainly matches the capitalist ideal of achievement. After all, sport does depend upon beating someone, proving yourself superior. For every winner, there is at least one loser.

Similarly the social construction of men in our society has produced a competitiveness particular to masculinity. The drive to success, to earn more, dress more expensively, to drive a faster car and so be seen with the most beautiful women is at the root of the images of maleness which surround us. Sport is very central to being a 'real' man. To be good at sport is to be strong, powerful, virile and macho. To be bad at sport is to be inadequate as a man. In sport you prove yourself more of a man than your opponents. If society was not so dominated by men and by the values of masculinity then competitive sport could not assume the huge cultural importance that it has at present. Overthrowing patriarchal domination would gradually transform social and cultural forms in such a way that competitive sport would have no place.

These are strong arguments. To be anti-sport is not simply to be negative. It is possible to argue for a non-competitive physical culture and for the development of non-competitive games. There are several books of children's games that do not involve competition and stress co-operation. But the main problem with the anti-sport arguments is that they assume there is one essential property called 'competitiveness' to which all sports can be reduced. This property is then condemned as being irredeemably capitalist and/or patriarchal. This book argues that competition takes many different forms. Boxing involves a different form than long jumping. Tennis in the park is different from tennis at the Wimbledon final. There is no single thing called competition that can be condemned or accepted.

The analogy with competition in capitalism is ultimately unhelpful. People are trying to beat each other in sport, but they are not trying to take each other over, or eliminate competition. There is no tendency to monopoly. Capitalist businesses aim to dominate their market totally. Total and permanent domination in sport renders a competition meaningless. The Football League clubs compete with each other but also depend on each other, for the structure of competition to continue. Competitive sport in a capitalist society does of course share the character of that society. But competition is not simply a product of capitalism. Similarly the fact that competitiveness is a distinctive masculine trait in our society does not mean that it is an inevitable male characteristic. Competitive masculinity is not a biological fact. It is a social construction. It can change and be changed. Indeed many would argue that it is in escaping from traditional notions of feminine passivity and becoming more self-assertive that the women's movement has been able to confront sexism and chauvinism. Just as assertiveness can be positive or negative in different contexts, competition can take positive or negative forms.

Although ultimately wrong, the anti-sport arguments do invite us to look more closely at the idea of competition. Desires to lift a heavier weight, swim the butterfly stroke faster, knock other people out, or throw 16 lb lumps of metal about are rather peculiar. They are social products, rather than natural ways of behaving. Certain forms of society emphasise competition. Others do not. If society is changed then the importance accorded to competition might well change too. There was extensive debate about this in the Soviet Union during the decade following the revolution. Many health workers argued for the importance of a non-competitive physical culture based upon health and fitness. The first Trade Union Games in 1925 barred the highly popular sports of weightlifting, boxing, football and gymnastics. The Proletarian Cultural and Educational Organisation fought for the rejection of competitive sport, which they saw as the product of a degenerate bourgeois culture. These tendencies were ultimately unsuccessful. Instead the Soviet Union turned to sport as a way of developing national fitness and identity, a policy that began to bring great international successes in the post-war era. The significance of this clearly depends upon broader political judgements about the Soviet system beyond the scope of this book. But it is worth noting that cultural change does not mirror political change in an automatic fashion.

Just as competition takes a variety of forms, so does sport. There is no single thing called sport, but rather a variety of competitive physical activities which we regard as sports. The word sport is a convenient label with which to generalise. To understand the development of sports in our society it is necessary to be more specific about the varied forms that sport takes. There are three rather different ways in which the word is used. First, to refer to games themselves – the sets of rules and principles that govern their playing. Second, the term also designates the social institutions of sport – the clubs, stadiums and governing organisations within which sports take place. The third meaning refers to the cultural and social settings and to the attitudes that constitute various sports. Football is not simply a game with rules, clubs and stadiums. It also has a complex culture. Street football, Sunday morning games, big crowds, buying programmes, eating peanuts, chanting, fighting between rival supporters, discussing the game and watching it on television are all part of football. To understand sport as a part of society we need to examine these three aspects and the relation between them more closely. The next two chapters give a brief account of the development of sporting institutions in England and the cultures that surround them.

2.3 Ruling English games

The last quarter of the nineteenth century was the crucial period in English sport. Many of the major sport institutions were formed then and the class control that would shape English sport in the twentieth century was consolidated. It is in this sense that the period 1875–1900 saw the formation of English sport as we know it today. This chapter outlines the social processes leading up to that formation. The following one traces the growth of sport in the twentieth century. The history of sport and leisure in England is in part the story of attempts by dominant classes to control the leisure time of subordinate classes and the story of attempts by men to control the leisure time of women. It is also the story of resistance to this control, marked by the persistent survival of popular activities.

Land ownership has always been a source of power. From the time of the Norman Conquest, the nobility enjoyed hunting for sport over huge tracts of land. Brutal penalties were imposed on peasants who killed for food rather than fun. The whole mechanism of hunting rights persists today with a thriving trade in shooting and fishing facilities in the Scottish highlands. Laws affecting leisure have frequently treated different classes differently. The hunting laws extended the property rights of the nobility to wildlife. The cruel sports of the common people – bull-baiting and cock-fighting – were outlawed in the nineteenth century, while those of the aristocracy – hunting and shooting – remain legal today. Gambling laws have generally clamped down on betting amongst common people while leaving the gentry free to wager. Periodic attempts were made to enforce regular archery practice at the expense of bowls or football.

The power of men to define the place of women has affected women of all classes. Responsibility for domestic labour tends to mean that women simply do not have leisure time in the way that men do. Domestic labour and child-rearing tend to be never-ending forms of labour. Upper-class women, freed of domestic labour by servants, had access to some forms of leisure but the rise of Victorian attitudes to femininity mitigated against physical activity. The influence of puritan and evangelical moral codes made it hard for women even to adopt suitable clothing for sport. Working-class women in the nineteenth century frequently had both paid labour outside the home and unpaid labour within it.

But all these pressures were resisted. Popular festivals were an important part of social life for 300 years, despite the power of the Puritan movement. Sports like bowls survived long periods of illegality. Women have persistently fought for the right to control their own lives. This chapter examines the rich tradition of popular festivals and feast days and the eventual decline of rural recreations and urban pastimes. It discusses the public school cult of athleticism and the re-shaping of sport in the nineteenth century. It offers an account of the formation of English sport and the crucial control exerted by men of the Victorian middle classes.

Pre-industrial festivities

England had a rich tradition of festivals and feast days, such as May Day, stretching back many centuries. Food, drink, dancing and sport were all part of the regular celebrations. Women and children often played as active a role as men. Many of the sports were violent; cock-fighting, shin-kicking, bull-baiting and dog-tossing all seem to have been popular. But recorded histories often disapproved of popular pastimes and so exaggerated the less savoury elements. There were many less violent activities. Running, stoolball, football, throwing at hoops, grinning contests and climbing the greasy pole have all been recorded as popular. Women often took part in stoolball, shuttlecock and smock races, in which the runner was awarded with a smock. The participation of women was often exploited for sexual display, as it provided a ready-made excuse for brief clothing.

One of the best-known celebrations was the Cotswold games. The games dated back to Saxon times but were revived with much success by Robert Dover in the early seventeenth century. They featured wrestling, dancing, smock races and backsword play. After running for around 200 years the strain of large crowds, rowdiness and gambling caused their demise in the nineteenth century. Bowls was a popular people's sport despite attempts to restrict its playing. An act passed in 1541 barred bowls for commoners, while allowing it for noblemen. Commoners were ordered to practise archery to boost the military power of the state. The act remained on the statute books until 1845. The phrase bowling alley originates from the use of high hedges to conceal sites for illegal games.

In the seventeenth century the rise of the Puritan movement was to pose greater challenge to popular leisure. The Puritan religious fundamentalism was bringing them into opposition with both the Crown and with popular activities. They were attempting to prevent physical activity and public gatherings on Sundays, which they felt should be devoted to religion. Under increasing pressure, from the Puritans on the one hand and anti-Puritan elements on the other, King

James I was presented with a petition protesting that the lower classes were being prevented from dancing and playing on Sundays after church. He responded by issuing the 1618 Declaration of Sports. This reasserted traditional rights and customs and the right of people to Sunday recreation. For the first, and really the only, time to date, sport and leisure was a major political issue. Continuing pressure forced King Charles I to re-issue the Declaration in 1633, but the days of his reign were numbered. The brief period of Puritan power between 1640 and 1660 saw a major clampdown on popular recreation. The Puritans attacked dancing for its carnality, football for its violence, maypoles for their paganism and sport in general for despoiling the Sabbath. They suppressed any sport which, like football, could be used to gather a crowd for seditious purposes and outlawed horse-racing, cock-fighting and bear-baiting. These strictures had much more effect on the common people than on country gentlemen who were able to continue sports debarred to others in the privacy of their own grounds. It is suggested that it was during this period that the lower-class sport of cricket was first taken up by the gentry. But popular sporting traditions often had deep communal roots and persisted through the repression to flourish again with the restoration of the monarchy in 1660.

A more serious threat to the pattern of popular recreations and festivals was posed by the long-term changes in the economic organisation of the countryside. The enclosure of common land, the growth of towns and the beginning of the transition to industrialisation caused a slow but drastic undermining of rural traditions. Traditional playing areas were swallowed up by enclosure, workers were forced off the land and into the towns and there were consequent upheavals in community and tradition. The survival of popular recreations in the eighteenth century came to depend increasingly upon the patronage of the local gentry. The involvement of the local gentry was a combination of paternalism and self-interest. The provision of festivals which permitted drunkenness and sexual licence was seen by the gentry as a safety valve and a form of social control. The great involvement of the gentry in betting led them to support sports like pedestrianism, which often featured races between the footmen of rival gentry. There was also a certain amount of political patronage of popular pastimes. The wider franchise meant election contests were now often accompanied by sports and festivities laid on by rival parties in an attempt to outdo each other. Festivals could, however, also be used for expressions of hostility to authority and often featured mock mayoral ceremonies in which the authorities were parodied. The person chosen as mock mayor was often a drunk or half-wit. He would be paraded around the area making speeches promising full employment, better wages and free beer.

The popular festivals of pre-industrial times were complex occasions. They were neither simply expressions of resistance nor means of social control. In their existing form they were threatened by the social transformation of industrial capitalism. Many of the features of present-day sport begin to make their first appearance from the early eighteenth century. The developing commercialisation, growth in spectators, offering of prizes, gambling on the result, emergence of professionalism and the development of a degree of spectacle and sensation were all features of the period.

All work and no play

From the middle of the eighteenth century the rise of industrial capitalism began to transform patterns of social life. The traditional forms of popular leisure were to be increasingly undermined over the next hundred years. The long process of enclosure and rural depopulation was already leading to the decline of the old rural festivals. The festivals and feast days of the new fast-growing towns were to be progressively squeezed out by the rise of capitalism.

The new urban working class found its leisure restricted in three ways. There was no space, there was no time and there was a powerful new ideology that disapproved of physical leisure for the working class. The new towns grew rapidly. Row upon row of tiny terraced houses sprang up unencumbered by civic regulation or concern about the environment. Very little provision was made for public open space in working-class areas. Capitalism brought a heightened rate of exploitation. Twelve- and fourteen-hour days, six days a week, left workers too tired for anything else but sleep. Public holidays were drastically cut back. In 1761 there were 47, and in 1825 40. By 1834 there were just four. Many of the traditional occasions for popular celebration had been eliminated. Popular recreation, undermined in the towns by lack of space and time, was also the subject of attack from a new set of dominant ideas. The Puritan tradition bore fruit in the form of the capitalist work ethic.

Previous attitudes had accepted the place of leisure and popular festival, if only as a safety valve or form of social control. The work ethic represented work as a virtue, idleness as a vice and physical recreation as a hindrance to study and productive labour. Amongst the bourgeoisie there was a developing hostility to the very idea of free time for the labouring classes. There were attempts to regulate leisure and keep holidays to a minimum. Calls were made for tougher laws and magistrates and for the establishment of a police force. This new attack on the people's leisure was reinforced with the authority of religion. The only free time available to working-class men was Sunday. Women, with their responsibility for domestic labour, could not even enjoy this brief respite. The evangelical movement, however, continued the Puritan hostility to pleasure and recreation on the Sabbath by working to restrict greatly the range of activities that were permitted or socially acceptable.

The campaign against cruel sports reached its peak in the early nineteenth century. Even this movement, which clearly had a progressive side, was primarily an attack on the leisure activities of common people. The 1835 Cruelty to Animals

Act outlawed bull- and bear-baiting. Field sports like hunting and shooting remained perfectly acceptable. Indeed the devotion of the aristocracy to their own particular forms of brutality was at a peak. They fought a constant battle to keep 'their' animals from the hands of poachers and trespassers. In this they had much assistance from the law. The use of automatic spring guns to shoot poachers was perfectly legal until 1827. Even after this date poachers could be transported for a third offence. During the early part of the nineteenth century offences under the game laws accounted for a third of all crime.

Renewed attempts were made to suppress popular sports like football and boxing. The evangelical movement continued its hostility to wakes and festivals and particularly to the outrageous spectacle of men and women dancing. The first half of the nineteenth century greatly heightened the distinction between the old aristocracy free to enjoy their sporting pursuits, a new bourgeoisie committed to the single-minded pursuit of profit and the working classes who must be protected from the temptations of leisure and pleasure.

The public schools and the Oxbridge blues

While the proletariat worked and the aristocracy played, a new cult was developing in the public schools of the mid-nineteenth century – the cult of athleticism. A fanatical devotion to sport, and in particular to team games, at public school and university was the crucible that eventually produced the formation of organised sporting institutions in the last quarter of the nineteenth century. The roots of this fanaticism for games lay in the reorganisation of the public schools in the 1840s. By this point the schools had become somewhat anarchic. Indicative of a peculiar combination of self-reliance and internal hierarchy, there was a large degree of self-government by boys, based on prefects and the fagging system. There were elements of a stress on team spirit – an emphasis on group loyalty, conformity and herd instinct – but the traditional pastimes of the aristocratic pupil were, with the exception of cricket, rather individual. Boating, hunting and riding were all popular. There was increasing concern about the degree of anarchy prevailing, the lack of control staff had over pupils and the extensive gambling, cruelty and 'immorality'.

But the schools were beginning to change with the full development of the Victorian middle class. This new wealthy bourgeoisie was anxious to gain social status for its male children through the public schools and it was these children who were to become the most enthusiastic devotees of the new cult for games. Team games were seen as a way of establishing greater social control over the boys' leisure time and also as a means of draining off excess energy and therefore repressing manifestations of developing sexuality. These games were at first introduced only reluctantly by staff but their popularity with the pupils and value in maintaining discipline soon secured them a central place in the curriculum.

A government enquiry into the public schools, the Clarendon Commission of 1861, recognised the value of games for 'character training' and saw cricket and football not just as means of exercise and amusement but also as ways of forming some of the most durable qualities and manly virtues. Games were also seen as a way of preventing immorality, by which they meant homosexuality and masturbation. The concepts of sport as a form of social control, as a way of developing character, as a way of defining masculinity and as a way of repressing sexuality have all left a deep mark on English sport.

The 1860s saw the emergence of the games master and the development of inter-house competition, soon followed by competition between schools. The cult became self-sustaining. Public school games players went on to be university games players and then often returned to teaching, where they played their part in popularising sport, influencing a whole new generation of pupils. This was a time of expansion in the number of public schools and recruitment became important. Extensive facilities for games became an important point of appeal to parents and much money was spent on acquiring and developing playing fields. Games were rapidly becoming more important than study in the schools and it was in this period that the distinction between the sporting philistine and the non-sporting aesthete became marked. There was a growing suspicion of excessive intellectualism and an interest in culture and the arts became regarded as effeminate and unmanly by many in the public school world. Only the games player was truly masculine.

The public school ethos under late Victorian capitalism was an odd amalgam. A tradition of Christian gentility combined with a sport-based concept of masculinity, and a belief that Darwin's 'survival of the fittest' principle applied to the social life as well as to the animal world. An emphasis on success, aggression, ruthlessness and the need for leadership combined with an altruistic courtesy in triumph, compassion to the defeated and stress upon fair play. The public school system had become an important part of the imperialist system as a whole, producing an officer class to rule the empire. Having been schooled in the virtues of sport for instilling discipline and team work, this officer class then spread English team sport, particularly cricket and rugger, throughout the empire.

But as well as an officer class, sent off into the empire convinced of the white man's right to rule, the public schools also produced the muscular Christians, who combined religion and sport, seeing the latter as a way of promoting the Christian ethos. They set out into the world convinced of the importance of sport and the need to spread its values amongst the lower orders. The association of sport and Christianity in this period was strong. During Victoria's reign, of 695 Oxbridge cricket blues, no fewer than 295 became Anglican clergymen. The muscular Christians were influential in the formation of many English football clubs, and in the development of cricket in the late nineteenth century.

Gentlemen and players

This section outlines the formation of the principal institutions of English sport in the last quarter of the nineteenth century. It was the period that saw the domination of sport by a class and by a gender – the men of the Victorian bourgeoisie – enshrined in organisational form. The great myth of English sport is that it was all dreamed up by Victorian gentlemen, drawing upon the noble amateur traditions of ancient Greece. There is very little truth in this notion and it serves only to confuse. England's major sports, athletics, football, cricket, golf, racing and even tennis, were all around in one form or another long before the late nineteenth century. Most of these sports had been engaged in at one time or another by both the upper and the lower classes. There was nothing very noble about the sports of ancient Greece. They were not specifically for the amateur – the Greeks made no distinction between paid and unpaid and many winners received substantial material rewards. They did not believe taking part to be more important than winning. The Greek games excluded women and slaves.

The distinction between the amateur and the professional, such a strong feature of English sport, was basically a Victorian creation and is little more than class distinction in disguised form. The term amateur came originally from early eighteenth-century France, where it meant a connoisseur of the fine arts. By the end of the century it referred to the so-called 'polite' arts of painting and music. By the mid-nineteenth century it was used more broadly to refer to gentlemen of leisure and taste – an amateur was a gentleman. It was in this form that the term first became widely applied in relation to sport.

The growth in public school and university sport and the formation of sport clubs were boosting the extent to which people were prepared to travel for competition. The growth of the railways from the 1840s transformed the nature of sporting competition. Matches between teams from different towns and different regions became much more feasible. But this gave rise to problems over rules. Different areas had evolved different variants of the same game. The need for standardisation emerged first in public school and inter-varsity sport. Standardisation required agreement over rules. But determining agreed rules could not be separated from the social authority to enforce them. It was the men of the public school and university world who, by virtue of their social power and influence, became the prominent figures in the formation of sport institutions.

At this point a distinction should be made. There was a whole set of sports such as athletics, football and rugby, whose governing bodies were formed between 1870 and 1900. In these sports the men of the Victorian bourgeoisie played a dominant role in the foundation of institutions. But some sports such as cricket, golf and racing had already established institutions. The Royal and Ancient Golf Club, the Jockey Club and the Marylebone Cricket Club were all creations of the eighteenth century in which the traditional aristocracy played a greater role. The most distinctive feature of the Victorian developments was the establishment of rigid distinctions between the professional and the amateur. The word amateur was first applied to sport in mid-nineteenth-century rowing. It referred to anyone who was not a waterman or otherwise employed on the water. But it soon became clear that it really referred to gentlemen as opposed to workers. The word was taken up by the Amateur Athletic Club in 1867. Its rules excluded from membership anyone who was a mechanic, an artisan or a labourer. This became a point of conflict within athletics and in sport generally. Battles over who could and could not compete, and to what extent payment should be allowed to compensate for lost earnings while playing sport, were prominent for the next 30 years.

The battle over the amateur/professional distinction was in reality a displaced form of class tension. Almost every sport had to find a way of handling it. Cricket and golf developed separate classes of player: the gentleman and the player, the full member and the artisan. Rugby split into two separate games, while football retained professional and amateur games under the same overall authority. Athletics, swimming and tennis simply outlawed professionalism entirely. Examining this period when institutions were formed and power consolidated reveals much about the variations between England's main sports.

Athletics played a key role in the development of amateurism. Various forms of athletics had existed for several centuries. The rural festivities of the sixteenth and seventeenth centuries featured running races. A tradition of rural athletic meetings in the eighteenth century became particularly strong in the north of England and Scotland with events like the Highland Games and the Border Games. Pedestrianism and the running of head-to-head matches for gambling was well established before the nineteenth century. In the nineteenth century it is known that there were both open professional athletics events, with prizes, and open meetings that were mainly middle-class affairs, with low-value prizes. The amateur concept arrived with public school and Oxbridge participation. A three-way battle developed over the Amateur Athletic Club's controversially explicit exclusion of mechanics, labourers and artisans. The London Athletic Club, which was building a broader lower-middle-class base, was challenging the AAC power over athletics. During the 1870s more working-class-oriented organisations began to emerge in the north. With chaos threatening, three Oxbridge men intervened. The social authority they were a part of enabled them to engineer a compromise. In 1880 the Amateur Athletic Association was formed. The barring of mechanic, artisan and labourer was dropped, but the distinction between amateur and professional became absolute. To compete for money put one forever outside the world of organised athletics. The enshrinement of the distinction between the amateur and the professional meant that gentlemen of leisure had a huge and permanent advantage over those whose work left little time for training and preparation. This proscription of the paid athlete was written into the constitution of sport after sport.

Football handled the class tension in a rather different manner. As a pre-industrial game it had a long chequered history, involving outbreaks of violence, attempts at suppression and the use of matches as a pretext for political agitation. It was more distinctly a people's game in that it never attracted much interest or patronage from the aristocracy. It was traditionally played in informal circumstances with mass participation, few clear rules, vast playing areas, very long games and an absence of referees. This form of football effectively began to die out with the rise of industrialisation, the enclosure of common land and the drift to the towns. While the new urban working class had neither the time nor the space for football, it was taken up by the public schools, where the first attempts to evolve an agreed set of rules took place. Several different forms of the game had developed between 1848 and 1863 and there were attempts centring upon Cambridge to formulate an agreed code. In 1863 the Football Association was formed, largely by ex-public-school men. The FA banned hacking, tripping and running with the ball, which led to the break-away of Blackheath and the emergence of rugby as a distinct game. The amateur dominance of both games was soon challenged by their growing working-class following. Each sport responded differently.

When football emerged from the public schools in its new codified form it rapidly became a highly popular working-class game. While many famous football clubs emerged from institutions like churches and schools, many others grew out of the workplace. Stoke City, Crewe Alexandra and Manchester United were all formed by groups of railway workers. Coventry City emerged from Singer's sewing machine factory, West Ham United from Thames Ironworks, and Arsenal from the Woolwich munitions factory. For its first eleven years from 1872 the FA Cup was dominated by the public school teams. But football was growing rapidly in the industrial midlands and north. It was attracting a large working-class audience and the income from spectators made it possible for the clubs to attract talented players with payments – illegal under the FA rules. Attempts to prevent the development of professionalism were unsuccessful and a showdown came in 1884 with the threat led by Preston to form a break-away organisation. Rather than lose their monopoly control, the FA decided to allow a limited degree of professionalism.

In 1888 the Football League, based on twelve clubs in the midlands and north, was formed. The rise of working-class football contributed to a gradual decline of middle-class interest, and the eclipse of public school teams in the FA Cup after 1882 led to the FA launching a separate cup competition restricted to amateur teams ten years later in 1892. The FA remained the supreme governing body of football but the greater working-class popularity of the game and the compromise with the league over professionalism meant that its control was less total than that of the AAA over athletics. The Football League and the clubs, however, were not controlled by the working class but predominantly by the industrial bourgeoisie. Most professional clubs had had humble origins but the financial base of the game was transformed by football's development as a spectator sport. Professional players were hired, stadiums were developed and the game rapidly became organised along business lines. By the end of the century the majority of clubs had become limited companies owned by their shareholders and controlled by boards of directors.

The emergence of professionalism in *rugby* was handled very differently. Like football, rugby grew rapidly in popularity. The Rugby Football Union was formed in 1871 in a Pall Mall restaurant by 32 clubs. By 1893 there were 481. The popularity of the game amongst the working class in Lancashire and Yorkshire led, as in football, to demands that players be compensated for lost earnings. This demand for broken time payments caused a showdown and in 1895 the northern clubs broke away to form the Northern Union, which in 1922 became the Rugby League. Initially the Northern Union was by no means in favour of complete professionalism. They insisted that players have a job outside rugby as the sport was supposed to be only a pastime, with no real financial reward. The split, which led to the development of two distinctly different games, was to cause a class polarisation. Rugby League remained restricted largely to the north and became as deep-rooted a working-class game as football. Rugby Union became, except in Wales, a sport largely based upon public schools, grammar schools, universities, and old boys' associations. It gradually replaced football as a public school sport, as football became increasingly identified with professionalism and with the proletariat. At the outbreak of the First World War rugby union games were suspended but football continued. Even though football games were used for large-scale recruitment into the imperial army, it became seen by the upper classes as an unpatriotic sport and its social status within the public school world was further diminished.

Sports like football, rugby and athletics acquired governing bodies only in the late nineteenth century. Other sports, such as cricket, golf and racing, had established institutions in the eighteenth century. But these sports were also to be transformed in the period 1875–1900. *Cricket's* supreme authoritative body, the MCC, dates back to 1787. But its control was relatively informal and undefined and the organisation of cricket as we know it today was as much a product of the late Victorian era. Cricket in one form or another had a long history as an informal folk game before being taken up by the aristocracy during the seventeenth century. This had two consequences. First, there was a growth in various forms of rural cricket under aristocratic patronage. Second, cricket became the subject of extensive gambling. The MCC emerged in the eighteenth century as an offshoot of an exclusive gentlemen's club, but cricket continued to be played in a variety of forms, from country houses to village greens. The importance of gambling contributed to the emergence of the first professionals. Upper-class men became keen to boost the chances of their teams by employing talented players.

These cricket professionals were often retained by gentlemen's cricket clubs. As well as providing talent for the club side in competition they were also expected to be on hand to bowl at the members in the nets whenever required. The growth of this possibility of employment in cricket was extended with the emergence in the nineteenth century of a professional touring team. William Clarke's All-England Eleven brought together some of the best professional cricketers and travelled the country playing local sides. Cricket was developing as a spectator sport and beginning to change from a pursuit of the gentry to a national game. The rise of the Victorian bourgeoisie produced a new stratum of country gentleman whose influence on cricket gradually became greater. As in other sports there was a new concern to mark clearly the distinction between the classes. The new county clubs were gradually coming to occupy a central place in the cricketing world. They occupied the middle ground between the populist travelling teams and the elitist country house game. As public interest switched from the touring professional circuses to the new county game, professionals had to come to terms with their new employers. In the last quarter of the century, as the County Championship developed, the authority of the amateur gentlemen over cricket was consolidated.

In this period, the conventions of separating gentlemen and 'players', i.e. professionals, grew into formal rigidity. Amateurs had their own dressing rooms, ate separately and entered grounds by their own gates. Their initials came before their surnames on scorecards, whereas professionals' initials came after. Professionals not only had to bowl at club members in the nets, they also had to help roll out the wicket. Athletics outlawed the professionals and rugby split into two separate games, but cricket contrived to create an internal caste system, echoing the class divisions of society as a whole.

Golf, in its early pre-seventeenth-century forms, was played by all classes of society, by men and women, mainly on the north-east coast of Scotland. During the eighteenth century segregation between three classes of players began to develop. These were the gentlemen of leisure, the artisans and traders, and the professionals – mainly club and ball makers. The development of competition required an agreed set of rules. The Royal and Ancient Club of St Andrews, another exclusive club, gradually became, like the MCC for cricket and the Jockey Club for racing, the recognised authority. At this stage golf was still played on common land and the courses, unlike the clubs, were accessible to all. During the nineteenth century the game spread to England and was taken up increasingly by the middle and upper classes. Tension between the various users of common land grew and the growth of private courses began. The new suburban middle classes were well placed to buy up the large tracts of land required for private golf clubs. Social exclusivity became an important part of the game's appeal. High subscription fees and vetting of potential members kept out the working class.

Some clubs did introduce special category membership for artisans. In exchange for limited access to the course, at hours not popular with full members, artisan members were expected to tend the grounds. They were given wooden huts, carefully hidden away from the opulent club houses that the full members enjoyed. In Scotland golf retained some of its working-class following and courses such as St Andrews, owned by the town, remained open to all. But golf in England rapidly became a badge of social status and a means of making and sustaining business contacts. As in cricket, clubs employed professionals to teach the game to their members. Golf professionals were given the rights to make money selling equipment in the club shop. Socially, however, this marked them as traders, inferior to the club members, and they were treated as such.

Even *boxing*, for a long time the prerogative of lower-class boxers, patronised by the aristocracy, became subject to the reorganising influence of the Victorian bourgeoisie. After a peak of popularity between 1800 and 1825 prize-fighting had been successfully outlawed. Its revival after 1867 was another product of public school and university enthusiasm for sport. The famous Queensberry Rules were in fact drawn up not by the Marquis of Queensberry but by a fellow student, John Chambers. The Marquis was approached to sponsor the rules to ensure their success. Chambers himself was a key figure in the university dominance of sport organisation. As well as devising the Queensberry Rules he rowed in and coached Cambridge boat race teams, staged a Cup Final, and started championships for athletics, cycling, boxing, billiards and wrestling.

The universities and public schools produced in the late nineteenth century a generation of men who played a dominant part in forming the institutions of many sports. But another important source of sport organisation was suburban life. The rapid growth of the cities had led to the development of areas of suburban housing for the affluent upper-middle class. This class developed distinctive forms of leisure. They played an important part in the growth of golf clubs and took up the newer game of tennis with great enthusiasm. The game of Real (or Royal) *tennis* had been popular with the court in the sixteenth century but had virtually died out by the Industrial Revolution. The new game of lawn tennis that developed in the 1870s was a reworked combination of real tennis, rackets and other bat and ball games. It rapidly supplanted croquet as the game to be played on middle-class lawns after lunch. The MCC had some early involvement in forming rules but lawn tennis was soon adopted by the All-England Croquet Club. After the first Wimbledon Championships of 1877, tennis rapidly became the major area of activity and the club changed its name to the All-England Lawn Tennis and Croquet Club in 1884. This club has retained great exclusivity. Together with the Lawn Tennis Association it dominates English tennis, which has consequently become another sport played by all classes but ruled by one.

Racing is another sport in which class relations were firmly inscribed at an early stage. British racing is ruled by the Jockey Club, one of the most exclusive clubs in the country. This self-electing elite of 110 men, answerable to no one, wields absolute power over racing. It controls the activities of trainers and jockeys and operates the system of stewards' enquiries. In the 1500 enquiries held each year, penalties can range from fines and suspensions to the ultimate power to warn off for life – that is, to bar someone permanently from all race tracks.

The most distinctive feature about the ruling of most English sport, however, is the use of a distinction between the amateur and the professional as a means of consolidating class power. The explicit exclusion of artisans in rowing persisted well into the twentieth century. The 1936 Australian Olympic Games team were excluded from Henley because they were policemen and hence artisans. Rugby Union developed 17 pages of stringent rules about amateur status, in which Rugby League players are totally excluded from Rugby Union, even if they are unpaid Rugby League players.

Women, of all classes, encountered a far greater barrier to full involvement in sport than did working-class men. English sport is one of the most distinctly male of all social institutions. Sport has been played more by men, watched more by men, and, crucially, controlled by men. It plays a significant part in the whole cultural image of masculinity. This is not a product of the nature of sport. It is part of a more general pattern in which social power is exerted by men over women. It is also a very specific product of the all-male upper- and middle-class world of the public schools and universities. The key institutions of sport emerged from this all-male world. Just as their organisational rules and underlying assumptions enshrined class dominance, so they also enshrined gender dominance in a lasting structured form.

Women of all classes were distanced from the world of sport, but in rather different ways. The middle of the nineteenth century was a period when leisure for working people was severely limited. But when the struggle of organised labour for shorter hours began to bear fruit after 1860 it was mainly men who benefited. The responsibility placed on women for domestic labour meant that less paid work time in the factory merely made for more unpaid work time in the home. Middle-class women enjoyed the leisure particular to those classes who could afford to employ domestic staff. However, the Victorian conventions held that women were frail, should behave in a ladylike manner and refrain from strenuous physical exercise. Women of the aristocracy were never so confined by the codes of Victorian gentility and had more access to and involvement in sporting pursuits. However, the sporting pursuits of the aristocracy were still very much their traditional pastimes, riding and the other equestrian sports, and the various forms of animal slaughter we call field sports.

For women who were able to overcome the obstacles to involvement in sport in the nineteenth century the next barrier was dress. The conventions of dress carried over on to the sports field. Long heavy skirts were the accepted wear for golf and hockey right into the twentieth century. Tennis was played in tight skirts with trains. The development of women's tees, nearer the hole, in golf was not simply an attempt to mark women's supposed lesser strength. It was also an attempt to discourage women from making full swings, which were seen as unladylike and inconsistent with the accepted full-skirted dress. There is a great irony here. The development of that symbol of masculine aggression, overarm bowling, has been widely attributed to women cricketers – the full skirts they wore made the conventional underarm bowling difficult.

The Rational Dress Society fought for more sensible clothing for women, both for sport and for everyday life. They commented in 1887 that the present style of dress made it impossible for women to walk properly. Their efforts were boosted by the spread of cycling as a popular pastime between 1890 and 1914. The popularity of cycling with women led to forms of dress that were less physically restricting. Early attempts to develop physical education for women had to struggle against unsuitable conventions of dress. The Bergman Osterberg Physical Training College pioneered women's physical education in this country. They developed the gym tunic and forbade corsets but had only partial success in changing accepted sporting dress. In 1912 the England hockey captain was ordered to lengthen her skirt. Ladylike respectability was still more important than freedom of movement.

Real changes in women's sporting dress did not come until after the First World War. The breakdown of Edwardian respectability and a transformation of social manners and morals meant women's clothes generally changed. In sport the popular successes of the athletic tennis star Suzanne Lenglen had a major influence. Her skirt, reaching just below the knee, was considered daring, but it soon became the accepted form of dress for tennis and ankle-length skirts became a thing of the past. Suzanne Lenglen is recalled in traditional histories more for this revolution in dress than for her tennis success. This is typical of the treatment of women's sport as peripheral and trivial.

Unsuitable dress was only the first obstacle. A larger problem was presented by male control of almost all sport institutions and the dominant feeling within these institutions was that women's sport was not something to be encouraged. The AAA was and is men only and wanted nothing to do with women's athletics. It was only in 1922 that a Women's Amateur Athletic Association was formed. The Baron de Coubertin, one of the founders of the modern Olympic Games, was shocked by the sight of lightly clad women engaged in strenuous activity. He felt their only role should be to crown the winner. Women were not allowed to compete in the Olympics until 1928. But the sight of exhausted women crossing the line at the end of the 800 metres was too much for the sensitive male souls of the IOC. Women were not allowed to run this length again until 1960.

Despite the many barriers women did achieve success in the early days of sport, even though their achievements were often hidden from history. One of the first famous woman athletes was tennis player Lottie Dod. She introduced speed, attacking net play and the smash to women's tennis. She first won Wimbledon in 1887 when she was 15 and won it four more times in the next six years. She never lost at Wimbledon and is believed to have lost only four matches in her entire tennis career. At 21 she gave up tennis for golf and won the English championships. She was a first-class archer, an international hockey player and also an ice skater. However, despite such achievements women's sport was still generally treated by the governing bodies and the press as a diversion, an inferior imitation of the real thing.

This chapter has outlined the way in which the institutions of sport were formed. The crucial feature was the rise of the bourgeoisie to a position of social authority in the nineteenth century. In the world of sport this enabled it to assume positions of power and influence in the governing bodies of most major sports. The rigid distinctions erected between the amateur and the professional were in the end rooted in class domination. The formation of these institutions on the base of public school and university sport made them also an expression of the domination of social life by men. This does not mean that no women or working-class people were involved in sport during this period. But such involvement was always within the bounds of authority exercised by the men of the bourgeoisie.

2.4 Playing under capitalism

In the last 60 years sport has grown into an international spectacle and a multi-million-pound business. This chapter examines the growth of that spectacle, the degree to which dominant sporting values have been resisted and the continuing resilience of popular forms of recreation. The first section traces the emergence of spectator sport and the growth of spectacle. The spreading of television to almost every home and the consequent economic transformation of sport by sponsorship is a central part of the process. The second section examines different ways in which the power of the dominant authorities to define and control sport has been challenged. Labour relations, the workers' sport movements of the inter-war years, and women's sport can all be seen as attempts to challenge dominant assumptions, not always successfully. The final section looks more closely at forms of popular recreation. Shaped as they are by the leisure industry, available facilities, accepted conventions of behaviour and by people's attempts to shape and control, within very different limits, their own lives, forms of popular recreation are bound to be contradictory.

Spectacle

Spectator sport

Between 1880 and 1939 sports rapidly developed as spectator sports with large popular appeal. The foundations of the mass spectacle, which has become the focus of much television coverage, were laid. The crowd appeal of many sports was realised and the process of paying admission formalised. With the growth of regular competition a fixture list was assured and the habit of spectatorship given a structure. The distinct separation of players and supporters helped give rise to a whole new culture surrounding sport – a fan culture in which stars developed. The emergence of a large-scale mass-circulation popular press, the spread of comics, the growth of working-class literacy and the later emergence of broadcasting all contributed to this emergent sporting culture. Massively supported rituals like the Cup Final became firmly established in public life.

Once national sport was established, international sport soon began to develop. The first modern Olympics had been held in 1896 but the real basis for international competition was laid in the twentieth century. By 1915 international bodies had been established for cricket, football, tennis and athletics. Sport spread out along the network of empire. International sport developed almost as a form of diplomacy, maintaining contact with friendly nations. It soon became a symbol of national virility to be successful at sport.

Spectating was not a new phenomenon. There had been a long tradition of large crowds gathering for sporting events before the 1880s. In the eighteenth century crowds of up to 10,000 were known to watch cricket at the Artillery grounds in Finsbury Park and crowds of 20,000 had been drawn to the Cotswold Games. In the early part of the nineteenth century, prize-fighting could draw 20,000 people to bouts. Pedestrianism was regularly watched by ten thousand or more. Racing, too, was popular. In 1824 17,000 paid to see a game of cricket at Sheffield.

But it was only towards the end of the nineteenth century, after the formation of sport institutions, the inauguration of nationally based competitions and the establishment of fixture lists, that spectator sport became an organised and regular feature of social life. The Football Association Cup Final, started in 1872, was watched by 2,000. By 1893 the crowd was 45,000 and by 1913 a phenomenal 120,000 crowded into Crystal Palace to see the match. From 1923 the competition found its permanent home at Wembley and an annual crowd of 120,000. (In the first famous Wembley final, over twice this many gained entry, many by climbing the walls.) Cricket's County Championship began in 1873 and after reorganisation in 1895 built its own regular audience. Athletics was slower to develop but began a boom after the First World War with crowds of 30,000 for the AAA Championships, in those days held at Stamford Bridge.

The inter-war period saw the emergence of new sports and the continued popularity of older ones. The popularity of the athletic French tennis player, Suzanne Lenglen, contributed to a growth in women's sport. Rowing, cycling, swimming and running were taken up by women in greater numbers. Gambling was becoming a major feature of working-class life, in increasingly organised forms. The popularity of horse-racing was supplemented by the introduction of greyhound-racing in the 1920s and the massive growth of football pools in the 1930s. The Betting Act of 1928 introduced the Racecourse Betting Control Board and the Totalisator. In the following year £230 million was gambled on the horses, not including the incalculable millions that changed hands in illegal off-course betting. Greyhound-racing was introduced in 1926 and by 1932 there were 187 tracks with annual attendances of around 18 million. Motorised sports introduced before the First World War continued to develop, although participation was largely restricted to the socially privileged. Dirt-track motor-bike racing was introduced from the USA in the 1920s and soon won a large working-class following.

Along with the growth in spectatorship went the development of a culture of sport on a large scale. The growth of the distinction between spectators and players and the development of full-time sport, whether played by professionals or amateurs, encouraged the emergence of star teams and individuals. The popular press, particularly after the First World War, began to devote increasing space to sport. When the BBC became a public corporation in 1927 it began to broadcast running commentaries on sporting events. For the first time major occasions like Cup Finals and test matches, and the exploits of star names who played in them, were relayed direct into the home. A whole range of comics and specialist magazines helped foster the growth of stardom as did the massively popular cigarette cards. Top sports people were household names as never before.

Sport, in becoming successful, had adopted regular formats, rationalised its organisation, evolved a form of division of labour and a dependence upon cash flow. In short, it had many of the features of any capitalist enterprise. Yet for the most part it was still organised as if it was a hobby. Athletics was run largely by spare-time voluntary effort. Tennis, cricket and golf were all based largely upon networks of membership clubs. Even football, that most successful of sporting enterprises, was not really run as a conventional business. Only the larger and more successful clubs had any real profit potential. There was a constant pressure for reinvestment not just in ground facilities but in that most intangible of assets, playing staff. Restrictions were imposed, by the Football League, on the payment of dividends to shareholders. Crucially the structure of football club ownership had not grown primarily out of the desire for profits. Football club owners were more interested in power and prestige in the community. Football was a way of becoming known and sustaining business contacts. Added to this was the desire to pursue schoolboy hobbies into adulthood.

English sport in general was dominated by a form of part-time amateur paternalism. This form of organisation was not without some positive features, despite its general anti-democratic character. It did ensure that money remained within sport rather than being reinvested outside it. This was important as the financial base of even the most popular sports had always been insecure. The governing bodies of many sports had mechanisms by which finance was diverted to the more impoverished parts of the game. The Football League system, for example, takes a levy of all gate money which is then distributed amongst the 92 clubs. In effect this means money goes from the more successful first division clubs to support the others. The main merit of this system is that it sustains and subsidises first-class football in areas that otherwise could not support a league team. Similarly the small clubs in many sports have depended upon money being diverted to them from more successful ventures. The power of governing authorities of sports has in the past meant that limited financial resources can be shared out fairly, although this is not always done.

This form of paternalist voluntary organisation was to become increasingly vulnerable after the Second World War. The rise of television turned sport into a whole new cultural form, with extensive marketing potential. Yet this process happened as sport itself was coming under increasing financial pressure. In the last 20 years the allied force of television and sponsorship has transformed sport and in the process undermined the lower of its traditional authorities.

Armchair viewing

Sport has always occupied an important space within the world of television. The BBC in particular has prided itself on its sports coverage, which provides an important element of its corporate prestige. Sport reaches a much greater audience via the screen than it ever has reached in the stadium. Nowadays, for most people most of the time, sport means television sport. The beginnings were slow. Britain's television service was fully launched in 1946. The pre-war experiments with television never reached more than about 20,000 sets. After the war the cost of sets was still high, and in the period of post-war austerity people were reluctant to buy them. Even by 1950 the new television service was still reaching only 340,000 homes. In the early 1950s, however, the growth in people's disposable income boosted set sales and by 1954 television had reached 3,250,000.

The arrival of commercial television in 1955 gave another impetus. The BBC was given a second channel in 1964 and both BBC and ITV introduced colour in the late 1960s. By 1968 over 90 per cent of homes had television. In 20 years television had gone from being the luxury commodity of a small elite to being the principal leisure activity for most of the population. Sport had been important to the BBC even in pre-television days. Radio commentaries brought sporting events into the home. The prominence of events like the Cup Final, the Boat Race, Wimbledon, the test matches and Rugby Union internationals had been enhanced by the attention given to them by the BBC. Television soon gave sport the same degree of attention. Sport offered a source of programming that was potentially both cheap and popular. In the late 1940s the BBC succeeded in getting coverage of many events simply by paying a facility fee of £25. Even by 1952 few events cost the BBC more than £250 to obtain. Sport authorities spent a lot of time worrying about the possible adverse effect of television coverage on live attendances and were slow to see the financial possibilities of television fees.

The imminent arrival of ITV was not taken seriously in many parts of the BBC, whose attitude was one of aloof superiority. The Outside Broadcast department were rather more alive to the threat of competition. Fees rose as the BBC set about securing their sport coverage by signing long-term agreements with a number of sport organisations. So ITV started with a number of disadvantages. The BBC had the contacts, the contracts and the technical expertise. ITV's system of separate regional companies meant that no single company could maintain extensive outside broadcast facilities. Coordination was hampered by the lukewarm attitude of some ITV chiefs to the audience potential of sport.

For many years the BBC held the initiative, even though ITV did compete over Wimbledon coverage with some success in the late 1950s. The BBC's dominance was reinforced by a government agreement that neither channel could obtain an exclusive coverage of six so-called 'national' events (the Cup Final, Wimbledon tennis, the Boat Race, the Derby, the Grand National and test matches). It was hard for ITV, hampered by regular ad breaks, to win audiences if both channels showed an event. The ITV companies soon realised that, with the exception of the Cup Final, if they could not have an exclusive deal the events were not worth covering. The gaining of a second channel gave the BBC an even greater advantage, enabling it to cover Wimbledon and test matches from start to finish. Sport was finding its fixed places on Saturday afternoon and Wednesday night. Regular Saturday night football soon became popular.

Sport, however, occupies an unusual place in the television schedules. While sport is quite popular it is rarely popular enough to be scheduled at peak viewing times. This is partly because it is less successful than other types of programme in gaining women viewers. So the regular sport programmes, *Grandstand* and *World of Sport*, *Sportsnight* and *Midweek Sport Special*, *Match of the Day*, *The Big Match* and the other football programmes, are all outside, or at best on the edge of, peak viewing time. But the picture is transformed at times of major events. The World Cup, the Olympic Games and the World Snooker Championships have an almost unique ability to win and hold huge audiences. These events also have a totally unique ability to hold large audiences at off-peak hours or late at night. So, during these major events, the regular schedules are torn apart to make way for liberal doses of sport.

Television has made watching sport a new form of shared national ritual. Over half the country watch the Cup Final. While the 1950s saw the Boat Race, the Cup Final and Wimbledon become national events in a new sense, the 1960s saw the growth of sport as a global spectacle. Developments in television and satellite technology gradually made it possible to relay an event in any part of the world live to every other part. The Apollo moon shots, American presidential elections, Olympic Games and World Cups have all been beamed around the world. Football matches in the 1978 Argentine World Cup were timed to fit peak viewing-time television in Europe. Major sport events have become subject to complex financial relations between multinational communications consortia. The development of elaborate television technology has great merits. Watching high-definition colour pictures of a live sporting event can be great fun. Merely adopting an attitude of puritan hostility would be silly. But television undoubtedly produces a very particular way of looking at sport. Because it reaches so many and because, along with sponsorship, it is also of great financial importance to sport, it has changed the nature of sport itself.

Television is, for better or worse, a mass medium. The bulk of its costs are in production rather than distribution. The real expense is in making the programme. Once made, it costs no more to send a programme to 40 million people than to 40,000. So there are great pressures to maximise the audience. With sport coverage, programme-makers are not primarily worried about sport fans. They will watch anyway. The audience they are most anxious about, most keen to appeal to, is the peripheral one. They want the programmes to appeal to people who are not sport addicts but will watch a sport programme if it promises to be entertaining. Sport fans also like entertainment, but the traditional characteristic of entertainment in sport is that it is uncertain and unpredictable. No promoter can guarantee an exciting match. The crowd would not expect this. The uncertainty of the entertainment value is what has distinguished sport from show business. But television needs to minimise this uncertainty. In order to hold the marginal audience it needs to be able to deliver entertainment even if the raw material is not promising. A striking feature of sport coverage is the time devoted to previews, post-mortems, interviews, discussion and action replays, as opposed to direct coverage of the event itself. If the match is bad maybe the amusing banter of the experts can placate us. If there are no goals, they will show us last week's goals again.

Television does not simply relay sport to us. It presents a particular view of sport, framed by its own selection of shots and the addition of its own commentary. It is a particular view, inviting us to look at events in a particular way. The attempt to reach, through entertainment values, a large audience means a constant attempt to forge links with that audience, to establish points of identification. So the coverage attempts constantly to engage our involvement in the stories of sport with endless speculation about what might happen and who will win. The focal point of these stories are the star characters with whom we are instantly familiar, thanks to frequent interviews and close-ups during the action. Our understanding of the action itself is rooted in the star system. The World Cup coverage told us a lot about the stars to look for in the teams of, say, Italy and Brazil. It did very little to explain the differences in style between the two as teams.

Television has constantly to distinguish between sporting events of greater and lesser importance. It has evolved a calendar of major events, repeated year after year, offered to us as the peak moments of the sporting calendar. Yet it is a very particular selection. Some events, such as the Boat Race, or Rugby Union internationals, have a prominence much greater than their public following would seem to warrant. Other highly popular sports such as cycling, swimming, netball, speedway and greyhound-racing get very little exposure. Television's selection is not, however, simply a result of the class background of its producers. The need to develop sports that work as small-screen entertainment is an important pressure. Television turned the obscure upper-class pursuit of show-jumping into a big audience winner. But it has done the same with darts and snooker, more working-class-based sports. Sports like squash and angling, on the other hand, have defied successful television. Television priorities constantly suggest to us that some sports are more important than others. Men's events are also constantly marked as being more important than women's. In tennis, athletics and swimming it is always the male events that come to occupy the central place. In the few sports where a greater focus is placed upon women, such as gymnastics and skating, television tends to emphasise the supposed 'aesthetic' qualities of grace, poise, elegance and timing. These sports are regarded as more 'feminine' and so women's participation is more acceptable. Even the values and qualities regarded as important in performers represent a particular way of seeing the world. There is a tendency to lay greater stress on the need for toughness, aggression and courage, as opposed to, say, balance, timing and dexterity. These attitudes are not peculiar to television. But in constantly relaying and reproducing them television perpetuates dominant gender stereotypes that serve to oppress women.

Television also directs our attention firmly towards British, or ideally English, involvement in sport. National events are given prime importance and victory is treated as a vital matter. Judgements constantly evoke national stereotypes – the Latins are fiery and temperamental, the Germans are efficient but cold and calculating, and so on. Somehow, though, the other nations never quite manage that perfect blend of skill and commitment captured by the bulldog breed of the Brits. It is our boys (and it usually is boys rather than girls) who are prepared to do it all, run and run and play from the heart. We admire the skills of the French and the Brazilians but when it's backs-to-the-wall time there's no substitute for work-rate. Television, then, does not simply show sport. It shows it in a particular way. It relates events as stories with star characters. It re-presents sport as spectacular entertainment. The underlying values reproduce stereotypical attitudes of men and women, of Britishness and of foreigners.

Most of us spend a large proportion of our leisure time watching television. Sport coverage occupies as much as a sixth of air time. So the way that television shows sport probably plays a part in shaping the way that we see and understand the world. It has certainly helped to change the face of sport. This is not simply because it pays money for coverage that most sports are glad to receive. Much larger sums are available in sponsorship money. Companies are keen to sponsor events that are televised. So a whole range of sports have been prepared to change the form of events to make them more attractive to television. The next section will outline the growth of sponsorship.

Pay up and play the game

The post-war period saw a substantial expansion of the leisure industry. Television became universal and the single most popular leisure activity. The record industry launched the long-playing record and the stereo hi-fi became an everyday device. Car ownership rose dramatically and mobility increased. Ordinary working people became able to take holidays abroad. Traditional sports began to lose popularity to newer diversions. Their organisations, dominated by an amateur paternalist approach, were slow to respond and failed to take decisive action. Change has instead been forced on the sports world by pressure from business interests who have been quicker to spot commercial potential. By the start of the 1960s several sports were in a poor state. Football had lost crowds all through the 1950s. Cricket was in a financial mess stemming from the steady decline in three-day county match receipts. Athletics was at the beginning of a decline in attendance that continued through to the 1960s. The popularity of Wimbledon was being undermined by the defection of many top stars to professional tennis. Only golf was relatively well off, benefiting from the adoption of the game by the upwardly mobile.

At the same time, thanks to television and the growth of international sport, top stars were better known than ever before. Opportunities to cash in on fame by grabbing lucrative fringe earnings were growing. In the 1950s a top footballer thought himself lucky to get the odd Brylcreem ad. Come the 1970s top footballers would need agents, tax consultants and offshore companies to handle their earnings. The last 20 years have seen a second transformation of sport in this country, as dramatic as that between 1870 and 1900. The economy was at first relatively buoyant, the leisure market in particular was growing, expenditure on advertising and promotion was rising and the spread of television had brought sport to a much wider audience. The traditional forms of sport organisation faced crisis. Their power and authority was threatened by economic forces they seemed unable to come to terms with.

Individual entrepreneurs like Jack Kramer, Mark McCormack and, in the 1970s, Kerry Packer picked upon the potential of the star system. Jack Kramer set up a professional travelling circus of tennis players in the 1950s. Top stars began to regard Wimbledon as a stepping-stone to a professional contract. Mark McCormack saw the promotional value of a sporting image. He made Arnold Palmer a millionaire by lending his name to sport clothes and golf equipment. These fringe earnings rivalled the prize money Palmer made from playing the game. McCormack turned his three golf clients – Palmer, Nicklaus and Player – into global stars. He devised his own tournaments, set up matches staged especially for the television cameras and became the dominant figure in world golf. His organisation, International Management Group, comprises several companies including Trans World International, which produces pseudo sports programmes like *Superstars*. He employs hundreds of people in several countries, handling stars from various sports. Recently he has begun moving into athletics in anticipation of professionalisation.

Kerry Packer's involvement in cricket was a more pragmatic venture. He wanted the exclusive television rights for test cricket in Australia for his own television channel. When the cricket authorities refused, he set about signing up dozens of leading world cricketers and presented his alternative test series, in competition with the official one. The cricket establishment was shocked to the roots. Cricketers in pink and blue flannels, white cricket balls, matches played under floodlights and on-pitch microphones were seen as an affront to tradition. After stormy battles – in and out of the courts – Packer got his television contract and wound up his cricket circus.

The economic forces represented by these brash entrepreneurs put the traditional sport authorities under considerable pressure. In particular the old hypocrisy of the amateur/professional division reached a crisis point. Cricket had abandoned the last vestiges of formal distinction between gentlemen and players in 1962. Tennis went open in 1967. Athletics has fought a rearguard action but it is now generally accepted that open athletics is the only way that the traditional authorities can retain control of the sport. There is already a lucrative professional road-running scene in the USA. The economic basis of sport organisation was changing dramatically. Sports have six main sources of revenue: admission receipts, advertising, sponsorship, television fees, membership fees and fund-raising. (Football clubs can also make money from the trade in human beings called the transfer system.)

In the 1960s sponsorship began to grow as a source of finance. In the 1970s it rocketed to massive proportions. Sport sponsorship was not a totally new phenomenon. As early as 1908 Oxo had the marathon catering franchise for the London Olympics, and gave every runner an Oxo Athletes' Pack, with samples of their product. The *News of the World* had sponsored athletics events for some years. But sponsorship money was not a major source of revenue for any sport. The first catalyst to growth came with the banning of cigarette advertising on television in 1965. Tobacco companies gradually realised that sport provided an alternative route to the screen. In 1966 less than £1 million went to sponsor sport events. By 1970 it was between three and five million pounds. The real boom then began. Sponsorship shot to £30 million by 1978. The tobacco companies have recently been joined by the finance houses and insurance firms like Cornhill and Prudential. Cornhill's banners appeared 7,459 times on television in 1981 as a result of cricket sponsorship. Its awareness level (the number of people who mentioned Cornhill when asked to name all the insurance firms they could think of) jumped from 2 per cent in 1977 to 17 per cent in 1981.

Cricket, racing, motor sport, athletics and golf became major beneficiaries of the sponsorship boom. Football held out for a long time, hoping for a huge offer for its major competitions. Eventually in 1982 the League Cup became the Milk

Cup. The new television sports like snooker and darts have attracted extensive sponsorship. Some tennis tournaments have benefited but Wimbledon continues to stand aloof. The All-England club, sustained by Wimbledon fortnight's mammoth income, is one of the few sport organisations that can afford to resist sponsorship. Sponsorship money, then, has become a large and tempting carrot for sport to nibble at. But though there is a lot of sponsorship money available, there are also a lot of sports trying to get hold of it. Around 90 sports in this country battle for a share.

Obtaining television coverage is a crucial part of this battle. Some sponsorship money does go to non-televised events. Coca-Cola sponsor grassroots swimming, Pernod sponsor petanque in an attempt to launch both game and drink in Britain and show-jumping can lure sponsors with its up-market following. But for the most part the large sponsorship sums go to events that are televised. This places television in a very powerful position. There are a few sports that are too popular for television to ignore – cricket, football, tennis, racing, golf and athletics, for example. These sports (with the exception of cricket) can hope that bidding between channels will make television fees worth having, even if not as high as they would like. As for the rest, television can pick and choose. There are maybe 90 sports that would love some television coverage. With only three real outlets, BBC, ITV and Channel Four, it is very much a buyer's market. If bowls authorities demand too high a fee, television will happily drop it and try table tennis instead.

So television gets much sport very cheaply. Sports are desperate to get coverage, not for the television fee, but because it opens up the possibility of sponsorship money. In order to get coverage a sport must offer something that will provide television entertainment. For many sports this has meant changes in rules, style and presentation. The growth of one-day cricket is just the tip of the iceberg. The changing face of sport is due in equal part to the growth of television and the increased penetration of sport by capital. Sport has become an important aspect of advertising, promotion and marketing, and hence questions of image have become central. Few sports have remained untouched by these pressures.

Since the introduction of the Gillette Cup in 1963, the one-day match has become a central part of cricket. Many argue that the standard of cricket has been adversely affected by the one-day game but its popularity with the crowd, the sponsors and with television make it vital financially. Athletics events are increasingly dominated by the pressure to present an array of stars and records. The public, reared on television, needs a Coe, an Ovett or an Alan Wells to lure it to the stadium. Once the spectators are there, promoters feel obliged to offer the sight of records tumbling, even if it means staging obscure and rarely run races such as the 4 × 800 metres relay featured at Crystal Palace in 1982. The fickleness of sponsors has placed the sport in a state of perpetual uncertainty. The AAA centenary year was marred by the sudden withdrawal of the

Championships sponsor, Nationwide, prompting a rush to find a replacement for the following year. Television's particular focus on track events and in particular the short middle-distance races is changing the form of athletics meetings. Televised events now rarely feature a 10,000 metres and sometimes not even a 5,000 metres. One wonders how a future David Bedford or Brendan Foster can emerge with no races to run. As in many sports, deals over brands of equipment are beginning to affect even the result of competitions. Poland banned their own crack high jumper Wzola from the 1982 European championships because he refused to wear the official brand of shoe. Britain's Steve Cram also had a row with officials during the championships when he refused to wear the official British shirt, which he found too hot.

Football has plunged on into deeper crisis pursuing the mythical family audience (a code word for middle-class consumers) with all-seated stadiums and executive boxes. The clothing firm Admiral changed the traditional football strips of many famous teams so that they could sell the new football strips in the latest colours to parents of boy footballers at inflated prices. Leading football clubs continue to pressure the BBC to allow shirt advertisements. Liverpool get £50,000 per year for selling their shirt fronts. Being allowed to wear adverts on television would triple this sum. Meanwhile Jimmy Hill continues to press for modifications to make the game more entertaining. The League decided not to outlaw the pass back to the goalkeeper, but have tried to clamp down on the professional foul. The main result is that during autumn 1982 so many were sent off that football looked like becoming a ten-a-side game.

Tennis has been transformed by the growth of the international circuit. With around 90 tournaments a year worldwide there is too much money chasing too few stars. In this sporting inflation the status of events becomes increasingly unclear. Is Lendl the true champ if Connors and McEnroe miss the tournament to play a lucrative, if leisurely, exhibition match elsewhere? Even the top events are being transformed to suit television. In the US Championships many matches, including the men's final, have been played at night under floodlights. This is ideal for peak-time television, though the tennis may suffer somewhat. The 1979 Tournament of Champions Final in New York between McEnroe and Gerulaitis was played out in rain to fulfil a contract with NBC. Tennis, like athletics, has seen a decline in competition between nations. Top stars are often reluctant to play in the Davis Cup when there are richer pickings elsewhere.

Sport has become in the last 20 years both a part of the world of television spectacle and a branch of the advertising industry. The star system dominates sport. The danger is that the more attention, exposure and money that are concentrated at the very top of the pyramid, the more impoverished, drained and sterile the lower levels become. When a mixed doubles between two couples (Chris Evert and John Lloyd v. Bjorn and Marianna Borg) staged in a tent in

Battersea Park can be labelled the Love Match and sold to television all over the world for vast fees, the sports scene seems to have been reduced to absurdity.

Resistances and alternatives

The development of international competition, the growth of sport as television spectacle and penetration by advertising and promotion have not encountered much resistance. Nor have clear alternative directions emerged. But certain aspects of the dominant power and values of the sport system have been challenged. The organisation of labour in sport is often primitive and inadequate but from time to time has attempted to challenge the power of the authorities. The workers' sport movement between the wars began developing an alternative sport system. The rise of women's sport has confronted the dominance of male-centred values in the sport world.

Labour

Like any form of productive human activity sport depends ultimately upon the employment of human labour, although not necessarily waged labour. The main features of labour in sport have been an advanced division of labour with the maintenance of rigid hierarchies and extensive use of cheap, casual and voluntary workers. Union organisation has in general been undeveloped, halfhearted, ineffectual or simply non-existent. The commercialisation of the last 20 years has given greater power to the top elite of star performers, without having much effect on others lower down. Most sports have featured a highly developed division of labour from the early days. There are owners, bosses, workers of varying levels of skill, casual labour and voluntary unpaid labour. The power of ownership is important to most sports, whether based on the board of directors as in football, ownership of horses, stables and facilities as in racing, or control over access to stadiums as in boxing. A lower level of labour carries out the owners' intentions by controlling the workforce. Managers in football, trainers in racing, committees and officials in many other sports control the nature of the performance.

The most prominent level of workers are the players. Their work is central to the sport as a commodity – it is their performance that attracts the public and the television companies, their labour that makes the economic system of sport possible. Only in a few sports are the players employed as wage labour in the normal sense. Football and cricket are the main examples. In sports like tennis and golf players compete to win prize money. Boxers negotiate fees for particular fights. Athletes are officially amateur and unpaid, but top athletes can receive large sums in illicit payments for appearances.

Most sports have a stratum of apprentices – people who are learning the trade. Like that of most apprentices their labour is particularly exploited. They are paid low wages and expected to do all sorts of menial tasks with no real relevance to the learning of skills. Apprentices in football are often expected to clean boots and dressing rooms and help out in ground repairs. There are no employment guarantees. Young footballers who fail to make the grade often find themselves on the street in their twenties with no qualifications and dismal job prospects. Most sports also depend on layers of back-up work – ground maintenance, upkeep of pitches, courts or courses, administration and office staff. Occupations filled by those hoping to make it as performers – gym staff, handlers and sparring partners in boxing, stable lads in racing – are often particularly open to exploitation.

Much of this labour is casual. Sports stadiums depend on vast crews of doorkeepers, programme sellers and stewards, who cannot be employed on a regular basis. A great deal of labour in sport is voluntary. The amateur tradition and shortage of money in many sports caused a dependence upon voluntary work. But even more financially secure sports, such as football and cricket, have often been able to rely on extensive assistance from supporters' clubs and members in providing stewards and help with cleaning and maintaining grounds. Officials also work on a generally casual and often voluntary basis. Referees, umpires, ball boys and girls and line judges all perform crucial sport labour. Athletics has a particular dependence on voluntary officials.

The hierarchies in this world have often been maintained in a very rigid form. An old phrase in football holds that 'Directors direct, managers manage and players bloody well play'. Rows between players and authorities are common. The growth in the economic earning power of top players and the increased importance of sponsors and agents have only heightened these tensions, as the traditional authorities of sport find themselves undermined from both sides.

Union organisation in sport has never been strong. The voluntary and amateur tradition and the high degree of casualisation, the organisation of sport in small units, the dominance of individualism and the degree to which players have to compete with each other to advance their careers do not encourage union organisation. As far as players themselves are concerned, it is not surprising that football, the most fully professional sport and the one with strongest working-class roots, should have the most developed union organisation in sport. Professional footballers first formed a union in 1898 but had to struggle for ten years to gain recognition. In 1909 the union affiliated to the Federation of Trade Unions and the Football Association immediately withdrew recognition, threatening life suspension of its members. The union called a strike which eventually collapsed despite some militant players going 14 weeks without pay, and it was forced to withdraw from the federation. In 1912 the union lost another battle in the courts when it contested the high transfer fee being demanded for an Aston Villa player. Its contention that the fee was preventing the player from moving to another club was rejected by the judge, who awarded Villa costs. The lack of effective union power meant that, soon after the First World War, the Football League was able to reduce the maximum wage from £9 to £8 a week.

After the Second World War, the Players' Union began to step up its campaign against the maximum wage and the retain and transfer system which gave clubs power to retain players against their will. A National Arbitration Tribunal in 1947 made some minor reforms and set up a joint standing committee with representatives of the Football League, Football Association and Players' Union. It recommended an increase in wage and bonus rates but once again rejected the union's main demands for abolition of the maximum wage and freedom of movement for players. Internal struggles within the union led to changes at the top. Jimmy Hill took over the chair from Jimmy Guthrie. The union became the Professional Footballers' Association and entered its most successful phase. Pressure on the maximum wage grew, culminating in the threatened strike in 1960. After long negotiations the authorities conceded defeat and the maximum wage was abolished.

The battle over the retain and transfer system eventually reached the courts in the famous Eastham case. In 1960 the Newcastle United forward George Eastham asked to be put on the transfer list and his request was rejected by the club. He appealed to the Football League, which ruled that it was a matter between the player and the club. Eastham refused to play for Newcastle and continued to fight, issuing a writ alleging that the club was depriving him of his right to earn a living at football. By the time the case reached the courts in 1963 Newcastle had backed down and Eastham had been transferred to Arsenal. Justice Wilberforce ruled that the rules of the Football League and the regulations of the Football Association concerning the retain and transfer system were an unreasonable restraint of trade. They were not actually illegal, but *ultra vires* – outside the law – and therefore were not legally binding.

This made some reform essential. The football authorities continued to resist complete freedom of contract and instead established an option system. This meant that the club had the option of renewing a contract but at the end of the second contractual period the player had the option of signing a new one or moving on at an agreed fee. The Professional Footballers' Association has continued to press for greater contractual freedom but never with the militant commitment that swept away the maximum wage system. The increased international mobility of top players in the 1970s has placed the system under further strain. The old monopoly power of the English football authorities has been undermined by the lucrative financial opportunities for players in Europe and in the United States.

The first attempt at organisation in cricket was made by a group of Nottinghamshire professionals in 1881. They demanded a formal contract of employment and the right to organise their own matches. The county refused, dropped the cricketers involved and thereby lost that year's championship. Cricketers never developed the same degree of organisation as footballers. This is partly because the game is less rooted in the working class, but more crucially because the workforce has an unusual composition – part amateur, part professional. This always left the professionals in a weak position.

The individual sports such as boxing, golf and racing have not developed organisations of a trade-union type. In amateur sports like athletics, there is no wage relation in any normal sense. There is no real contract or agreement over the labour of athletes. This has increasingly led to friction between the authorities and top athletes. As the authorities are not in any sense employers they have no real power to force athletes to compete. So they cannot guarantee to sponsors that stars will turn up.

In the last 20 years the top stars in a number of sports have become more powerful as their status has increased. But players' organisations are now more often like professional associations than trade unions. They are efficient at protecting the interests of the elite but usually lack the total commitment to solidarity needed to fight for better conditions at all levels of the hierarchy. In tennis and golf, organisations of professional players have gained a significant degree of control over the game at the highest level. Women tennis players have found greater need for solidarity in their attempts to get a more equitable share of available prize money. Organisation in both these sports is dominated by top American stars. In this country top cricketers secured a substantially better deal in the wake of the Packer affair when it was realised that the only way to ward off another Packer-style assault on test cricket was to increase players' earnings. But it was mainly the test players who benefited. The ordinary county cricketer does not earn much above the average industrial wage. (People in sport have a very short effective working life. Apart from snooker players, careers are generally over by the age of 40.)

Top athletes are organised together in the International Athletes' Club. Athletics is in a state of transition, with widespread undercover payments and open athletics just around the corner. The athletics meeting sponsored by Coca-Cola and organised by the IAC is generally the most star-studded and usually the most successful of the British season and this could be taken as an indication of the potential power of the top athletes. Certainly the traditional athletics authorities are in the midst of crisis. The commercialisation of sport in the last 20 years has encouraged an individualised attitude to contracts. Top stars and their agents can negotiate huge earnings from a position of strength whilst people in the lower levels of sport are hard pressed to protect their basic interests. In particular the conditions of behind-the-scenes work essential to most sport remains generally poor and exploitative.

Workers' sport

One alternative to large-scale professionalised spectacle is suggested by the workers' sport movement. These organisations developed as deliberate alternatives to bourgeois dominance of sport and gained great popularity in the 1920s and 1930s, although they were less successful in Britain than on the continent. Workers' sport had its beginnings and its greatest successes in Germany, growing initially out of the Social Democratic Party in the 1890s. It sought to provide alternative cultural experiences, based on proletarian values rather than bourgeois ones. By the beginning of the First World War there were 350,000 people in workers' sports organisations, but the real growth came in the 1920s.

By 1928 the workers' sport movements, still largely under SPD control, had two million members. Various organisations published a total of 60 newspapers read by 800,000 people. In 1928 the communists split to form their own organisation, which had over 100,000 members by 1931. Both organisations were smashed by the Nazis in the early 1930s. The movement generated a considerable degree of autonomous organisation. The German Workers' Cycling Association established a bicycle factory run on co-operative lines in the late 1920s. Workers' sport also flourished in Belgium, Austria and Czechoslovakia. The Austrian Workers' Swimming Association gave 100,000 free swimming lessons in 1930. Membership of the Czechoslovakia labour sports movement reached over 200,000. Similar organisations in Belgium, Denmark, France, Switzerland, Finland and Norway all had over 20,000 members. In Britain the movement had less success. A National Workers' Sports Association formed in 1931 grew only slowly, although a series of workers' tennis tournaments was held at Reading Tennis Club in the 1930s. Workers' Wimbledon!

The movement had a strong commitment to internationalism. Many sporting visits were made and a series of Workers' Olympics was held as a counterpoint to the imperialist-dominated Olympics. The Czechs hosted a Workers' Olympics in Prague in 1921 and, whereas the official Olympics of 1920 excluded defeated countries Germany and Austria, the Prague games included them as a gesture of international working-class solidarity. A Socialist Workers' Sports International was established and soon enrolled 1,300,000 members. By 1931 its membership topped two million, of whom 350,000 were women. The International organised the first official Workers' Olympics in 1925 in Germany, attended by 150,000 people. This was followed by a second event in Vienna in 1931 which involved 100,000 competitors from 26 countries. A third Workers' Olympics was held in Antwerp in 1937, but the projected fourth games in Helsinki were cancelled after the outbreak of war.

A People's Olympics scheduled for Barcelona in 1936 was cancelled after the opening parade when the fascist uprising began. But many athletes remained to fight in the battle for Barcelona and the ensuing civil war. But the internationalism of the workers' sport movement was marked, as was politics more generally, by tensions between communist and social democratic organisations. A separate organisation, the Red Sports International (RSI), set up in Moscow in 1921, spent much of the 1920s locked in a power struggle with the Socialist Workers' Sports International. The RSI fought for an international sport organisation that, under communist control, would be an active part of the class struggle. The SWSI was more interested in creating a socialist cultural organisation. The RSI became involved in international sport festivals in Moscow in 1928 and Berlin in 1931. It was not until after the rise of the fascists in Europe that the two organisations began some degree of co-operation. By then, of course, it was too late.

After the Second World War this degree of internationalism could not re-establish itself in the face of the cold war. But workers' sport organisations in several countries provided an important base for post-war developments. In Czechoslovakia the Proletarian Sports Federation opened the way to the development of a socialist physical culture. After the war in West Germany the occupation powers effectively prevented the re-emergence of a politicised workers' sport movement. The German Democratic Republic, on the other hand, through the organisation Free German Youth, provided lavish sport facilities to win political support. This policy, and the emphasis on mass participation, had a great deal to do with the startling success of the GDR in international sport in the 1970s. Finland still has a workers' sport movement, separate from the state sport organisations, with its own network of sport centres. This separate history dates back to the expulsion of socialists from the bourgeois sport organisations in the wake of political struggles in 1917. The expanded scale of sport in the post-war world and the enormous cost of provision and organisation, together with the general decline in international socialist links, has inhibited any revival of autonomous workers' sports organisations.

Women in sport

The image of sport is heavily masculine. So even the participation of women represents a challenge to the dominant values of the sporting world. Increasingly the advances in women's sport, both in numbers of participants and in standards of performance, are challenging the notion that women's sport is a poor relation to the real thing. Many factors have kept women out of sport. Parents teach basic physical skills like ball sense more effectively to boys than to girls. Education treats boys and girls differently. Girls are led to attach less importance to physical activity and facilities are often inadequate. The entry into adolescence introduces girls to notions of femininity that depend on physical passivity. The pressure on girls to help their mothers around the house restricts leisure time. This burden is frequently replaced by marriage and the greater burden of serving a husband and raising children. Sport facilities have often been designed without consideration of women as participants. Few women are active in sport organisation and so their voice is not heard nearly enough at policy level.

Despite all these factors, women's sport has seen major advances in the last 20 years. In 1960 women were still barred from marathons and the longest distance commonly run was 1500 metres. Today thousands of women regularly run long distances. Women's tennis and golf have become established professional sports. The myth of female frailty is firmly under assault. But it has still to be decisively dislodged. Education has a complex place in the development of women's sport. The introduction of compulsory physical training in schools was an important break away from Victorian notions of female frailty and did expose girls to organised physical movement. But the separate traditions in male and female physical education have reinforced traditional views of gender difference. It is not just that many sports are boys only. Even in mixed sex sports like athletics many events, such as pole vault, triple jump and even races from 400 metres and longer, are often barred to girls. Attitudes to sport in school are still heavily influenced by the notion that girls' bodies are less able. In fact there are no medical or physiological reasons why girls cannot take part in as wide a range of sports as boys of the same age.

But traditional notions of femininity are powerful. Many girls drop sporting activity early on in secondary school. Many women's sports developed in the context of taboos over physical contact between women. Netball, for example, involves less physical contact than basketball. In America a specially adapted form of half-court basketball was devised in the belief that women could not possibly be expected to do so much running. These attitudes are further entrenched by the male dominance of sport organisation. The Sports Council has always been at least 90 per cent male. The current council of 23 has only two women, and of 18 principal officers only one is a woman. In the nine regions there is only one woman principal regional officer. Only 8 per cent of the other officials are women. Facility provision is often dominated by the attitude that sport is for men. Pat Gregory of the Women's Football Association has been refused pitches by a local authority. Some authorities would appear to discriminate in favour of male teams at weekends in the belief that women can play during the week. Like most public facilities, the average sport centre has no proper provision for childcare. Many of the myths about women and sport are now being exposed. There are no medical reasons to prevent women's participation during all phases of the menstrual cycle and there is some evidence that regular exercise and fitness may reduce period pains. Periods can cause fluctuations in performance but records have been set and medals won at all stages of the cycle. In general there appear to be no medical reasons for reducing normal sporting activity in the earlier stages of pregnancy. Again, physical fitness tends to mean easier deliveries.

Since women have begun participating in sport in increasing numbers standards have improved dramatically. Women's world swimming records are rapidly catching up those of the men. The women's world 1500 metres record time would have won gold in the men's 1968 Olympic final. The women's world 400 metres record is within 18 seconds of the men's. Norwegian Grethe Weitz has run the marathon in two hours twenty-five minutes, only fifteen minutes slower than the fastest men. Over 100 women have now run the distance in less than two hours fifty minutes. It is now widely believed that women can perform better than men in ultra-long-distance events requiring stamina, because women's bodies are more efficient at burning fat reserves. Cross-channel swimming records are currently held by women, as is the all-comers' record for walking the 840 miles between John O'Groats and Land's End. Cyclist Beryl Burton, now in her 40s, still competes successfully with men in long-distance events. In racing women were barred from all races except the Newmarket Town Plate until 1972. Since 1925 they have won that race 50 per cent of the time. In 1975 women jockeys were allowed in flat racing but it took the Sex Discrimination Act before they were allowed in steeple-chasing the following year. Since then women have won 250 steeplechases.

But it is important to avoid the trap of comparing women's sport and men's sport, as if women's sport is important only when performances come close to men's. Women's sport should be seen in its own right. It all too seldom is. While there have been great changes in many sports, women are still treated as second-class citizens. Women golfers in Britain between the wars who wanted to turn professional found it impossible to get jobs. Nowadays the women's golf circuit in the United States consists of 40 tournaments with total prize money of around three million pounds. But the sport still exists in the context of dominant sexist values. As a recent promotion stunt for women's golf a magazine featured photographs of top women golfers in the costumes and poses made famous by Hollywood stars like Jean Harlow and Marilyn Monroe. Traditional values and attitudes still remain very powerful. Golf journalist Liz Kahn was thrown out of the men-only Royal and Ancient Clubhouse in 1978 while trying to report the Open Championship. At many golf clubs women are either excluded or given lower subscriptions with restricted access to the course and other limitations on membership. Real open opportunity for women in sport will require many changes, a genuinely non-sexist educational system, an undermining of dominant attitudes about the inferior physical abilities of women, a greater responsibility taken by men for domestic labour, more social provision for childcare and more women in positions of influence in sport organisation. The rising prominence of women's sport provides a base from which to attack the traditional masculine domination of sport. But the battle has still to be won.

Popular recreation

Recreation under capitalism is bound to be riddled by contradictions. Just as leisure itself is determined by the pattern of work, so forms of recreation are determined by the forms of social organisation that make them possible. The ownership and control of open land, the development of the education system, the pattern of local authority provision, types of commercial provision and the publicity given to different activities all shape the forms of recreation available. But people still make choices. They opt for some activities rather than others. They set up organisations to regulate and develop particular activities. They shape their own leisure, although always within limits. Take skateboarding – a massive, if short-lived, fad in the late 1970s. Skateboarding was made possible in part by technological development, providing more sophisticated wheels and flexible suspension. It was adopted by the street culture of early adolescence and the craze was fuelled by publicity. Huge numbers of boards were sold and a lucrative trade developed in protective helmets and pads. Street accidents led to a demand for skate parks. Commercial interests and local authorities both responded. As provision improved the craze began to run out of steam. Manufacturers, stuck with over-capacity in little plastic wheel production, began promoting roller skates. A new craze, combining roller skating and listening to music on the new Walkman portable tape recorders, began. Forms of recreation are not simply the outcome of freely exercised choice. But neither are they simply forced on people by a state intent on social control, or by entrepreneurs seeking profits. Recreation patterns are complex because all these factors are involved. This final section discusses some of these complexities.

Education

Most people first encounter organised physical activity at school. So the education system plays a formative role in shaping recreation habits. The spread of universal education from the late nineteenth century heavily influenced the development of recreation in this country. There has never been one single dominant tradition in physical education but rather a number of strands. Because the growth of state education took place alongside a continuing private sector, lower and upper classes were exposed to different traditions of physical education. As men and women physical education teachers received different forms of training, boys and girls were also exposed to different traditions.

The development of physical training in the board schools of the late nineteenth century stemmed in part from a desire to keep an eye on children during break times and to keep them away from bad company. It was partly a form of social control. But the early development of physical education was half-hearted. The 1870 Education Act allowed PT (physical training) for boys but did not prescribe it. An inspector's recommendation was needed before a school could adopt PT for girls. A lot of early physical training was based upon military drill, despite considerable and growing opposition from many teachers. The state's concern to have fit workers was partly based upon the desire for a fit army, especially since the Boer War, when there had been considerable alarm about unfitness and malnutrition amongst troops. Much of the support for drill-based PT came from military sources. Boys in the private and public schools played games that were supposed to train them for leadership, while the schools for the poor adopted forms of physical training and drill that would produce obedient and fit followers.

The opening of the Bergman Osterberg College in 1885 heralded a different tradition in the physical education of girls and women. The founder, Mme Osterberg, wanted women to be taught by women and the men she initially engaged to teach cricket, tennis and vaulting were soon replaced by former students. A tradition of therapeutic gymnastics developed with an emphasis on health, grace and beauty.

Poor facilities were a big problem. In 1912 600 elementary schools had no playgrounds while a further 2,836 playgrounds were inadequate. The church schools had successfully opposed moves to enforce the improvement of facilities in the 1902 Education Act. The state began to take recreation more seriously in 1906. The Education Act of that year talked of the importance of games in building physique and moulding character. It emphasised the potential improvements in health and *esprit de corps*. It said that the spirit of discipline, corporate life and fair play were acquired largely through sport. So sport and recreation entered the education system as a fairly explicit tool for turning humans into subject citizens. But as so often, an expansionist aspiration eventually fell foul of a policy of contraction.

After the First World War a massive programme of government cuts inhibited the further development of physical education. Training courses for PE teachers were ended in 1923. There was to be no special training for men in physical education for ten years. But games and sport were still often seen as useful for engineering consensus, papering over social division and preventing conflict. Prime Minister Stanley Baldwin said in 1926 that the greater the facilities for recreation, the better would be the health and happiness of the people and 'the closer will be the spirit of unity between all classes'. The ruling-class delusion that sport is a magical panacea with the ability to erase class conflict is powerful. The massive unemployment, economic collapse and social deprivation of the 1920s and 1930s gave rise to a renewed interest among establishment figures in leisure provision. In 1925 a National Playing Fields Association was formed under the presidency of the Duke of York. Successful financial appeals led to the establishment of 800 playing fields over the next few years.

Concern over fitness brought closer connections between the physical education and medical professions. A British Medical Association report of 1936 said that 40 per cent of people between 14 and 40 needed, but did not get, regular physical recreation. With fear of war growing, a *National Fitness Campaign* was launched, without conspicuous impact. There was a renewed attempt to use recreation as a disguised form of military training. In a 1937 debate Aneurin Bevan denounced the need to evoke national well-being to fund recreation, saying that individual well-being was a sufficient justification.

The Second World War left its mark on physical education. The use of assault courses in military training spread downwards into the schools. Primary schools developed 'jungle gymnasia' and secondary schools took up circuit training. After the war there was a gradual expansion in provision. A number of tensions between different traditions continued in importance. The battle between training and recreation, between proponents of military-style drill and advocates of games for recreation and enjoyment, continued. An increased interest in dance and movement in girls' physical education teaching sharpened the debate between those who saw physical education as tied primarily to competitive sport and those who emphasised individual body movements. The development of the outward-bound schools and the Duke of Edinburgh award schemes in the 1950s represented a return to a more aristocratic tradition of individualism. These schemes were supposed to foster courage, initiative, self-reliance and leadership. This note of macho rugged individualism was in some degree opposed to the already well-established emphasis on team games.

In the 1960s and 1970s a new set of tensions in the syllabus developed between the adherents of the traditional sports – football, rugby and cricket for boys, hockey and netball for girls – and the introduction of newer and more novel ones. The improved level of educational provision brought basketball, volleyball, trampolining, tennis and many other sports into more common use. The growth of multi-cultural education brings new problems for physical education teachers, who are going to have to respond to demands that traditional Asian games be provided for and also come to terms with the Muslim and Hindu attitudes of disapproval towards physical activity for girls. Underlying many of these tensions are two conflicting attitudes about physical education: one that it has some benefit for society as a whole, the other that its benefits are primarily individual. But perhaps the most tangible effect of organised games at school has been to put many people off sport for the rest of their lives.

Leisure between the wars

The inter-war years saw the growth of many existing participation sports and the development of new ones. Fitness-centred activities like hiking and cycling grew enormously in popularity. They attracted larger lower-middle and working-class involvement and generated a range of autonomous organisations. The spread of municipal provision extended the popularity of swimming, tennis and bowls. New commercially run ice rinks became popular. Cycling had enjoyed continued popularity since the late nineteenth century and the development of the safety cycle and the pneumatic tyre. The group cycling trip was well established.

There was a new level of interest in physical activity and fitness, and a whole range of organisations – YMCA, YWCA, Boys' Brigade, Scouts and Guides – had expanded their physical recreation programme. The influence of religious, military and imperialist ideas in these organisations is well known. It is much harder to know how much these ideas appealed to members. Many may well have joined to use the organisations' facilities without subscribing to the ideas they peddled. Hiking, rambling and camping grew enormously in popularity. The Youth Hostel Association was formed in 1930. By the following year it had 73 hostels and 6,000 members. It grew throughout the 1930s and by 1939 had 279 hostels and 83,417 members. The new London County Council Evening Institutes introduced classes in physical exercise, gymnastics and swimming.

The Keep Fit Movement, launched by women in the north-east, had 127 women turn up for its first class in 1929. By the following year it was running nine classes for about 500 people a week. The Women's League of Health and Beauty was launched in 1929. By 1933 it had 30,000 members and an incredible 120,000 by 1937. It appears to have developed a distinct political inflection. During an Albert Hall performance in 1933 it staged a mime symbolising the reconciliation of capital and labour (an interesting contrast to the workers' sport movements thriving on the continent at this time).

During this period, much leisure activity seems to have centred around the lower middle and working class, outside the traditional structures of organised sport. There appears to have been a widespread interest in active physical leisure, but generally in a non-competitive form. People often set up their own organisations and activities, separate from both state and commercial outlets. But cultural-political organisations like the workers' sport movements do not seem to have attracted much support in Britain. Mental and physical activities are more compartmentalised in this country. So coherent interaction of activity and ideas is limited. Sport and politics are seen as very different aspects of social life.

Fun in the 1970s

The relative affluence of the post-war era transformed leisure activity. The spread of television and car ownership, and the growth of the record industry in the 1950s and 1960s, encouraged more passive forms of leisure. The great outdoors no longer beckoned as it had in the 1930s. The new focus of leisure time was the family home. The acquisition of material goodies – fridges, hi-fis and the like – was an important part of home buildings. The do-it-yourself industry grew to service the new passion for home improvement. But these developments have, in the 1970s, reversed. A new enthusiasm for physical leisure has arisen. People have become more concerned with fitness and health. The well-documented link between smoking and heart and lung disease has finally begun to make some inroads into smoking habits. (The tobacco companies still market their more lethal blends in the third world with undiminished zeal.) Hostility to processed foods, particularly bread, has had a growing impact on eating habits. Nonetheless, over-consumption and unhealthy products are still major killers.

This new enthusiasm for fitness and exercise has a contradictory character. The passion for exercise is largely confined to the middle class and has spawned a thriving health and fitness industry. Track suits are now high fashion, a form of sport chic. But the fitness boom also breeds criticism of passive consumption. Getting more exercise, eating sensibly and leading a more active life lead people to see more clearly the harmful aspects of the food, drink and media industries and of passive forms of leisure. The new interest in fitness has shown itself most obviously in the huge growth of running. The development of the jogging craze in America was treated largely as a joke. It certainly had its comic aspects. People jogging alongside highways sometimes passed out from the fumes. When jogging crossed the Atlantic much of the early advice passed between runners was concerned with how to deal with the smirks, sniggers and cat-calls of non-runners.

The immense success of mass fun-runs and gigantic people's marathons have gradually shown that the enthusiasm for running is more than a craze. Last year in Britain 100,000 people ran in marathons up and down the country. Many times that number probably run regularly for exercise or fun. The new fun-running undermines many of the dominant values of sport. The marathon used to be represented as the ultimate challenge, the Everest of athletics. Only highly-trained men were capable of completing the course. Women were not even allowed to run the distance. This mystique has been shattered. The distance has now been run by thousands of ordinary people after a year or so of part-time training. It has been run by men and women of all ages. A 78-year-old man finished in the 1981 London marathon. It has been run by people recovering from heart attacks, diabetes and cancer. Women have had great success. Joyce Smith, who is 44, has been an athlete most of her life but took up the marathon only three years ago. She finished the last London marathon in two-and-a-half hours, within twenty minutes of the fastest man. Her performances have inspired many other women to take up running. 1400 women ran in the 1982 London marathon. Few things have so effectively undermined the myth of female frailty. Large-scale popular running is also not very competitive. Everyone runs to his or her own standards and if people compete it is largely against their own limitations. Runners give each other a lot of mutual support.

The people's marathons have broken down the sharp divisions between spectators and participants too. Because the runners are so obviously ordinary people rather than highly-trained full-time athletes, many spectators realise that they too could run. Many who watched in 1981 ran in 1982. Runners often refer to the immense support and encouragement they get from the crowd. The giant marathons are certainly a form of spectacle, but not of the normal star-laden variety where all focus is on the winners. Television commentators soon found out that the people's marathons cannot be treated simply as a race. Taking the spotlight off stars breaks down the normal distinction between the elite and the grassroots. Usually we are encouraged to see top athletes as a different breed of humankind. It is hard to go on believing that if you have run the same course in the same race, even if it did take you an hour longer. Running can be a spontaneous, simple and unstructured activity. It can be done anywhere, singly or in groups. It needs no elaborate equipment. There is no need to be subject to the rule of a coach, manager or boss figure. It is a highly effective way of keeping the weight down, the muscles in trim and generally staying fit. Many people also find that it feels good to do and feels good afterwards. The benefits are not all physical. Regular runners talk of feeling more alert, being more able to relax, sleeping better and feeling more self-confident.

Of course there are negative aspects to the whole running phenomenon too. The macho-competitive element is still present. The concept of running a marathon has become rather over-dramatised. You aren't a real runner until you've done it. The very popularity of marathon running has had undesirable effects, such as the premature involvement of child runners. Eleven-year-old Cheryl Page was banned by the AAA from running in the London marathon. Many doctors believe that excessive forms of exercise by growing children can cause bone damage and malformation. There is concern that the marathon boom could trigger a wave of child runners, pushing their bodies too hard.

The marathon business has become very commercialised too. Trade names emblazon everything that moves. Public relations firms jostle to get their clients on the screen. Application forms for the London marathon are accompanied by an enclosed leaflet advertising New Balance Shoes. People are now so anxious to get into the limited entry marathon that the procedure is surrounded by queues for the post, threats of lawsuits, allegations of bribery and the likely development of an illicit market in entry permits. ßA whole new sector of the sport clothing market has opened up. Once it was possible to have a pair of plimsolls, a white vest and shorts and a tube of vaseline and be a world-class runner. Now, if you believe the adverts, no Sunday jogger is complete without a pacemaker digital watch, a runner's radio, a waist pouch, a security wrist band for keys, weighted training gloves, special reflective bands for night running and a personalised computer training program. Training shoes and track suits sell for anything up to £90 each. And, if you're really serious, a special aerobic exerciser, consisting of a face mask and a couple of back cylinders, will simulate the beneficial effects of altitude training. It will also set you back around £100.

The conditions in which popular recreation takes place are established by the nature of the economic system and the network of social institutions built upon it. In a capitalist society any popular leisure activity is also going to be highly commercialised. Change within sport alone cannot have dramatic results. But, if a more humane, more egalitarian and less oppressive form of sport is worth fighting for, then it is important to examine the existing organisation of sport and possible alternatives. The next chapter looks at state policy towards sport and the existing patterns of provision. The final one suggests the issues that socialists need to consider if they are to argue for alternatives.

2.5 Sport and the state

In many countries the state has developed a systematic policy towards sport and put it into practice. Cuba is an excellent example. This has not happened in Britain. The recurrent pattern has been one of *ad hoc* improvisations, carried out by a variety of separate, largely voluntary organisations, with unco-ordinated plans and persistent financial problems. This chapter will examine the Sports Council and the problems of a state policy towards sport. I have outlined the development of sport in England in terms of shifting patterns of dominance. The aristocratic patronage of the eighteenth century was replaced in importance by the rise of sport institutions dominated by sections of the upper-middle class of the late nineteenth century. These predominantly amateur-paternal sport organisations dominated English sport until the post-war era. From the early 1950s the growing internationalisation of sport, its penetration by capitalist commerce, the effect of television and the associated growth of sponsorship gave birth to a new form of patronage – the economic patronage of sponsorship. Only in the last 20 years has the state played much of a role.

The state intervenes in the field of sport and leisure in three main ways. First, it tries to ban certain activities. I have already mentioned attempts to outlaw bowls and football in the sixteenth and seventeenth centuries. There was the wave of anti-cruel-sport legislation in the nineteenth century. Bare-knuckle boxing remains illegal and a new lobby is under way to ban boxing altogether. Second, the state regulates and licenses activities. The most notable example is the control of betting and gaming. The whole social practice of gambling, and hence horse-racing and greyhound-racing in their current forms, is in no small part determined by state legislation. The 1960 Betting and Gaming Act brought the off-course betting shop into being. In 1953 there had been 4,000 arrests for street betting in London, but by 1967 there were a mere three. A vastly profitable and legal industry had been created. Third, the state provides facilities. The long fight by the labour movement gradually forced the reductions in working hours and increase in public holidays that made leisure time a possibility for urban workers. Conservative concern with social control and liberal pressure for social reform led to a growth in municipal provision of parks, wash-houses and swimming pools. But the scale should not be exaggerated. In 1909 there were more public hard courts for tennis in Hamburg than in the whole of England.

The rise of the Sports Council

State involvement in leisure was largely *ad hoc* and local from the mid-nineteenth century until the 1930s. The first impetus towards a central coherent organisation grew out of concern over national fitness. The international capitalist crisis of the 1930s had caused severe cuts in public spending and unemployment for between two and three million people. Children left school at 14 but could obtain unemployment benefit after 16 only by attending the compulsory Junior Instruction Centres. The rise of fascism in Europe prompted British establishment figures to compare the nationalistic fervour of fascist youth movements with the supposed listless, apathetic state of Britain's youth. Within the ruling classes, both those who admired and those who feared the rise of fascism felt some need for action. These half-formed feelings combined with the growth of a consciousness about physical culture stemming from the medical and physical education professions. The many existing voluntary bodies also felt the need for a forum to co-ordinate activities.

The Central Council for Recreation and Training (as it was then called) was formed in 1935, through the initiative of Phyllis Colson, a physical education organiser. It had royal patronage and the support of the Board of Education. It brought together organisations of sport and physical education, along with a large medical presence. The declared aim was 'to help improve the physical and mental health of the community through physical recreation by developing existing facilities for recreative physical activities of all kinds and also by making provision for the thousands not yet associated with any organisation'. The government was also prompted to act by concern with fitness. It formed a National Fitness Council, which had a brief and unhappy life. The outbreak of war eventually defused the paranoia over national fitness. After the war the CCPR was to turn its attention to the provision of facilities and, in particular, to the development of National Recreation Centres.

The CCPR was an independent body, but most of its income came from statutory grants. So in the late 1940s and 1950s it featured in post-war reconstruction, along with the growth of the welfare state and the expansion of state intervention, in the mixed economy. Its most significant achievement at this time was the establishment of seven National Recreation Centres. These provided residential facilities for a variety of sports. The centres mainly served more committed sports people and part of their role was to raise standards at the highest level to boost British chances in international competition. The physical education world was becoming increasingly concerned with preparing for international competition. English assumptions of sporting dominance were shaken when Hungary's footballers beat England 6–3 at Wembley in 1953. English sporting administrators felt threatened by the growing power of both America and the communist countries in international sport. There was a reaction against the traditional amateur-paternal ethos.

The CCPR set up the Wolfenden Committee in 1957 to recommend ways in which statutory bodies could help promote the general welfare of the community in sport and leisure. Confusion between developing an elite and serving the general interest is a typical feature of English debates over sport policy. The Wolfenden report, *Sport and the Community* (1960), found that there was an overwhelming case for statutory financing of sport. It expressed concern that sport, which then came under the Minister for Education, was a low priority. The report recommended the establishment of a sports council of six to ten people to control expenditure of around £5 million per year. A distinct political consensus was developing. In the 1959 election campaign both major parties were against a minister for sport but in favour of a sports council along the lines of the Arts Council. But the victorious Conservatives then did little. Lord Hailsham, given special responsibility for sport, increased government expenditure, but dragged his feet over the proposed sports council.

Labour came to power in 1964 committed to a sports council but, as a statutory body required legislation, they initially set up an advisory council. Seven years of uncomfortable negotiation followed as the relationship between this advisory council and the CCPR was worked out. The problems were a reflection of a typical desire on the part of the British state to prevent institutions appearing to be state controlled. A Minister for Sport would be answerable to parliament, whereas a quasi-independent council, even if appointed by the government, would be outside the parliamentary political process. By 1968 a compromise had been arrived at. In 1969 Denis Howell, the Minister with responsibility for sport, was moved from the Department of Education and Science to the Ministry of Housing and Local Government. Sport funding was no longer a part of the education budget. It acquired greater status as a result.

The 1970 Conservative government resolved to establish a statutory and executive sports council which would disburse funding. This would effectively take over many of the functions of the CCPR, which was offered the option of self-destruction. There was strong feeling in the CCPR against this and in the event the Sports Council took over the full-time staff and resources of the CCPR, which then restructured itself into an independent forum of sport organisations. The character of the two organisations has been very different. The Board of the Sports Council is appointed by the Minister and so is a quasi-autonomous part of the state. The CCPR is somewhat more democratic, being composed of representatives of the various governing bodies of sport.

The Sports Council and sport in the 1970s

The new executive Sports Council was established in 1971 by Royal Charter. Its brief again reflected the conflict between the needs of the elite and the grassroots. It was supposed to develop knowledge of sport and physical recreation in the interests of social welfare and to encourage the attainment of high standards in conjunction with the relevant governing bodies. The prevailing wisdom in the early 1970s was that leisure time would increase, participation would rise and that there was serious under-provision for sport and recreation. Given a legacy of chronic under-provision, and an uphill struggle for adequate funding, the most significant advance has been the expansion of sport centres. In 1964 there was just one purpose-built sport centre in the whole of England and Wales. By 1972 there were still only 30. By 1978 there were 350.

The prediction of rising rates of participation has proved to be true. So, in a sense, with over three million people on the dole, has that of increased leisure time. As funding has become progressively tighter, the emphasis has switched from the provision of new facilities to the maximum exploitation of existing ones. In recent years the Sports Council has begun to identify low-participation groups – the disabled, the over-50s, and women, especially those with young children. The final chapter questions the ability of the Council to deal with the problems it identifies. Since the mid 1970s, the inner cities have increasingly been seen as areas of special concern. The drive to develop sport facilities in these areas stems partly from a progressive liberal reformism. But it is also clear that many policy makers see inner-city sport as a way of defusing social tension, as a form of social control. Since the riots of 1981 it has suddenly become much easier to obtain funding for inner-city projects. Nothing loosens the purse strings like panic.

State policy and social reality

No political party in Britain has a clear policy for sport. The Liberals have just produced an extensive document on the arts but nothing equivalent on sport. Conservative Central Office told me that 'we don't generate policy when we're in office'. The Labour Party support the right of access to common land, oppose apartheid in South African sport and oppose the sale of sports grounds into private hands. The SDP are still working on it. Other parties of the left and right have little to say on the subject. So policy is formed by a combination of Sports Council action, ministerial whim and – crucially – local authority policy and spending patterns. Up until around 1976 the expansion proposed by the Sports Council was in relative harmony with the aims (as opposed to the actual practice) of government policy. But commitment to expanded provision has come under increasing pressure. Restrictions on state spending threaten public provision. At the same time the rise of sponsorship is re-shaping sport in ways that bypass the Sports Council. Privatisation increasingly threatens public sport facilities.

The Sports Council's response is totally inadequate. Its current strategy advocates a budget rising from the current £22 million to £46 million in 1987. Realising that this prospect is fairly remote, it outlines the effects of limited growth and standstill budgets over the same period. Yet the strategy fails to highlight the crisis in public provision, does nothing to pinpoint the causes and is of no help in fighting cutbacks. At a time when the gulf between rich and poor in sport is widening, the Sports Council not only has no effective strategy but fails to recognise that there is a problem.

Public spending cuts affect sport provision in many ways. Few new facilities are planned. Old ones are threatened with closure. Staff cuts reduce opening hours. Lower spending on maintenance leads to collapse of facilities. Poorly maintained tennis courts drive people away, reducing revenue and encouraging further staff cuts. In some places cuts in ground staff have encouraged vandalism. Mobile security services have then been called in – a depressing manifestation of the growth of a law and order society. Higher fees reduce use. In Wandsworth swimming pool and weekday tennis fees have doubled in the last year. The CCPR estimated that in 1980 £20 million was lost in spending on sport and recreation. In the same year the Thatcher government offered £50 million as an inducement to move the Olympic Games from Moscow.

In sport, as in the health service, an impoverished public sector sits side by side with a booming, and expensive, private sector. Major spectator sports already cast their eyes mainly at the affluent end of the market. Football has thrown resources into the provision of elaborate executive boxes. For £120 Keith Prowse offered a top-price seat at Wembley. The price included a champagne reception and a four-course meal. But the highlight was a buffet party with Jimmy Tarbuck afterwards. For an outlay of £6,000 Abbey Executive Services will provide 20 Wimbledon Final Day tickets, along with a luxury lunch, limitless wine and strawberries and cream. But it is not just spectator sports that are being transformed. Private clubs thrive on the boom in physical leisure. At the Cannon Sports Centre in the City of London city executives' subscriptions of £350 per year are often paid by their bosses, who can claim part of the cost against corporation tax.

Of course a large proportion of sport and recreation provision has always been in private hands. Our two major spectator sports, football and cricket, have always jealously guarded their facilities against encroachment by the public. The premier tennis facilities are maintained for the year-round benefit of a tiny elite, on the huge profits of Wimbledon fortnight. In the mid 1950s, when only 47 of Britain's 130 athletic tracks were in public hands, Finland had 500, and Sweden 800 for a population of seven million. At a time when open land is being gobbled up by property developers, school recreation grounds, seen as surplus to requirements, are also being sold for development.

Privatisation poses a greater threat to public provision. Local authorities are increasingly prepared to offload their traditional responsibilities for short-term gain. Privatisation is a new form of asset-stripping in which assets belonging to us all are sold to private capitalists at knock-down prices. The much touted increase in efficiency that privatisation is supposed to bring is largely a myth, as those unfortunate enough to live under the Wandsworth Tories are currently discovering. Privatisation results in either a worse or a more expensive service, or in greater exploitation of workers. Often it means all three. Any hope of public accountability is also lost. Already some boroughs, such as Hillingdon in London, are experimenting with a form of halfway house on the road to privatisation, whimsically referred to as an entrepreneurial partnership. The Manor Leisure Centre near Peterborough, complete with sports hall, cricket and football pitches, swimming pool and tennis courts, has been put up for sale. After closing tennis courts in Carshalton Park at weekends to save overtime, the London borough of Sutton then made three out of five available for exclusive private use. Richmond Park golf course currently breaks even and thus pays for itself, providing a highly popular public service. But the government are determined to privatise it.

Private enterprise has its eyes on the potential profits in this field. Commercial Union, Dunlop, Debenhams, MacAlpine and Watneys have formed a consortium, Cavendish Leisure, to promote the privatisation of swimming pools. Their strategy is to blame restrictive practices by NALGO and their claim that admissions at pools cover only 18 per cent of the costs suggests that they would charge a lot more. They will probably get ministerial support. A campaign last year to get public swimming baths to open early in the morning failed to gain Minister of Sport Neil MacFarlane's backing. MacFarlane does, however, appreciate the value of early-morning swimming. He swims 20 lengths every morning – in a private pool. Unfortunately the Sports Council shows little awareness that these developments constitute a problem. Its current strategy seems to involve active encouragement of entrepreneurial partnerships.

The Sports Council has consistently failed to give any encouragement to progressive forces. On the two most public aspects of sports policy, apartheid and tobacco sponsorship, the Council has tried desperately to avoid taking a clear position. On apartheid, the report of its recent fact-finding tour does little to convince readers that the Council is in the forefront of the battle to maintain the spirit of the Gleneagles agreement. On tobacco, it is reluctant to take a stand against such a major source of money. Its discussions have no doubt been aided by the presence on the Council up till 1982 of Sir James Wilson, chairperson of the Tobacco Advisory Council. The Sports Council is a profoundly undemocratic body. It is run by a board appointed by the Minister and accountable only to him. It is also heavily male-dominated and until very recently has done little to acknowledge, let alone alleviate, the factors inhibiting women's involvement in sport. Its recent prestigious international conference, Sport and People, had not a single woman speaker, apart from the closing address by the organiser. It has lost touch with the grass-roots of sport. It has evolved a strategy incompatible with the current economic situation and has failed to acknowledge fully the threat to past achievements.

2.6 Arguments for socialism

This chapter offers some suggestions for transforming the structure, organisation and values of sport. It draws on the socialist critique of sport discussed in Chapter 2. But it rejects the view that the whole institution of sport is simply incompatible with socialism. Instead it argues that competitive sport is a more complex, varied and adaptable activity than its critics suggest. The first section argues the need for a genuinely egalitarian sport system, with adequate facilities and finance. A case is made for social ownership and democratic control. The second section examines areas where discussion is needed to clarify the way ahead. The place of elite sport, and of national sport and the nature of competition in sport, should be debated more openly. Dominant ideas and values do not change overnight. Nor can they be legislated away. Support for socialist principles must be won. The third section discusses the problems facing those arguing for a socialist transformation of sport. We need a strategy for making socialist ideas popular.

Sport for all

The first aim of any socialist strategy ought to be the achievement of an egalitarian sport system with adequate facilities available to all. The Sports Council's own slogan, 'Sport For All', provides a fine starting point. It expresses an egalitarian intention, but one that can be realised only through socialism. Only with social ownership of resources under democratic control could we have genuine sport for all. Socialists should seize on the contradictions lying behind this slogan and press those within sport to see its implications. The rhetoric of the policies behind Sport For All expresses admirable principles. But good intentions must founder if they fail to confront social reality.

We live in a society with massive inequalities of wealth and income. A small proportion of the population owns and controls a vast proportion of the country's land, property and production. Giant commercial enterprises have great power to define the whole field of leisure. So the achievement of Sport For All depends on broader social changes. But it is still important to spell out the preconditions for achieving

Sport For All. First, we need to define what is meant by the phrase. Then we need to develop a strategy for the provision and financing of adequate facilities. This book will argue that this requires an extension of social ownership. Finally, we need to build in democratic control at all levels.

I take Sport For All to mean that the means of sporting activity should be available to everyone in the forms and at the times that people can best use them. It does not mean that everyone has to be involved in sport. People have a right to take other forms of physical exercise or shun exercise altogether, however irresponsible this may be! Taking Sport For All seriously involves confronting sexism and racism. Positive discrimination is needed to undo a long history of white male dominance. Dominant stereotypes of sporting activity must be combated. Posters advertising sport halls frequently feature boys but not girls and white but not black or Asian children. But the fight for genuine opportunity for all involves more than being non-racist and non-sexist. It means actively confronting the legacy of past practices that have perpetuated racism and sexism. Positive discrimination is needed to involve more women and black Britons in the running of sport. There is a need for far more women and black sport teachers and motivators. Action must be taken to ensure that schools and sport centres always have as good facilities for girls and women as they do for boys and men. The need for change here is closely linked to broader struggles. The fight for crèches in sport centres is part of a broader struggle for full social provision for the needs of pre-school children.

The degree to which these problems are recognised within sport administration varies greatly. The regional strategy of the Greater London and South East Council for Sport and Recreation has worthy intentions, although its ability to promote them effectively in the present economic climate is doubtful. By contrast, the regional strategy of the West Midlands mentions the problems of mothers with young children but has virtually nothing to say about women on the whole. Change in sport, and attitudes to it, depend in part on education. The practices of physical education are outside the scope of this book. But education could play a major role in undermining the notion that sport is for the boys. To date education has tended to reinforce gender roles and attitudes to sport. Attitudes to race are rather different. Black children who show an ability for sport are often encouraged at the expense of pressure to maintain their academic studies. The underlying stereotype is that black people are only good at sport, not academic work. The notion of sport as a way out of the ghetto has brought material success for an elite few, but is a dangerous cul-de-sac for thousands more.

The struggle to change attitudes will mean little without adequate facilities. Despite the work of the Sports Council in the 1970s, we are still very short of local multi-purpose sports halls. Britain has only one indoor athletics track. France has twelve and West Germany five. Our 64 indoor tennis courts compare unfavourably with the 1,200 in France. Since the Second World War Holland, France and West

Germany have each spent three times as much per head on sports provision as Britain. Yet there is great social value to be obtained from money spent on sport. A fit healthy population is a great social asset, and spending on sport has hidden benefits for public spending as a whole. The radical solution to the problem of the high cost of health service provision has always been to place much greater emphasis on prevention. Discouraging alcohol and tobacco abuse, and encouraging healthy eating habits and regular exercise, could eventually transform the pattern of health care. Cuba places great emphasis on the benefits of physical activity. Babies are introduced to exercise through play almost from birth.

Sport funding could be improved in a number of ways. Thousands of millions are spent each year on gambling. A small portion is taken in tax, but none of it is earmarked specifically for sport. In 1981 betting duty on the football pools netted £184 million. A mere 12 per cent of this would be almost enough to double the Sports Council's grant. But there is no sound reason why the hugely profitable betting industry should remain in private hands at all. Many countries operate state lotteries. If we are to have gambling (and many argue that like tobacco and alcohol it cannot be legislated out of existence) then let us at least use the profits constructively.

At present, certain areas of sport get substantial funds through tobacco sponsorship. The great irony is that a physical activity like sport should be supported by such a physically destructive product. The argument in favour of tobacco sponsorship has always been that some sports depend on it. This argument is somewhat spurious. Even cricket is now getting as much help from the finance houses and insurance firms as it is from tobacco. If money has to go from tobacco to sport let it be through a levy on tobacco company profits. This principle – that those who threaten health and fitness should pay for its promotion – is perfectly viable, even in the heart of capitalism. Long Beach in California levies a tax on local oil-drilling companies to pay for sport and recreation facilities in the area.

One broader strategy option is to take into public ownership not just unprofitable sectors but precisely those profitable ones which could help support other areas. It is bizarre to have an impoverished sports system amidst industries growing rich by selling rackets, clubs, bats, track suits, jogging shoes, swimwear and other sporting paraphernalia. But the problem of facilities is not simply one of finance. It is also one of social organisation. The economic climate has forced the Sports Council to switch emphasis from the provision of new facilities to the more efficient use of existing ones. School facilities, for example, should be made available for community use at evenings, weekends and during school holidays; unfortunately this still happens fully only in a minority of cases. For too many years it has been all talk and no action. The crisis now facing education authorities from cutbacks in state spending and falling rolls ought to force fresh thinking. School facilities are community facilities. The fall in pupil numbers provides a perfect opportunity to bring school and community closer together. The enormous amount of recreation land in private hands presents a greater problem. The utilisation of private playing fields is appallingly low. There is no social justification for fields standing empty day after day, week after week. Open land is rapidly becoming more scarce and should be controlled for the social good.

Facilities alone are no good. They are there to be used. There is a great shortage of teachers and motivators – people able to encourage physical activity. Sport authorities in this country have only recently begun to appreciate the value of motivators. Countries that have put more resources into supporting this role have generally seen a significant increase in participation rates. Much of this work can be on an informal basis. In China, factory workers can attend coaching clinics and workshops in exchange for coaching their workmates when they return. This is a valuable social principle, based on sharing knowledge rather than treating it as private property.

Social ownership of facilities would have other advantages. Take the case of football, for almost a century the most popular spectator sport in the country. At the highest level, the Football League clubs are structured like capitalist enterprises, but controlled mainly by businessmen for influence or as a hobby, rather than for profit. Their product, football, has a large working-class audience, with no power over the sport often regarded as 'theirs'. Football is currently in financial crisis, with clubs as famous as Wolverhampton Wanderers coming close to bankruptcy. The causes are complex and those in and around the game endlessly debate the respective importance of high wages, spiralling transfer fees, hooliganism, quality of football, professional fouls, too much television coverage and the changing face of society. Underlying it all is a pattern of financial mismanagement with roots in the late 1960s and early 1970s.

A moral panic over hooliganism led many in the game to think in terms of appealing to a more affluent consumer. They saw the way ahead in terms of all-seated stadiums, executive boxes complete with colour TV and cocktail cabinet and the mythical 'family audience'. Grandiose plans were put into motion up and down the country for expensive new stands. Meanwhile gates continued to fall steadily through the 1970s. While gates declined, expenditure rocketed. Millions were borrowed to erect new stands. Transfer fees spiralled towards the million pounds per player level and competitive bidding drove wages up rapidly. Clubs borrowed heavily and landed themselves with huge interest payments at a time of falling revenue. Rising interest rates made things worse. Football clubs have few tangible assets. Players' values are too erratic for financiers to rely on. Grounds and stadiums may be worth a lot but their value can be realised only by ceasing to play. Football could become an asset-strippers' playground – particularly where grounds are in urban areas suitable for property development.

Football can still attract around 20 million people a year and television fees of £2,500,000 for a year's league matches alone. But it is unable to sort out its own financial problems. The passionate desire for success leads directors towards self-destruction. The financial collapse of Chelsea in the mid 1970s, brought about by huge interest payments for their £2.5 million stand, failed to prevent other clubs from following like lemmings the same route. The fall-off in crowds during the 1970s has been mainly amongst working-class supporters. This is hardly surprising when most clubs seem bent on ignoring the terrace fans to concentrate on their new executive box-dwellers.

One solution is for local councils to buy grounds and then lease them back to the clubs. But from a council's point of view this makes sense only if it is also going to control the use of the ground. Football's stadiums have always been notoriously under-used. Local authority control could lead to a more rational use of their resources. A more radical step would be to encourage multi-sport clubs on the continental model. There, successful football clubs are often part of larger organisations. The financial strength of football helps support other sports, which in turn generate additional revenue in receipts and bar and restaurant takings. The famous Spanish club Real Madrid run teams in many sports and are highly successful at basketball.

If multiple sport clubs were owned and controlled by their members then sport could be democratised. Club users could determine policy. Resources could also be exploited more efficiently. In a sport centre attached to a football club, all-weather floodlit pitches could be used by the club in the morning and open to the community in the afternoon and evening. Gymnasia, swimming baths, equipment and storage space could all be shared in this way. Many sports in Britain have been dominated by small elites who have jealously guarded facilities and protected their own privileges. In cricket, tennis and golf working-class people are treated as interlopers and gate-crashers. The rich pickings of major occasions such as Wimbledon and the Open Championship should be used to boost sporting opportunities for ordinary people instead of maintaining the privileges of those wearing the right school tie.

The whole concept of social ownership has been seriously undermined by the negative image of the nationalised industries. While not all the hostility to nationalised industries is fair, they are for the most part large, hierarchical, inefficient bureaucracies that have done little to transform capitalism. New proposals for social ownership must be radically different – decentralised, non-hierarchical and subject to the control of workers and users. In the case of sport, proposals must avoid the danger of control by a faceless state. The idea should be to give power to those who work in and use sport centres, recreation grounds, swimming baths, football clubs and so on.

There are many benefits of social ownership. A more rational financial organisation would allow for a degree of cross-subsidy at present impossible. The inward-looking isolation of different sport organisations could be broken down by multi-sport clubs. A much closer relation between organisers, top performers, grass-roots participants and spectators would be possible. New structures of control would be crucial. Otherwise social ownership could generate new elite-controlled cultural bureaucracy. Sport must be thoroughly democratised at all levels. Sport centres run by committees elected by workers and users of the centres could provide a basic network. (Many sport centres in the Netherlands are run on this basis.) These centres could in turn send delegates to a network of regional councils and a national council, which, unlike the present Sports Council, would then be controlled by the people it was set up to serve. Single-sport organisations could benefit similarly from a democratised structure.

In summary, a basic socialist policy for sport might contain four elements:

- An egalitarian intention. Genuine Sport For All, with positive discrimination to counter existing structures and attitudes;
- Adequate facilities and funding to make Sport For All possible;
- Social ownership of stadiums, sport centres, recreation land and the subsidiary leisure industry;
- Democratic control of sport facilities and at all levels of sport organisations. These facilities and organisations should be controlled by those who work in and use them.

What sort of games?

The strategy outlined so far would be unlikely to succeed without broader changes in society. It would transform the organisation of sport, but not necessarily have much impact on its nature. Here changes are not a matter of legislation. The cultural patterns, habits and values embodied in particular sports will not necessarily be altered simply by new forms of ownership and control. Cultural change is a slow and complex matter. There is no clear agreement among socialists about developing more progressive forms of sport. But there are a number of areas of potential change, where further debate could be useful. I have singled out four. First, the place, if any, of elite sport within a general Sport-For-All strategy. Second, the place, if any, of international competition between nations. Third, the whole question of competition. Fourth, the degree to which different sports should be encouraged or discouraged by differential funding.

An attack can be mounted on the whole role of elite development in sport. The pyramid form of sport organisation, in which a disproportionate amount of money, time and resources is spent nurturing small squads of top athletes for prestigious international competition, can be seen as fundamentally incompatible with egalitarian principles. No special privileges should be available to those who excel. The inflated importance bestowed by the media on international competition has led to heavy spending to buy international success. Certainly a tension exists between the demands of the elite and the needs of the grassroots. This is not confined to Britain. Communist countries such as the USSR and the German Democratic Republic can claim, with rather more justification than Britain, to have developed genuine sport for all. Yet they lavish far more care on their elite athletes than does the British state. Sport in the GDR has become a highly specialised profession for which those who show prowess are systematically groomed from an early age. The problem is one of the place of specialism. Industrialised society features a highly developed division of labour that will not simply wither and die from the first days of socialism. Socialism continues to depend on the development of special areas of knowledge, skill and expertise. A much less rigid division of labour in, say, the health service would be highly desirable. But the need for specialist doctors would remain. Are athletes so very different?

Greater participation in sport increases interest in watching skilled athletes perform. In the cinema industry many people watch films but few make them. Far more people should have the opportunity to make films but this does not mean that one day everyone will make films and no one watch them. One of the strengths of sport is that it is possible to be both a participant and a spectator. The pleasure in playing and the pleasure of watching enhance each other. And part of the pleasure of watching lies in a sense of physical skill and control that comes only with specialist expertise. Are we to give people with an aptitude for sport any less right to develop their talents than we would give to, say, musicians or electronic engineers?

I do not believe there is any easy answer to this question. International sport is so deeply embedded in the system of global relations that countries are caught up in its system of values irrespective of their own political philosophies. Elite sport at the international level has become a site for the struggle to establish national prestige. Cuba and the German Democratic Republic have both used elite sporting development to establish their legitimacy on the world stage. Sport played a significant role in the GDR's long battle to be recognised as a separate nation. China has adopted the slogan 'Friendship Before Competition'. Yet it is beginning to dip its feet into the international pool, after many years' isolation in protest at the Western inclusion of Taiwan in world events. All these countries have had to negotiate the conflicting demands of developing an elite and extending sporting opportunity at the grassroots. Both the USSR and GDR have provided sport opportunity on a massive scale while also investing in an elite that has won substantial international success.

The problem in Britain is not so much that neither aim has been achieved. It is rather that there has been no clear public debate; no attempt to establish a precise policy about where resources should go and what the priorities should be. Britain's athletes have recently had unparalleled success and the Sports Aid Foundation has been able to raise thousands for the elite squad. Public interest has rarely been higher. Yet facilities for young athletes remain woefully inadequate. It is crude to argue that all money should be spent on grassroots sport and none on an elite level. But it is essential to determine where the balance should lie. The provision of sporting opportunity should certainly take priority over the enhancement of national prestige.

Nationalism has always been a problem for socialist analysis. National sport, as a manifestation of nationalism, presents similar problems. National sport has proved a highly successful element of bourgeois ideology. A popular cultural activity is linked to national identity, an unproblematic unity over and above political difference. It creates a largely artificial sense of national-belongingness, an imaginary coherence. It masks social divisions and antagonisms, offering a unity which we all too easily fall in with. National sport promotes that beguiling desire that England should win. We see through it and yet are part of it. National sport fosters a xenophobic attitude to foreigners – it is us against them. It helps to circulate unreal expectations of our own merits and derogatory stereotypes of everyone else. Yet more remains to be said. The world is structured by national divisions which are not simply imaginary. But for international sport their prime significance is perhaps symbolic. So the success of the communist countries in international sport has to be explained away. It has continually to be derided, ascribed to drugs or fanaticism, or to dehumanising assembly-line methods. The massive successes of the GDR, out of all proportion to its relatively small population, make the Western media particularly uneasy. The GDR women's team, which won more medals at the Montreal Olympics than all other women combined, has been described in a British paper as 'battery huns'. The role of sport in Cuba's self-image, and in its prestige in Latin America, is important. The Cuban sporting system has won the admiration of many Western coaches, notably Ron Pickering. A popular national figure like boxer Teofilo Stevenson is part of the national identity. It is dangerous to see national sport simply in a negative light. Political battles are fought with symbols. There are dangers in allowing the right to capture the power to define national identity.

Judgements about the relation between national sport and nationalism cannot be made without considering the particular social context. National sport plays a different role in developing and post-colonial countries from that which it has in imperialist powers. Similarly its role in industrialised communist countries is rather different from its role in capitalist countries. Take the case of Scottish football, which has a large following among working-class Scots. The massive popularity of football in Scotland is allied to its position as a nation within the British state. So the annual England/Scotland game assumes a massive symbolic importance – a contest between a subordinate nation and the dominant state. Every second year, the soft south is invaded by the northern hordes. The whole ritual, from the waving of yellow flags with rampant lions and 'Remember Bannockburn' slogans to the booing and whistling that drowns out *God Save the Queen*, is a complex mixture of sporting fervour, expression of national identity, class consciousness and political struggle. The jeering and booing of the national anthem has become such an embarrassment that sport authorities have tried to defuse the hostility by using a separate Scottish tune. But they have stuck to the traditional *Scotland the Brave*, in opposition to the fans' own loudly expressed preference for *Flower of Scotland*.

International competition does not, however, necessarily mean competition between nations though. The Olympic movement itself, flawed from the start, and further perverted by super-power competition and media spectacle, nevertheless had internationalist potential. Olympic competition was originally supposed to be between individuals rather than nations. The organisation of teams on a national basis was originally merely for convenience. But the whole set of rituals – parading of teams with national flags and medal ceremonies with flags and anthems – soon arose. The festival became an occasion for boosting national prestige. Newspapers and broadcasting further emphasised the national element by relaying comparative medal tables. Yet there is another kind of symbolism in the Olympic movement to do with internationalism, coming together and peace. The five interlocked rings on a white background that make up the Olympic flag express the unity of the continents as opposed to nations. The concept of the youth of all nations mingling in the Olympic Village is internationalist in conception, even if the reality may be fraught with tension, rivalry and overcrowding. The best moments in Olympic festivals have been when the spontaneous has broken through the organised, swamping formality. At the closing ceremony of the Commonwealth Games the athletes, bored with the endless pomp and interminable speeches, broke through the cordons to dance around the track, supplanting the rigidly orchestrated television event staged for the aggrandisement of Brisbane, with something closer to the spirit of a people's festival. One solution might be to replace formalised national sport with less formal contacts between groups and teams from different countries. There may be much to learn from the internationalism of the workers' sport movement of the inter-war years.

Competition presents another set of problems. To reject, as this book does, the argument that all competition is bad is not to accept that all forms of competition are equally acceptable. Competition can take grotesque, unpleasant and distorted forms, or friendly, co-operative and casual ones. There is also a spectrum between these extremes. Distinctions need to be made between competition between individuals, between teams, competition against records and events where individuals merely compete against their own limitations. Many undesirable aspects of competition have already been singled out. The widespread use of drugs to improve performance is one prominent example. Anabolic steroids heighten muscular development at the long-term expense of hormonal disturbance and impairment of sexual functioning. Puberty-delaying drugs are believed to be administered to girl gymnasts. Some Finnish runners have been widely reported to use blood-doping techniques, whereby quantities of blood are removed from the body to be returned to it shortly before a major competition. The growth of violence, be it the deliberate foul to cause injury in football and rugby, or the excess use of the whip in racing, has become a point of public concern. Rows over judging and refereeing decisions have grown to such a pitch that in sports such as gymnastics, tennis and motor-racing behind-the-scenes political battles have sometimes become more competitive than the sports themselves. Much of the fanaticism over winning can be traced to the enormous distinction made between winners and losers. Increasingly winning means access to great material rewards and international stardom, while losers fade quietly from the scene. Since the Moscow Olympics Coe and Ovett remain megastars. Yet how many remember Jurgen Straub, who actually finished ahead of Ovett in second place in the 1500 metres? One underlying message of the world of sport is that winning is everything and losing is nothing, even if losing is coming second. This is the logical outcome of bourgeois culture. Winning is equated with success and happiness. Losing is equated with failure.

But competition also has a positive side. It can go hand in hand with co-operation, friendship, mutual support and genuine human aspiration. It can also be fun. Teamwork involves co-operation and all team games require co-ordination, working together alongside competition. People develop close friendships in sport even though they are rivals. The development in China of a sport system under the sign 'Friendship Before Competition' is an attempt to change the emphasis of the values inscribed in sport. Athletics events often involve strong mutual support along with rivalry, as anyone who has watched a triple jump or pole vault can tell. The finish of the first London marathon, when the two leading runners crossed the line hand in hand, was more than a bit of showbiz kitsch. It was a spontaneous response to the spirit of an event in which, for once, taking part really was more important than winning. Even at the highest level sport can be performed with great enjoyment and mutual respect. It can also be real entertainment as opposed to mere spectacle. We need to explore ways of promoting the positive aspects of competition and diminishing the negative ones which often predominate at present.

This in turn means adopting a whole new policy towards the funding of sport. At present there are no principles as to the kinds of sport which it might be desirable to encourage. In a rationally planned society decisions have to be taken about what kind of activities to support with community resources. Arguing for socialism means arguing that some activities are more appropriate in a humane, caring and egalitarian society than others. Funding is limited and therefore the decisions as to its allocation involve choices. These choices should be taken in the context of clear policies. Women's participation in sport is low. The tradition in state funding has been that low participation is simply an indication of low demand. If few women play sport then most do not want to play, so little attention is paid to providing for them. Recent policy documents break with this tradition in singling out low-participation groups for attention. These proposals will remain good intentions until they are translated into action. Sports centres with proper facilities for women, full social provision for childcare, the employment of women motivators, could all increase the level of women's participation. A more consistent sport policy could go further.

Faced with demands for funding from, for example, archery, bobsleigh, curling, cycling, lacrosse and trampolining, the alternative to spreading the jam evenly, and therefore thinly, is to have a policy. Some sports are more worthy of support than others. It is surely absurd that this country, which has little regular snow, and no tradition in winter sports, save that of a small stratum of the aristocracy, should spend state money in a futile attempt to gain international success in winter sports. On the other hand, it is clearly undesirable that swimming, a mass popular sport and one of the few as popular with women as with men, should still suffer from under-provision, closure of pools, reduction of opening hours and creeping privatisation. A rational policy would also have to be imaginative. It would need to identify sports that could become popular if facilities existed. The danger at the moment is that the new high-tech sports, boosted by the entrepreneurs of the leisure industry and taken up first by the affluent young middle class, are seen uncritically. Socialists must have grave doubts about the wisdom of state funding for sports such as ballooning, hang-gliding and parachuting. There are sports that should be encouraged because of cheapness, accessibility and potential appeal. The advocates of korfball, a form of handball, point out that it is one of the few team sports in which men and women compete on equal terms. A policy committed to transforming the gender imbalance in sport participation should take this sort of claim seriously. Participation is also low amongst ethnic minorities. Participation amongst Asians is particularly low and it is time that sport policy recognised that not everyone wants to play the games invented by the English. When state funding goes to a whole range of oriental martial arts it is hard to justify not funding traditional sports from India and Pakistan.

There are pitfalls to be avoided in this approach. It would be a naive mistake to determine funding simply on the basis of the class image of particular sports. This book argues that sports cannot be assigned a class-belonging like a number plate. The emergence of tennis from middle class suburbia does not mean that there is something inherently middle class about the sport itself, merely that it was the bourgeoisie that controlled the facilities, ran the game and determined the values and social rituals within which it took place. This pattern was modified, but not substantially altered, by the spread of municipal provision. An attitude to archery, lacrosse, squash, or crown green bowls, speedway and greyhound-racing cannot be determined simply according to the apparent class base of the sport. More complex questions are involved that socialists have yet to explore.

A different set of issues is raised by sports that might be proscribed. All states have found the need to proscribe various sporting activities. Britain has barred not only cock-fighting and bear-baiting, but also bull-fighting, which is permitted in Spain and Portugal. The British Medical Association has recently launched a campaign to outlaw boxing. It is indeed difficult to see how a sport based centrally upon the attempt to cause more physical damage to an opponent than he can to you can be compatible with socialist principles. But this does not necessarily mean advocating prohibition. If boxing was banned could martial arts be left unrestricted? The implications have yet to be explored.

Hunting, based on cruelty to animals and the private ownership of vast tracts of land, is a far clearer case for abolition. Yet, if hunting is banned, what justification can be found for allowing angling? The argument that deer and foxes feel pain but not fish is unimpressive. I would not like to find myself impaled on a giant hook after taking a bite of cornflakes. I see no reason why fish should feel differently. We are cruel to a whole range of animals in the name of agriculture. But this is no reason why we should claim a licence for further cruelty in the name of sport. It seems to me an entirely inadequate defence of both boxing and fishing to say that they have a large working-class following. There is a great danger of hypocrisy if the logic of socialist principles is not followed through to its inevitable conclusion.

A radical approach to policy formation should also consider the form of sport events. One implication of the critique of elite sport and of the separation of different sports is that it would make sense to switch from major single-sport events to multi-sport, multi-ability people's festivals. There is a lot of scope for the promotion of such events by local councils. All the questions raised need further exploration. If a distinct socialist approach is to emerge, the issues of elite sport, nationalism and internationalism, forms of competition and types of sport to encourage will need discussion. The need is not for glib over-simple policies but for a continuing debate that takes the real complexities on board.

A culture of sport

England played an influential part in the formation of many sports. Its forms of organisation have been copied all over the world. Varied and rich cultures surround different sports. But there is little public discussion of sport and society. This country has produced no reflective philosophy of sport. Everything about sporting activity is taken for granted. The media report sport with great professional skill but discuss it with a crass lack of seriousness. Newspapers relay results efficiently and delight in trivial controversy, but are timid and uninformative about the organisation of sport. Television sport takes up as much as one-sixth of air time and is for the vast majority of the population the public face of sport. The technical sophistication of living colour and slow-motion replay is remarkable. So is its failure to produce informative sport journalism. Britain has no weekly sports newspaper, no equivalent to the French journal *L'Équipe*. Since the demise of *Sportsworld* the only monthly magazines covering a range of sports are house journals such as *Sport and Leisure* (the Sports Council) and *Action* (the Physical Education Association). Most sports publications are glossy magazines aimed at single sports. They are heavily constrained by the advertising imperative. So up-market sports, which appeal to affluent consumers, are best served. Water sport, motor sport, golf and tennis are covered by a wide range of titles. The journals that exploit the new boom in popular running all emphasise equipment – the best shoes, track suits and so on – in both articles and adverts. Many sports journals owe their success to the growth of spending on leisure and sport goods.

There is no place in which a dialogue between socialists interested in sport and sports people with a socialist outlook might develop. If progress towards the sort of transformations suggested in this book is to be made, then a site needs to be found to develop the discussion. For sport to develop it must be forced out of its self-imposed ghetto. Sport is not separate from social life as a whole, nor is it separate from cultural life. It is not a natural activity which cannot be changed and need not be discussed. There is scope for a new form of local centre. It could contain library facilities, exhibition space, meeting space, workshops with community-owned tools and equipment, cafés, nursery and laundry facilities and sport provision. Such centres, democratically run, could provide an alternative to privatised use of leisure time, and a way of integrating sport into social life generally. If a people's culture of sport is to emerge it needs to be built from below. It must not be based on a new level of cultural bureaucracy. Cuba has over 50,000 people actively involved in voluntary sport councils. These people are not simply functionaries who do the leg-work. They do not just organise events. They also work in factories, farms and offices to make sport popular. They produce media material – film and television items, posters and press reports. They are not officials but motivators. Their activity is given a framework by the socialist organisation of the society. Sport policy in this country has recently begun to place more emphasis on the role of motivator. But motivation will succeed fully only if it is allied with adequate provision and an overall strategy for making sport an integrated part of full human development.

In short, real change in the nature of sport depends on a broader socialist transformation. But that does not mean that developments in sport provision should be ignored. On the contrary, any chance of developing multi-activity local centres and promoting genuine people's festivals should be pursued. The Regional Recreation Strategy of the Greater London and South-East Council for Sport and Recreation contains a number of outline plans for new facilities. Two are of great interest: the possible redevelopment of Battersea Power Station and Alexandra Palace as sport and community centres. In the present economic climate these plans are unlikely to gain state support. If they did, they could still become rather over-priced, semi-privatised leisure centres for the affluent. But, properly funded and democratically controlled, they could become pioneering examples of a new form of community centre – a people's palace. There are many problems to be overcome, problems that apply to the whole concept of community centres. But it is an idea worth fighting for. Fighting cuts and privatisation is not enough. We need a positive alternative to struggle for. This should not be a return to the bureaucratised drabness of the municipal tradition. It should revitalise people's relation to their facilities. Hopefully the need to argue for socialist policies in an arena that reaches those involved in sport is obvious. The underlying rationale of this series of books is the need to make socialist ideas popular. We cannot afford to talk only to the converted.

2.7 A guide to reading*

There are countless thousands of books about sport, the great majority of which are biographies of great names, memories of great moments or coaching manuals. Some of these are of great merit, many others are hastily produced ghost-written attempts to cash in on fame. To keep this guide short I have concentrated on three areas of specific interest to readers of this book: socialist accounts of sport, histories and information about policy.

There are three socialist accounts of particular interest. *Sport, a Prison of Measured Time* by Jean-Marie Brohm (Inklinks 1978) is the most elaborate critique of the whole institution of sport as such to appear in book form to date. *Sport, Culture and Ideology*, edited by Jenny Hargreaves (Routledge and Kegan Paul 1982), is an excellent collection, with contributions on youth culture, football hooliganism, women and sport, sport in the Soviet Union, apartheid, drugs and television sport. *Beyond a Boundary* by West Indian Marxist C. L. R. James (Stanley Paul 1963) is a remarkable book, which weaves together autobiography, cricket, politics, literature and art and asks, 'What do they know of cricket, who only cricket know?' Essential reading for anyone interested in sport.

There are several books that develop critiques of sport. *Rip Off the Big Game* by Paul Hoch (New York: Anchor 1972), *Football Mania* by Gerhard Vinnai (Ocean 1973), *From Ritual to Record* by Allen Guttman (New York: Columbia University Press 1978) and *The Name of the Game* by Fred Inglis (Heinemann 1977) are the most relevant to Chapter 2.

There are a number of accounts of the struggle against apartheid in sport. *The South African Game* by Robert Archer and Antone Bouillon (Zed Press 1982) has a detailed explanation of the South African sport system. *Apartheid, the Real Hurdle* by Sam Ramsamy of SANROC (International Defence and Aid Fund for South Africa 1982) outlines the political struggle to isolate South African sport and South African attempts to undermine the boycott. *Don't Play with Apartheid* by Peter Hain (Allen and Unwin 1970) relates the story of the highly successful campaign to stop the 1970 cricket tour by South Africa. The recent rise of black people in British sport has been documented in *Black Sportsmen* by Ernest Cashmore (Routledge and

Kegan Paul 1982). The book contains many interesting interviews but concentrates, without offering any reason, almost exclusively on men.

The history of sport is poorly documented. Most general histories tend to ignore sport, while most histories of sport are little more than reminiscences of great occasions and top stars of the past. The books listed here are an exception and consequently a major source for anyone interested in the development of sport and leisure. *Sport and Society, from Elizabeth to Anne* by Dennis Brailsford (Routledge and Kegan Paul 1969), *Popular Recreations in English Society 1700–1850* by Robert Malcolmson (Cambridge University Press 1973) and *Leisure in the Industrial Revolution* by Hugh Cunningham (Croom Helm 1980) are all useful accounts of the development of sport before its reorganisation in the second half of the nineteenth century. The rise of public school sport is examined in *Athleticism in the Victorian and Edwardian Public School* by J. A. Mangan (Cambridge University Press 1981). *Physical Education in England since 1800* by Peter McIntosh (Bell and Hyman 1968) traces the emergence of distinctive ways in which sport and physical activity have been handled in schools. Brian Dobbs's *Edwardians at Play 1890–1914* (Pelham 1973) is a valuable account of the place of sport in this pre-war period. For a general history covering the whole period to the present day, *This Sporting Land* by John Ford (New English Library/Thames 1977) makes a useful introduction.

Only a few histories of specific sports place events in any kind of social context. Among the more useful are *English Cricket* by Christopher Brookes (Weidenfeld and Nicolson 1978), *The People's Game* by James Walvin (Allen Lane 1975), *Association Football and English Society 1863–1915* by Tony Mason (Harvester 1980), *Golf in Britain* by Geoffrey Cousins (Routledge and Kegan Paul 1975), *The Official Centenary History of the AAA* by Peter Lovesey (Guinness Superlatives 1979) and *The Complete Book of Athletics* by Tom McNab (Ward Lock 1980). *Only a Game* by Eamon Dunphy (Kestrel 1976) is a remarkable diary of a football season, far more revealing about the game than sport autobiographies. As an antidote to the perennial hysteria over 'football hooliganism', *Football Hooliganism: The Wider Context*, a collection of pieces edited by Roger Ingham (InterAction Inprint 1978), is a source of alternative explanations. There is interesting material on the historical origins of British football in *The Sociology of Sport*, edited by Eric Dunning (Cass 1976).

So far there is a regrettable absence of book-length accounts of women and sport in this country, although there are articles and papers. *Sport, Culture and Ideology* (already listed) contains some material on women, sport and leisure. Margaret Talbot's review paper *Women and Leisure* (Sports Council/SSRC 1980) has references in the broader area of leisure. Historical sources include *The Nineteenth-Century Woman, Her Cultural and Physical World* by Sara Delamont and Lorna Duffin (Croom Helm 1978), *Hidden from History* by Sheila Rowbotham (Pluto 1973) and *English Costumes for Sports and Outdoor Recreations* by P. Cunnington and A. Mansfield (Adam and Charles Black 1969). *Catching Up the Men* by K. F. Dyer (Junction 1982) contains a detailed examination of the narrowing performance gap between women and men in top sport. There is a lot of material about women and sport in America, much of it in the tradition of functional sociology. One of the better books is *Women and Sport, from Myth to Reality* by Carole Oglesby (Philadelphia: Lea and Febiger 1978).

More information about the sport system in other countries is available mainly in article form, but two books worth examination are *Sport under Communism*, edited by James Riordan (Hurst 1978), and Don Anthony's *A Strategy for British Sport* (Hurst 1980). James Riordan has also written extensively about sport in the Soviet Union, in *Sport in Soviet Society* (Cambridge University Press 1977) and *Soviet Sport* (Blackwell 1980).

Football is the only sport with a developed form of trade union and a history of organised struggles over pay and conditions. For information about this, try *Soccer Rebel* by Jimmy Guthrie (Davis Foster 1976), *Striking for Soccer* by Jimmy Hill (Peter Davies 1961), *On the Spot* by Derek Dougan and Percy M. Young (Stanley Paul 1975), *Hardaker of the League* by Alan Hardaker (Pelham 1977), *The Football Revolution* by George W. Keeton (David and Charles 1977) and the *Chester Report on Football* (DES 1968). The brief account of workers' sport organisations between the wars offered in this book is based upon two articles in *Journal of Contemporary History*, vol. 13, no. 2, April 1978.

Despite the prominence of television sport there is as yet no comprehensive study in book form. Football coverage is discussed in *Football on Television*, edited by Edward Buscombe (British Film Institute 1975), and there is a paper on *Television Coverage of Sport* by Roy Peters (available from Centre for Contemporary Cultural Studies, University of Birmingham 1975). Otherwise the main accounts are in biographical form, perhaps the most interesting being *Cue Frank* by Frank Bough (Macdonald Futura 1980). Now this book is finished I hope to write up my own extensive research into television sport.

There are two books of relevance to the discussion of sport policy, the official history of the CCPR, *Service to Sport*, by H. Justin Evans (Pelham 1974), and Don Anthony's *A Strategy for British Sport* (already listed). Otherwise information about policy is largely in the form of official reports, documents and research papers. In particular anyone interested in sport policy ought to look at *Sport in the Community: The Next Ten Years*, the current Sports Council strategical plan. Each regional Sports Council has also recently published a *Regional Recreation Strategy*. The Sports Council and the Social Science Research Council have jointly published a range of research papers, including material on women, youth, ethnic and elderly leisure patterns and private and state leisure organisation. A complete list of reports, documents and leaflets published or distributed by the Sports Council is available from the Publications Department, The Sports Council, 16 Upper Woburn Place, London WC1H 0QP.

* *Blowing the Whistle* was aimed at a general reader, and the series house style dispensed with the usual references to sources. Consequently, I have included the guide to reading from the original edition, which helps to highlight the extensive growth in publishing on the social and cultural dimensions of sport that has taken place since 1983.

2.8 Afterword

NOTEBOOK

Alternative Bestsellers

A selection of London's bookshops reports on what has been selling well in the capital this week. Brackets indicate position last week; figures in bold the number of weeks in the list, not necessarily consecutive.

Fiction

1 (1) **18** **The Color Purple** by Alice Walker (Women's Press, £3.95) A novel of pain, hope and celebration is the form of a young black woman's letters to her god. This year's Pulitzer Prize winner still outstripping the opposition.

2 (2) **6** **Tar Baby** by Tony Morrison (Granada, £1.95) By the author of 'Song of Solomon', a magical novel explores the history and complexities of black freedom struggles through the eyes of a black woman academic in Paris.

3 (-) **1** **Adah's Story** by Buchi Emecheta (Allison & Busby, £2.95) Collects 'Second Class Citizen' and 'In The Ditch' into one volume: the story of a young Nigerian woman coming to this country and finding the going tougher than expected.

4 (-) **14** **Braided Lives** by Marge Piercy (Penguin, £1.95) Powerful, introspective novel of women's emotional history.

5 (-) **1** **Paris, America** by Gertrude Stein (Brilliance, £2.50) Good to see Gertrude back in the charts. First British paperback of 1940 edition, with a new introduction by Jean Straus.

Non-Fiction

1 (1) **3** **Womansize** by Kim Chernin (Women's Press, £4.50) American feminist critique of the tyranny of slenderness.

2 (-) **1** **The Fragrance Of Guava** by Plinio Apuleyo Mendoza (Verso, £2.50). Mendoza in conversation with Gabriel García Márquez.

3 (-) **1** **Sweet Ramparts** by Deighton et al (Nicaragua Solidarity Campaign, £2.95) A collection of essays on 'Women in Revolutionary Nicaragua', providing a perspective on change since the revolution.

4 (-) **1** **Style Wars** by Peter York (Sidgwick & Jackson, £4.95) A belated paperback of York's witty analysis of punk, and post-punk, raisons d'être.

5 (-) **1** **Blowing The Whistle** by Garry Whannel (Pluto, £2.50) In the 'Arguments For Socialism' series, a useful primer on sport and the Left.

Figure 2.8.1 The Alternative Bestsellers list.

It is hard to assess the impact of the book on the market. It sold out its initial print run, and appeared, briefly, in a *Time Out* Alternative Bestsellers list (along with Alice Walker, Gertrude Stein and Peter York). It became key reading on sports studies courses about the time that the book ceased to be in print. It has remained on key reading lists, and this was a major impetus for this new edition. I imagine far more people have read it than were able to buy it, never the ideal situation for a penniless freelance, as I was then. Many people since have been kind enough to tell me that it had an influence on their thinking.

It is never comfortable for an author to reflect on the strengths and weaknesses of previous work, as I have been invited to, and indeed feel impelled to do, here. Re-reading it, I recognised all the faults of youth – naivety, gaucheness, brashness – along with some of the merits of youth – combativeness, and disrespectfulness. More seriously the book is parochial, and British centred, in a way that is far more striking now than it would have been then. Of course partly this was a consequence of the address of the book to policy issues in the British context. My own account, in the introduction to this volume, probably reveals much of the context of this parochialism. It came out of a sensibility shaped by engagements with the specific British conditions of politics, culture and sport policy. There has since been a growing imperative for analyses that cross state borders, that acknowledge globalising processes, that take into account issues of perspective and positionality, diaspora and hybridity raised by post-colonialism. Indeed much recent work in the sports studies field has taken on this task. Publishers are increasingly keen to press authors to write books saleable in more than one market. There are, of course, dangers in over-generalisation and loss of cultural specificity; and a continuing need for culturally specific embedded and grounded analyses.

The politics of the book may have echoed the tactical preoccupations of a small, young, middle-class leftist metropolitan intelligentsia, but in retrospect, this strata lacked the strategic vision to grapple with the complex political manoeuvring that was required to secure a longer term position within the opposition to Thatcherism. The defeat of the radical socialist moment of the early 1980s and the rise of Third Way politics should be a salutary warning that practical socialist analysis needs to pay attention to strategies for policy, and to ways of winning, building and holding broader support for a radical and alternative agenda. The experience of the 1980s and 1990s should have taught us that sniping from the sidelines is never enough. Many people within sport organisations and local authorities were engaged in micro-struggles over resources and policy. I met some of them around the period of writing the book, as I was working on a radio series about sport and politics. In retrospect, it is a shame that more of this detail did not find its way into the book. From outside, institutions can seem like seamless monoliths, agents of oppression, ideological state apparatuses. The left, and possibly the book, devoted far too much energy to merely casting ill-aimed stones at the concrete carapace of institutional power. We should remember that institutions are rarely so seamless, so uniform. They are forged through struggle and contestation, they are riven with internal contradictions, they are a site of continuing struggle, and there are people within who need and deserve support and a different kind of relation with those outside. I think now of those who fought to keep swimming pool prices subsidised, those who established women-only sessions to encourage more British-Asian girls to swim; those who tried to block the sale of school playing fields. Those who tried, as did Labour's GLC in the early 1980s, to introduce innovative sport policies against the grain of the brass-buttoned blazerati of British sport were part of the broader struggle for more egalitarian and democratic forms of provision. They fought a lonely fight, and must all too often have felt marginalised. The book could usefully have reflected more of this. While the book paid lip service to struggles against sexism and racism in sport, it did not fully get inside these issues, and did not succeed in offering an analysis of their relationship to the broader context of race and gender politics, or indeed of politics generally.

I would claim the book had its strengths and passages that are still pertinent. I would still insist on the distinction between politics *and* sport, and politics *of* sport. It seems to me important that there are people prepared to engage in sport on its own terms, to struggle to change and alter its own internal politics (race- and gender-based campaigns, the campaign to give fans a greater say in the way clubs are run in football, pressure on local authorities to continue to serve a social role in sports provision, campaigns against commercialisation, etc.). I still believe the bread and circuses view to be profoundly wrong; we should never discount the real pleasures of sport both as participant and as spectator, and even, or especially, as viewer. The book spoke out against the rather one-dimensional analysis of sport then prevalent on the left. This still holds. The historical sections, I still believe, constitute clear, if over-simplified, introductions to the material formation of the institutions and practices of sport, in their contradictory trajectory into modernity. Of course they were only introductions – one hoped a reader would go and read Dunning, John Hargreaves, Jennifer Hargreaves, Mangan, Holt, Brohm, Gruneau and James. But all readers need a starting point. Above all the discussion of commercialisation and of the erosion of welfare statist notions of sport for all by the introduction of public–private partnerships, written as they were in the early years of a transformative process, serve to draw our attention to the enormity of the changes that have occurred.

The book was part of a broader tendency in which the new cultural studies fed into a new cultural politics. In many ways the cultural politics/cultural studies project has had extraordinary successes. It has been part of the growth of a self- reflective awareness of the meanings embedded in popular culture. Decoding and deconstruction have moved from being rather obscure intellectual methodologies to being part of the ways in which people constantly read and interpret the universe of signs they exist within. To listen to young people talking about advertising, style or brand image reveals as much. But the fears voiced by some about the dangers of the institutionalisation of cultural studies turned out to be prescient. Cultural studies moved from being a critical irritant within established disciplines to being constructed as a subject in gradually academicised, institutionalised and, to an extent, depoliticised forms. As universities have become starved of resources, and staff–student ratios have risen, the institutional pressures on staff have become greater. Careerism and the pressure to publish have distorted the focus and quality of scholarly production. The policies of senior management have been characterised by a growing philistine hostility to research except where 'practical', and geared to 'endusers', ideally with a financial return to be made. In consequence there has been a devaluing of forms of intellectual productivity that engage with broad audiences (except those highly specialised and semi-mythic 'end users'). There is little professional kudos in writing for non-academic audiences – it does not score research points, and points, as any fool knows, mean prizes.

Municipal socialism was defeated in a series of dramatic public political battles, most notably in London and Liverpool. The rout of the left, the destruction of union power, the halt of the 'forward march of Labour', the collapse of Eastern bloc communism and consequent implosion of Western communist parties contributed to a mood of soul searching, debates over tactics and strategies and the reconfiguring of the political landscape. The magazine *Marxism Today* had its finest moments during this period, prompting a lively and open debate about the 'new times'. Identity politics, sexual politics, racial politics and ecological politics were amongst the fragments that some hoped to nudge towards a new rainbow alliance. Meanwhile Neil Kinnock was cleansing the Augean stables of the last traces of militancy, and as it turned out, preparing the property for its Blairite makeover. There have been, it must be said, dramatic advances in the UK around the politics of race, gender, sexuality and identity. In the Britain of the 1950s, in which I grew up, it was routine to see signs offering flats for rent which specified No Irish, No Blacks and No Dogs. Homosexuality and abortion were illegal, contraception difficult to obtain and the pill yet to be invented, divorce involved scandal and humiliation, children born 'out of wedlock' were stigmatised as 'bastards'. The cultural landscape has been transformed in my lifetime. The political agenda now is a different one from that in 1983.

In Part 2, I try and explore sport from the perspective of this new cultural landscape and in relation to the new political agenda. The main sections in Part 2 of this book concern pleasure, commercialisation and commodification, spaces, globalisation, celebrity and masculinity, national identity, and politics. First, though, to conclude Part 1, I have chosen to include in this volume two pieces that I published in 1994, around halfway between the year of the original *Blowing the Whistle* and this present book. They address two themes that developed in my work after *Blowing the Whistle*: the relations between the ideological and economic dimensions of sport, and between the pleasures of sport and its commodified forms. I chose these two papers for two main reasons. First, because they appeared in relatively obscure places, and have not been as well read as some other, in my view lesser, pieces I have written. Second, because in their concerns with both performance and commodity, with both ideal and reality, with both aspiration and result, I think they catch something of my own ambivalent responses to sport – the hopes and the disappointments, the joys and the sadnesses, and the exultation and the disillusionment.

3   Profiting by the presence of ideals
Sponsorship and Olympism

(Originally given as a paper to the International Olympic Academy in 1992, transcribed and published as Whannel, G. (1994) Profiting by the presence of ideals: Sponsorship and Olympism, *International Olympic Academy: 32nd Session*, pp. 89–93, Olympia, Greece: International Olympic Academy.)

> Ideals are like the stars – we cannot reach them, but oh, how we profit by their presence.
>
> Richard Pym, the father of the hero of John Le Carré's *The Perfect Spy*[9]

> CARS LOVE SHELL
> How can I say I love – How can I say 'I love you' after hearing 'CARS LOVE SHELL'? Does anyone understand what I *mean*?
>
> Jerry Rubin[10]

Jerry Rubin was drawing attention to the way that advertising appropriates language, and drains it of its emotional force, and ultimately of its meaning. I think there is a real danger that this is about to begin happening in the Olympic movement. In promoting their products, the major Olympic sponsors seek to draw upon the language of Olympism, the Olympic ideals and the Olympic spirit. In doing so they may serve to drain those ideals of their force. I am very aware, in writing this, of two English clichés – 'don't bite the hand that feeds you', and 'he who pays the piper calls the tune'. Let me say right away that it is not my intention to attack the very concept of sponsorship. I am not that kind of idealist – sponsorship is not going to go away, and the revenue it provides has great potential value to sport institutions, if used wisely. However, I think we have to recognise that those who pay the piper might at the least tend to influence the piper's repertoire. Indeed no less an Olympian than Seb Coe, certainly no enemy of commerce as such, has warned that those who pay the piper are tending to want to rewrite the symphony.[11] It is now widely accepted that the Olympic Games has been transformed by television. The huge advertising market in North America, and resultant competition between the networks for Olympic rights, has produced hundreds of millions of dollars in revenue for the IOC. Television has provided the Olympic Games with a global audience. Television has also, I would argue, transformed the cultural dimension of the games, exerting an influence over the programme, the schedule, and the presentation of the Games.[12]

Through this process of globalisation the Olympic rings have become a universally recognised symbol. The Olympic Games connotes excellence. It is no surprise that global corporations have realised the advantages of commercial involvement with Olympism. For the IOC too, this made sound sense. The Olympic Games was becoming too dependent on American television revenue, and needed to broaden its base.[13] ISL devised the TOP programme, which has now produced a whole new revenue source of growing importance. On the face of it, there should be less concern over the impact of sponsorship. Unlike American television, which hopes desperately for Games sites in time zones that allow live coverage in peak time, sponsors have no need to be overly concerned with the choice of site. As long as no arena advertising is allowed, sponsors do not intrude into the visual spectacle. Finally, television revenue comes predominately from the single American network that has won the rights, and this network is in a position to exert focused pressure. By contrast sponsorship is spread among a dozen companies, who may have very different needs. Any pressure they may exert to change the Games is rather more diffused.

The problems arise when one considers the image of Olympism, the state of Olympic idealism, and the degree to which images and ideals are inevitably transformed by their reproduction in the more commercialised context. It has been suggested that what ISL markets is not the Games, but the Olympic Idea, as symbolised by the five rings. Juergen Lenz, formerly of ISL, points to the unique global reach of the Olympic Games, and is fond of saying that 'there are only four things that travel across borders: sports, music, violence and sex. And it's difficult to find sponsors for violence and sex.'[14] Sport is of particular value – not only does it reach a global audience, but reaches all ages, all classes and (despite a higher proportion of men) both genders. In addition, it signifies youth, health, fitness, and success, extremely desirable elements for many advertising campaigns. Indeed the enthusiasm with which tobacco companies have invested in sports sponsorship suggests that the less healthy the product the more keen it will be to sponsor sporting events. The Olympic Games offers all these desirable properties, along with excellence, guaranteed and symbolised by the five rings – the world's most instantly recognisable logo (rivalled only by McDonald's golden arch). So there is a potential contradiction between the imperatives of commerce and the traditions of Olympism. Surely warning bells should start to ring when we hear that the French sponsors of the 1992 Winter Olympics were grouped together in an organisation that was named Club Coubertin. I want to examine two aspects of the interaction between commercialism and idealism: the use of Olympic sport as a marketing tool; and the recasting of elements of Olympic idealism in advertising.

Marketing sport and its values

There is a growing tendency for sport to be seen as a marketing tool – Kodak refer to the Olympic Games as a worldwide marketing opportunity. Sponsors are part of the Olympic Family, and the family is increasingly involved with corporate entertainment, the marketing of souvenirs, the distribution of promotional freebies, and the battle for commercial exclusivity. Corporate hospitality is an increasingly visible feature of major sport events like the Olympic Games. The very visible presence of a strata of pampered guests, whose interest in sport is sometimes less than intense, has done little to enhance the image of sport's governing authorities in the eyes of ordinary sport fans. TOP sponsors get some free tickets, accommodation and privileged access to Olympic sites. *Time* took 300 people to Albertville and planned to take around 2,000 to Barcelona. EMS were believed to have budgeted for $3 million in hotel rooms, $250,000 in Winter Games tickets and almost $100,000 in dinner cruises. Despite the huge investment EMS are making in Olympic sponsorship, they hope to make a profit from added sales of Express Mail, and from marketing of T-shirts, key chains and other Olympic linked souvenirs. They have arranged for the marketing of more than 300 items including a $299 colour TV and a $174 porcelain eagle.[15] How much control does the IOC now have over the quality and tastefulness of such souvenirs?

Bausch and Lomb will offer each competitor a pair of Ray Bans, in their words 'thereby incorporating them into the official uniform of each National Olympic Committee'. Every medal winner will be presented with a pair of gold, silver or bronze Ray Bans in recognition of their achievements, and Bausch and Lomb comment that 'A visit to the Athletes Village would show clearly that Ray Ban is the athletes' preferred choice of sunglass' – surprise, surprise. The Olympic Family is now becoming swollen with its adopted corporate children – EMS claimed that three and a half million postal employees are now a part of the Olympic Movement. And like other well publicised families, the Olympic Family devotes much energy to taking care of the family businesses. The Visa advertising campaign features shots of top sports performers in gruelling exertion and the voice-over says, 'But if you think he's tough, wait till you see the guys at the ticket window if you don't have your Visa card. Because Visa is the only card they'll accept. Visa – it's everywhere you want to be.' In the USA the Visa advertisement says 'wait till you see the guys at the ticket window if you try and pay with American Express'. So don't leave home *with* it, and Access, your flexible friend, is no good either. American Express hit back with a spoiler campaign, trying to link themselves with the Games, and the commercial battle produced an acrimonious legal contest. This is hardly in the spirit of taking part being more important than winning. Indeed the ability to freeze a competitor out has become a major motive for Olympic sponsors such as Visa, Coca-Cola and Kodak. Research indicates that Visa's profile has overtaken American Express and is now level pegging with traditional sponsors such as Philips and Kodak. American research after the 1984 Olympic Games showed that 83 per cent had positive recall of sponsors advertising, 43 per cent said that Olympic sponsorship enhanced their opinion of a company, and 33 per cent said they would buy a brand sponsoring the Games.[16] Significantly, all these percentages were even greater among the more affluent.

Corporate images and Olympic ideals

Companies are increasingly seeking to link their image to the Olympics. In doing so they are drawing on and appropriating the themes of Olympism. Golden memories, the Olympic spirit, youth, festivity, and athletic aspiration and innovation provide a lexicon of elements from which advertisements can select and juxtapose, in order to recast products in an Olympian glow. A Kodak ad links a series of personal images with more famous sporting ones, with the voice-over proclaiming: 'from special personal moments to great moments in history – one brand of film more than any other captures the full colour and naturalness of life. Kodak Film – let the memories begin.'

The Express Mail Service tells us to 'save these stamps and you capture the Olympic Spirit – Ask for them now at your Post Office and keep that spirit alive!' The assistant postmaster general, in charge of the Olympic promotion, says the Olympic symbols belong on the stamps because they stand for speed and excellence, qualities that the mail service and the Olympics share.[17] Olympic festivity is becoming increasingly entangled in commercial promotional strategies. In 1984 Coca-Cola made plans to 'paint Los Angeles red' with the Coke trademark. Concentrating on main roads within a five-mile radius of each of 23 venues, they bought billboards, store front signs, and sidewalk benches.[18] In promoting their involvement with the same games, McDonald's hamburger chain distributed more than 300 million Olympic theme game cards.[19] Earlier this year, at Albertville, Coca-Cola boasted that their vending machines and billboards would light up the Savoy valleys like a fireworks display. Of course this merely makes a place look like downtown of any big city. What happened to cultural distinctiveness – come to think of it what happened to real fireworks?

Coca-Cola are of course the longest standing Olympic sponsor and they draw on this in trying to make their own links between Olympic quality and the qualities of their own product:

> There's a feeling in this country. It's in the Olympics and wherever people reach deep down inside to do their very best. It's a thirst for greatness. The same kind of greatness that has made Coca-Cola the world's favourite soft drink and part of the Olympic dream for 60 years.[20]

Are we happy about equating Paavo Nurmi, Jesse Owens, Emil Zatopek, Fanny Blankers-Coen, Dawn Fraser, Peter Snell, Alberto Juantorena, Mark Spitz, Nadia Comaneci, Marita Koch or Carl Lewis with a fizzy drink made from sugar and water? Another Coke ad proclaims that 'when the Olympic day is over, the Olympic spirit continues', over shots of fashionable and stylish young people drinking Coke and concludes 'That's the Olympic spirit and Coca-Cola has always been a part of it'. Youth has indeed always been a central element in the Olympic spirit, but youth internationalism should not be restricted to the slim, stylish and affluent. In attempting to make a connection between their products and Olympism, campaigns at times descend to absurdity. A series of 3M ads, using the slogan '3M: Innovation working for you', might better be titled 'the sublime and the ridiculous'. Comparing a series of innovations in sport and stationery, they link Sonja Henje and ice dancing with Scotch Tape, the Fosbury Flop with Scotchguard protector, and Olga Korbut's backward somersault on the beam with the invention of Post-It notes.

Contradictions and corporatism

In this fusion of corporate capitalism and Olympic idealism, contradictions inevitably emerge. The IOC has to manage a festival of youth rooted in an idealist philosophy, which has become a global spectacle, creating sporting stars, generating advertising revenue, boosting corporate profits, and agency income. Express Mail Services plan to spend $122 million on Olympic promotion and hope for revenue of $177 million from stamp and merchandise sales, and increased use of the parcel service.[21] Do I seem to remember a principle about no one profiting from the Olympic Games? It is no surprise that the concept of amateurism has been rendered redundant, irrelevant and laughable. It has become untenable to allow agencies, corporations and networks to profit, while at the heart of the spectacle, sportsmen and women are supposed to remain hermetically sealed away from commercial reward.

It is not so long ago that Lord Killanin was able, from Olympian heights, to warn the world of the need to 'unite in peace before a holocaust descends'.[22] More recently a set of stamps, featuring the Olympic rings and the American flag, was launched in a ceremony saluting Olympic medallists, Olympic hopefuls and the families of Desert Storm military personnel. It is a little hard to see quite how this fits the project of peace and international understanding.[23] *Time* with *Sports Illustrated* are now a TOP Programme sponsor. *Sports Illustrated* plan a special Olympic issue, and, uniquely, *Time* plan an extra issue as an Olympic preview.[24] But how can we fairly judge the journalistic neutrality of publications reviewing events they are sponsoring? Giving one news organisation privileged status does little to promote journalistic integrity, and the row between Visa and American Express has done little to promote the co-operative ethos.

A recent conference on food, the *International Consensus Conference on Food and Nutrition*, was sponsored by Mars and held under the patronage of the IOC

Medical Commission. A video report of the conference uses clips from doctors and scientists and ordinary people. None of them specifically praise Mars but the cumulative effect is to suggest the following argument – carbohydrates are an important element in diet; both simple and complex carbohydrates have a role; sweets are one useful source of simple carbohydrates. Now nutrition science is not my field and I wouldn't presume to make extensive comment on this. I understand that there is a perfectly valid case that simple carbohydrates are a useful source of quick energy for athletes in training who may not want the bulkier complex carbohydrates.[25] The fact is that the research I was referred to in the course of my necessarily limited enquiries in this area was part-funded by Mars. I am not questioning the integrity of the research, but just as I don't want research on global warming to be determined too much by funding from ICI, nor do I want our understanding of nutrition to be structured by confectionary manufacturers. It is not a case of manipulation of research findings, but rather an issue of how research priorities and research agendas are established. In Western society obesity, diabetes, heart disease and tooth decay are all causes for concern. We have to ask if it is appropriate for non-essential sugar-based products to position themselves at the heart of Olympism. What might we think of a conference on alcoholism sponsored by brewers or on heart and lung disease sponsored by a tobacco company?

One characteristic theme in corporate advertising is the suggestion that the corporation cares extend beyond the balance sheet. So chemical companies proclaim their concern for the environment, banks boast of their ability to listen, and soft drink manufacturers hint at their desire for universal harmony. Ricoh's campaign slogan is 'making a world of difference' and their ads proclaim that

> The Olympic Facsimile network is just one example of Ricoh's advanced technologies and social commitments are drawing people closer. For that is not just a corporate goal but a responsibility. Our social role goes beyond developing and marketing state of the art products. With our support for cultural and sporting events we are creating new opportunities for communication and quite simply raising the quality of life.[26]

Perhaps I shouldn't say too much on this as I was able to fax my acceptance of the invitation to this conference, and I'm sure it was received, safely, on a Ricoh. Indeed the fax, unlike the Coke, is both genuinely useful and progressive. In this sense, it does have real organic links to the Olympic ideals. The fax machine also, famously, enabled Primo Nebiolo to inform the world of his appointment to the IOC one minute after it was made.[27] But this social responsibility cannot become limited to those who can afford a FAX. Indeed the world is peopled largely by those who can barely afford bread, never mind a Coke. Where do they now fit into the Olympic dream? For their images do not appear in the montages of sleek stylish world youth enjoying harmony and fizz that Coke and other advertisers are showering us with.

Does any of this matter? I think the answer to this question depends upon how one assesses the relevance of Olympism as we head for a new millennium. The Olympic Games has always aspired to being more than just a sporting event. If Ronald McDonald runs out to perform the ceremonial kick-off at the next World Cup in 1994 in the USA, I suggest to you that few will be seriously shocked.[28] The World Cup has no pretensions to be anything other than a modern commercial global spectacle, run on rationalist lines. It has no lofty ideals. By comparison the Olympic Games has always been more than a sporting event. It has a whole complex apparatus of rituals, symbols, traditions and ideals. Ever since the first modern Games in 1896, the Olympic movement has been set on a collision course between idealism and materialism, a conflict brought to a head by the processes of spectacularisation, commercialism and globalisation that television helped to trigger.

The battle is constantly being fought out. The refusal to permit arena advertising is, it is sometimes suggested, an example of the strength of tradition and the determination to resist erosion of idealism by commerce. The only other major event to take such a principled stand is the Wimbledon Tennis Championship. In fact, as the highly successful marketing of Wimbledon has demonstrated, the very exclusion of commerce, by giving the Championships a 'special' aura of being above commerce, ironically greatly enhances its commercial value. By the same token, the IOC are well aware that refusing arena advertising, in helping to mark out the 'special' properties of the Olympic Games, gives them an enhanced value to sponsors.

Some in the IOC are now eager to permit arena advertising, and Nebiolo wants to introduce advertising on the number bibs.[29] This, in the short term, would produce more sponsorship revenue. In the long term, however, it might ultimately undermine the high level of prestige attached to the Olympic Rings. There is a need for caution on two pragmatic grounds. First, arena advertising will signal to the world that the Olympic Games is just another heavily commercialised event like all the others. The commercial value of the aura will be devalued. This process is in fact already well underway – in allowing sponsors to utilise elements of Olympic idealism in their advertising, the Olympic movement could be inadvertently engaged in selling the family silver. Second, the faith of corporations in the power of sport sponsorship is not necessarily a permanent feature of advertising economics. The Olympics offers rare access to the global market, but there are not many corporations who market products to a global market. ISL has not yet succeeded in marketing all of its product categories. The advertising industry is in the midst of a crisis of confidence, as outlets proliferate and markets fragment, causing one analyst to comment that 96 per cent of all advertising is wasted but no one knows which 96 per cent.[30] The IOC could find that sponsorship revenue provides an unstable base, although as long as major corporations such as Coke and Pepsi, Visa and Amex, Kodak and Fuji are prepared to slug it out, this seems unlikely.

With reference to the pending court case concerning American Express, Richard Pound of the IOC has said 'when the only thing you have to sell are the aspirations of youth and five rings, then misappropriation of intellectual property becomes a very serious matter'. But whose property is it? Do the IOC own the aspirations of youth – and do they have any right to sell them to Coca-Cola, Visa, Mars or the others?[31] A quote is relevant here:

> Ideals are like the stars – we cannot reach them, but oh, how we profit by their presence.

It was a favourite saying of Richard Pym, the father of the hero of John Le Carré's *The Perfect Spy*. Pym was a liar, cheat and con-man. He had great charm and tried almost every dodge going, but for some reason it never occurred to him to sell the stars to sponsors. Modern sport was formed in the context of capitalist consolidation and expansion, international sport grew out of the imperialist networks of the European powers. Television helped transform international sport into a global spectacle, and multinational corporate capitalism has further boosted this process of globalisation. The central contradictions for the Olympic movement are, and always have been, those between idealism and materialism, between utopianism and pragmatism, between festivity and spectacle. These oppositions are not easy to reconcile or transcend, and will continue to constitute the terrain upon which Olympism must reproduce itself. Well, I've at least managed to please the sponsors by mentioning most of them, and as we know any publicity is good publicity.

4 Sport and popular culture

The temporary triumph of process over product

(Originally published as Whannel, Garry (1993) Sport and popular culture: the temporary triumph of process over product, in *Innovations*, 6(3).)

In this article I want to address questions that have concerned me for some time; specifically, what pleasures are involved in the consumption of sport, and what role do heroes, as figures for identification, play. First, however, it is necessary to explain briefly the sense in which I am using the concept of popular culture. I am operating with a definition of popular culture derived largely from the work of the Open University course team who devised a popular culture course in the early 1980s. Broadly speaking, they argued that popular culture should be understood neither as the authentic culture of the people, nor as commercialised mass-produced artefacts, but rather as the result of processes of struggle and contestation between cultural practices generated from below and imposed from above (Bennett 1981). While many cultural products have emerged from the practices of ordinary people to become popular, this production cannot take place separate from the process of mass production and distribution. In the era of mechanical production, mass culture and globalisation, language and meaning are themselves not neutral. It is no longer possible to conceptualise a folk tradition that can carry on un-influenced by, and in ignorance of, the world of Madonna, Michael Jackson, or Maradona. However, the alternative mass culture model of a domain of mass-produced cultural products imposed on a passive unthinking indiscriminate audience is not tenable either. Popular culture has to address its audience – it has to relate to their real lived experience, their lives, in some meaningful way, precisely in order to become popular. This need means that popular cultural production can never be totally controlled by producers – its success always also depends on striking the public nerve – articulating the right elements at the right moment in time for the right audience. In short, popular culture needs to be understood as a site of struggle, and as a field of complex and contradictory meanings (Bennett 1981).

Sports such as cricket in England, cycling in France, baseball in the USA, and football in much of the world are aspects of popular culture not simply because they are popular but because the rituals and practices associated with them grew out of, and are etched into, the everyday life of the people. However, in the era of mass production, popular culture is also a commercialised form, organised from above and sold in the marketplace. Football clubs, sport governing bodies, television companies, sportswear firms and sports agents are not for the most part popular-democratic bodies: they are not forms through which ordinary people can organise and control the processes of sporting production. Sport, like other aspects of popular culture, is the site of a struggle; and at stake is the power to define the nature of social reality – in this case the forms that popular sporting pleasures can take. Sport, however, is exceptional in one way. Of all popular cultural forms, sport has historically been one of the most gender specific. Many major sports have been the product primarily of male players, and male organisers, and have tended to win audiences that have been largely male. Modern sport had its formative moments during the second half of the nineteenth century and its governing bodies to this day are marked by this origin in their patriarchal structures and attitudes.

So this account of the pleasures of sport is inevitably an analysis of cultural practices that are largely male-defined. Indeed the cultures of sports spectating around sports such as football and cricket are specifically exclusive. Girls and women are marginalised, not simply by virtue of their smaller numbers, but by their gender. The cultural norms at play typically frame them as lacking expertise. Knowledge and understanding of sport is held to be a masculine competence. However, as in most areas of sport study, more detailed research is needed, as there are clearly significant differences between sports. Athletic crowds have a more even gender balance and expertise seems not to be seen as the property of men alone. The rapid growth of women's sport in the last 20 years has challenged the established structures of male dominance in a number of sports, and is one pertinent instance of popular culture being inevitably a site of struggle.

Sites of struggle

These struggles can take many forms, from the most politically concrete and economistic, to the more symbolic, ideologic and apparently innocent. I will try and sketch out four aspects of struggle: concerning power, social control, the nature of the audience, and pleasure and reality. From the earliest days of modern sport, the shape and form of sporting organisations was determined by the extent of the power of the dominant class and the degree to which it needed to negotiate and compromise with other classes in order to maintain its power over the institutions of sport. The changing definitions of amateurism, the battles over broken-time payments, the establishment of professionalism, and the marginalisation of women's sport are all instances of the ways in which the paternalism of governing bodies was challenged by subordinate groups, with varying degrees of success. The English Football Association, for example, could only maintain their overall control of football by compromising and allowing professionalism within the Football League. Rugby, by contrast, dominated by a more traditional fragment of the English upper middle class, refused to compromise, and lost their overall control, resulting in the emergence of an alternative version of the game in Rugby League. The fight for genuine sporting opportunity for all has always had to battle against the limited availability of funding and low political priority accorded to sport.

People have, in a range of ways, challenged the private property rights invested in sport and leisure. Ownership of land, fishing rights, private golf clubs, and privileged access to club-controlled venues such as Wimbledon (tennis) and Lord's (cricket) have all been the subject of contestation, most famously in the campaign for public access, which culminated in the mass trespass on Kinder Scout in 1932. The history of women's athletics can be told in terms of the struggle against the patriarchal power of bodies such as the IAAF and the IOC who continue to restrict the range of events in women's athletics. Black sportsmen and women in the USA had to battle against segregation both on the pitch and in the stadia. Research has demonstrated the tendency for black people to be stacked in certain positions in team games, whilst being under-represented in others, and whilst in many sports black performers have a high visibility, very few have become captains, coaches, managers, or officials.

If power has been one aspect of struggle within sport, another has been over social conventions – the nature of behaviour at sporting events. Sporting crowds have always had a tendency towards the celebratory, the rowdy and the carnivalesque. The presence of large numbers of ordinary people from subordinate classes has invariably been seen by the dominant class as a potential challenge to law and order. So the various sub-cultures that have generated noisy chanting and singing, the carrying of signs, the painting of faces, drinking, fighting and passionate commitment have generally found their behaviour circumscribed by laws, rules, policing and the differentiated architecture of sport arenas (fences, pens and enclosures etc.). This opposition is not simply between a dominant class committed to order and restraint and subordinate classes who are characteristically rowdy and uncontrolled. Elements of subordinate classes have frequently expressed desire for 'law and order', and elements of dominant classes have frequently embraced forms of partial anarchy whether expressed through rugby club disorder or through the ultra-pure free market ideologies of some extreme right conservatives.

Such battles underpin the notion that what is really at stake is the power to define. In the more recent era, when television and sponsorship have combined to transform the political economy and the cultural practices of sport, this issue has become ever more pertinent (Whannel 1992). The issue of 'whose game is it anyway?' has become central. Where the central opposition was once that between fans and authorities, new complexities have been added by the extension of sport into living rooms worldwide. Live spectators now only provide a small proportion of revenue. So in a sense the spectacle is really provided for the TV audience. However, sponsors too have to be satisfied that the event delivers sufficient in the way of star value and spectacle to justify their investment. The corporate clients, entertained in executive boxes and hospitality tents, fed on salmon, champagne and strawberries, also have to be satisfied, even if their interest in the sport is frequently, and observably, less than intense (usually because they are in tents and not in their seats).

Ordinary live spectators could be forgiven for occasionally getting the feeling that they are being used as extras in a television production. Spectators at some indoor events find themselves herded into specific parts of the arena to form a backdrop for the cameras. After NEC bosses complained at empty seats during the Seoul Olympics, organisers had to hand out free tickets to create the right image. English football fans not only have to forgo their traditional standing terraces, but at some clubs are being charged (through expensive bond schemes) to finance the elaborate new stands that, for the most part, they didn't want in the first place. In short, as spectacularisation and globalisation take a hold, live spectators are finding even the limited power they had to define their cultural experience being eroded. The massive growth of football fanzines in England has produced a new emerging discourse of localist authenticity in opposition to global consumer culture.

The enthusiasm that sport generates speaks volumes. There are around 20 million admissions each year to professional football in England. For people to endure poor facilities, inadequate views, overpriced admission, meagre catering, squalid toilets, officious security and general rudeness in such vast numbers is clear evidence that there are pleasures on offer that exert a significant pull factor. In the world of capitalist rationality, where cultural production is subject to careful market research and precise calculation, sport offers a rare domain of uncertainty. In the quest for excitement sport offers a performance that always threatens the unexpected. Unlike a fictional product, it can never be totally contained. Indeed it is these tensions between predictability and uncertainty, improvisation and system, flair and work-rate, performance and product, that give sport much of its appeal.

Realms of pleasures

How then to analyse these pleasures more precisely? The issue is replete with problems both of theory and of method. Pleasure has both a psychological and a social dimension. Forms of psychoanalysis from Freud to Lacan have attempted to identify basic mechanisms that produce within us the sensation of pleasure. Applied to popular culture, this has produced significant insights (Marcuse 1955; Mulvey 1975). Laura Mulvey (1975) analysed narrative cinema in terms of the dependence of its visual pleasures on scopophilia and voyeurism, producing a spectacularisation of women for the male gaze. Influenced by Mulvey's work,

Duncan and Brummett (1989) discuss TV sport in terms of fetishism, voyeurism, and narcissism, and Margaret Morse (1983) argues that sport discourse is unique in that its object is the male body. I have commented on this work elsewhere (Whannel 1992) and in this piece I want to focus on the social dimension of pleasure. Psychoanalytic accounts alone, if not augmented by more socially grounded analysis, can sometimes tend towards a trans-cultural, trans-historic reductionism, in which ideological domination stems from entry into language, or from acquisition of gendered subjectivity (Hall *et al.*, eds, 1980: 117–76). The social dimension of pleasure needs to be analysed with reference to particular cultural forms, with their specific histories and modes of production and consumption. Cultural studies is nothing if not eclectic, and I propose to draw here on three separate elements: Richard Dyer's concept of utopian sensibility, Roland Barthes's concept of *jouissance* and Bakhtin's concept of the carnivalesque.

Richard Dyer's analysis of entertainment suggested that part of the pleasure was associated with the presence of a utopian sensibility, which he analyses in terms of five categories: energy, abundance, intensity, transparency and community (Dyer 1978). *Energy* consists of the capacity to act vigorously, using human power, activity and potential. *Abundance* involves the conquest of scarcity, having enough to spare without a sense of poverty of others; and an enjoyment of sensuous material reality. *Intensity* concerns the experience of emotion directly, fully, unambiguously and authentically, without holding back. *Transparency* refers to a quality of relationships – between represented characters (e.g. true love) or between performer and audience (e.g. sincerity). *Community* references togetherness, a sense of belonging, and a network of phatic relationships (i.e. those in which communication is for its own sake rather than for its message). Each term is counterposed to its binary opposite: respectively scarcity, exhaustion, dreariness, manipulation, fragmentation. So the utopian sensibility in representation is set up precisely in opposition to, and establishing a distance from, the grim realities of everyday life. *Scarcity* means poverty, and the unequal distribution of wealth. *Exhaustion* is produced by work, alienated labour, and the pressures of urban life. *Dreariness* is produced by the monotony, predictability, and instrumentality of the daily round. *Manipulation* is experienced from all sides – advertising, bourgeois democracy, sex roles, etc. *Fragmentation* is the consequence of job mobility, rehousing and redevelopment. Entertainment, with its utopian sensibility, offers a magical resolution, a better world.

How might this enable us to account for the pleasures of sport? First we need to be precise about what is meant by sport. This, of course, risks descending into a philosophical labyrinth. So let me say briefly that my concern in this article is with sport as popular culture. I focus more on those sports that can be considered more centrally part of popular culture, by virtue not simply of their popularity but also because of the degree to which they are part of the cultural fabric of the everyday life of the people. While it is relevant to consider both participation and spectatorship, Dyer's theory is primarily a theory of the relation between performance and audience. Consequently my focus is more upon elite level sport – that is to say sport that is produced partly for an audience, rather than simply for its own sake. For all practical purposes it is now impossible to separate popular culture from media representation, so I shall consider both the live spectator and the television audience.

Energy: the display of physical energy is of course, to echo a journalistic banality, what sport is all about. The exuberant speed of sprinters and tennis players, the stamina of long distance runners and grand prix drivers, the physical power of boxers or rugby players, the work-rate of footballers; the display of physical energy is a fundamental component of sport. Abundance is experienced in the sheer size of crowds, the spectacular profligacy of major events, and especially opening ceremonies, and in the display of sensuous material reality. This latter is most prominent in those aestheticised events – the pole vault, gymnastics, skating, diving and skiing – where attention becomes focused on the sensuous properties of the human body in performance. Intensity as a category directly describes the experience of being in a sports crowd. Anyone who has stood behind the goal at a major football match will have no problem recognising 'experience of emotion directly, fully, unambiguously, and authentically, without holding back' as a fair description. Transparency is most apparent in the approval given to the notion of commitment. The big-hearted player, who runs himself into the ground; the performer who never gives up, who gives her all, is always likely to win the heart of the crowd. The most popular performers are often those who establish a relationship with the crowd. The wave to the crowd after a goal is a crucial part of the football ritual. Indeed players now customarily greet their own supporters with waves beforehand in the warm-up, and rounds of applause at the end. Athletes and motor racers perform laps of honour. After victory comes communion with the crowd. By contrast players who are 'insincere', who don't try hard, who hide, who approach performance in a cynical way, soon lose the affection of the audience.

Community is an important part of the experience of being in a crowd, and in the identification between a crowd and the team or individuals they are there to support. A feeling of belonging-ness is a significant element in the experience of regular spectatorship. Many people who stand at football have made their way to the same spot year after year, often to meet friends only encountered at the match. This helps to account for the massive degree of popular resistance to the notion of all-seated stadia. Territory – occupying it, defending it, and attacking and invading that of others – was a key element in the growth of the terrace subcultures of the 1960s and 70s. Sport clearly involves networks of phatic relationships. The cheers and the chants of crowds are a means of opening channels, of announcing 'we are here'. The Mexican wave, that most strange and all-embracing ritual, is divorced even of partisan affiliation – it doesn't support one side or the other, it demands universal involvement, and ultimately celebrates the collective presence of the crowd. This belonging-ness appears both in the grounded form built on localism, and regular partisan commitment; and also in the more transitory experience of the 'big event'. At times it seems that the signs of commitment are a crucial element in the continuing reproduction of that commitment. In the symbolic call-and-response of the relation between audience and performer, the crowd will call 'Vinnie, Vinnie, give us a wave' and with luck Vinnie will respond with a toothy grin and an air punching wave. What could be more phatic …?

Indeed, because a sports crowd is generally more active, more involved, and more integral than that for a play or a film, in some ways the sport audience is more of an organic part of some of the components of the utopian sensibility like intensity, transparency and community. A film audience merely observes these elements, a sports crowd enacts them. So sport offers a brief escape into a utopian world, separate from and different from the drabness of everyday existence. Like the theatre and the cinema, the sports arena is a bounded universe. To enter it is to leave the every day and enter a magical domain. It is no accident that the best sports stadia are those that allow no glimpse of the world outside.

In discussing the pleasures of reading fiction, Roland Barthes distinguishes between *plaisir* and *jouissance* (Barthes 1975). *Jouissance* does not readily translate into English, as Stephen Heath has pointed out. It embraces enjoyment as legal/social possession (enjoying certain rights), pleasure, and, specifically, sexual pleasure. Barthes identifies two different ways in which writing can work upon the reader. First, the text of pleasure (*plaisir*) contents, fills, grants euphoria, the text that comes from culture and does not break with it, and is linked to a comfortable practice of reading. Second, the text of bliss (*jouissance*) imposes a state of loss, discomforts (perhaps to the point of a certain boredom), unsettles readers' historical, cultural, psychological assumptions, the consistency of tastes, values, and memories; and brings to a crisis their relation with language. Attempts to align *jouissance* with progressiveness and *plaisir* with reactionary qualities do not work. In most cases the two tendencies are present in most texts, in differing balances and with different interactions (Mercer 1981).

Clearly sport and sport spectatorship provides moments of *plaisir*. A victory or a good performance offer contentment, and can grant euphoria. But because sport does not conform to expectation or convention, precisely because it is uncertain, it can also provide brief moments of *jouissance*. It may be, however, that the concept of *jouissance* is inadequate to the peculiar intensity and range of relationships involved in football spectatorship. Nick Hornby in *Fever Pitch* (Hornby 1992) describes the devotion of Arsenal fans as 'entertainment through pain' and the constant exposure to defeat, disappointment and failure means that, in terms of sexual pleasure, football spectatorship has a distinctly sado-masochistic cast. It is worth noting in passing that sexual metaphor is common in sporting language. Morse (1983) refers to American football, with its deep penetration, and end zones. Easthope (1987) talks of snooker's deep screws, and kisses on the pink. Tudor comments of English football that 'compared to many continental cultures we subscribe to an orgasmic theory of football; the foreplay only has meaning if it is climaxed with goals' (Buscombe, ed., 1975). It is surely no coincidence that young lads in England typically describe sexual success as 'scoring'. Sport, as a form of display, has an erotic dimension at once instantly visible and deeply repressed. Most sports place the body on display, make it available as a form of visual spectacle, yet the erotic power of such display is rarely alluded to and even aesthetic beauty is only referenced in those few 'aestheticised' sports, such as ice skating and gymnastics.

However, *jouissance* is to be found in the uncertain as well as the erotic. The surprise victory by the underdog, the hole in one, the world record, the hat trick, all potentially disrupt, and unsettle, our expectations. Bob Beamon's famous long jump world record in 1968 was so utterly unprecedented, in breaking the previous record by over a foot, that the crowd took a while to take it in. Beamon himself briefly fainted when the reality of his performance hit him. The moment of celebration on the terraces following a goal briefly disrupts point of view and produces an almost orgasmic euphoria in which strangers may embrace. The USA's dramatic last putt victory in the recent Ryder Cup and Denmark's totally unpredicted football victory in the European Championship provide a somewhat disorientating excitement. *Jouissance* temporarily unhinges us from our convention-bound expectations. When England won the World Cup in 1966, in Ken Wolstenholme's now famous phrase, 'some people are on the pitch, they think it's all over ...'. The enthusiasm for pitch invasions at moments of triumph is in part an index of *jouissance*. The moment of joy can only properly be celebrated by a carnivalesque assault on the audience–performer barrier.

The application of a concept of the carnivalesque developed from the work of M. Bakhtin (1968). Carnival involves mimicry, instability, transgression, the refusal to define and specify, ambivalence and ambiguity. It typically involves the development of new meanings through bricolage, and challenges the authority of social laws (Thompson 1983). Carnival is a rebellious event, a play without a stage, a world turned upside down, a mixing and confusing of categories, and a dissolution of opposites (Bennett 1983). Bakhtin saw carnival as an anticipation of a people's utopia of pleasure, a vibrant and changing form living only in the street theatre of the people. But Eagleton has noted that this populist utopianism has limits: carnival is licensed; it is a permissible rupture, incorporative as well as liberating (Eagleton 1981). Clearly sport crowds frequently exhibit aspects of carnival; such as the wearing of team colours, fancy costumes, and painted faces, singing and swearing in ways not conventional in other settings, and utilising artefacts such as inflatable objects, or giant hands with pointing fingers. Pitch invasions and clashes with police challenge the authority of social laws. The desire to invade the pitch is a symbolic dissolving of barriers between performer and audience. At the end of football matches players now often applaud the crowd. At major events the crowd, with their singing and chanting, costumes and banners, become part of the show. This phenomenon, always particularly striking at the English FA Cup Final, was also visible when Wimbledon, for the first time forced to allow play on the middle

Sunday, found the Centre Court full of ordinary tennis fans instead of the usual more privileged strata. West Indian cricket crowds, Italian motor racing fans, Australians on the Hill at Sydney Cricket Ground, Liverpool fans on the Kop, the Italian Ultras, all exhibit carnivalesque elements. Of course, spectators do not necessarily see themselves as engaged in carnival, and there is, it seems to me, a pressing need for more focused research on this theme.

Popular heroism and the brief triumph of process

Terry Lovell (1980 and 1981) draws on Raymond Williams' elusive and allusive term, structures of feeling, in speaking of structures of pleasure. Soap operas, for instance, offer the female audience validation, reassurance and utopianism (Dyer, Lovell and McCrindle 1977). If the pleasures of sport watching have a structure, then identification is central to it. Research by Wenner (1989) suggests that watching to find out the fate of a favourite team or individual was the strongest motivation for watching, followed by a liking for the drama and tension. While there are clearly aesthetic pleasures in merely watching a sport performance, the real intensity comes from identifying with an individual or team as they strive to win. Taking sides appears important to the experience of watching sport, even where no obvious local regional, national or emotional affiliation offers itself. Hence the search for a figure to identify with is not simply nationalism, but is evidence of the need to secure an appropriate figure for identification in order that the pleasure might work. Within this domain of popular pleasure, heroes clearly play an important role. Identification is absolutely central to the consumption of sport, indeed it is hard to make full sense of sport without identification. By identification here I mean firstly a partisan identification with the fate of one performer or team; and secondly an attachment to the way that performer approaches the task.

While there are a range of forms of identification both with teams and with individuals, with clubs and with countries, not all star performers are also popular heroes. My concern here is with a particular type of popular hero, one that is fully heroic in defying expectations, achieving the impossible, transcending limitations, or at least threatening to do these things. The invented word 'Bothamesque', as a description of sporting performance, will have little meaning to most continental readers, but in England this reference to the buccaneering skills of cricketer Ian Botham has clear and comprehendable connotations. Such heroes, in their spectacular performances, their ability to create drama, and often, in their off-field exploits, represent the victory of improvisation over system, the victory of the individual over authority and the triumph of the pleasure principle over the reality principle. Popular heroes transcend limitations, preconceptions and systems. Feats like Roger Bannister's four-minute mile, long jumper Bob Beamon's phenomenal world record in 1968, or Denmark's victory in the 1992 European Championships catch our imagination because they defy our expectations. The exceptional abilities of Martina

Navratilova, Marita Koch, or Paul Gascoigne are inspiring because they extend our sense of the possibilities of the human body. Great performances transcend the accepted limitations of the body (Beamon) and, occasionally (Miruts Yifter, Roger Milla), the ageing process.

Such performances can produce brief moments of *jouissance*. Above all they represent the temporary triumph of process over product, the moment when the spontaneous inspiration of performance escapes, fleetingly, the tendency of capitalist commodity production to transform all such cultural processes into calculated packaged objects for consumption. When cricketers and boxers appear in pantomime, when sport stars wear dark glasses in winter for promotional purposes, when grand prix drivers slip hats on to advertise tyres during interviews, or when football teams change shirts before receiving trophies, there is every reason to feel cynical. But sport performance itself always carries the magical promise of inspiration and improvisation. It holds out the possibility of remaining playful, of grasping pleasure and of holding reality at bay. In the field of struggle that the popular culture of sport constitutes, such moments of inspired performance symbolise a rare victory for people over the limitations that confine us.

References

Bakhtin, M. (1968) *Rabelais and his World*, Cambridge, Mass: MIT Press.

Barthes, Roland (1975) *The Pleasures of the Text*, London: Jonathan Cape.

Bennett, Tony (1981) Popular culture: defining our terms, in Unit 1 of *Popular Culture*, Open University Course U203, Milton Keynes: Open University.

Bennett, Tony (1983) A thousand and one troubles, in *Formations of Pleasure*, London: Routledge.

Buscombe, Edward (ed.) (1975) *Football on Television*, London: BFI.

Duncan, Margaret Carlisle and Brummett, Barry (1989) Types and sources of spectating pleasure in televised sport, in *Sociology of Sport* 6(3), Sept 89, USA.

Dyer, R., Lovell, T., and McCrindle, J. (1977) Soap opera and women, in *Edinburgh International Television Festival Programme*, Edinburgh.

Dyer, Richard (1978) Entertainment and Utopia, in *Movie* 24, London.

Eagleton, Terry (1981) *Walter Benjamin or Towards a Revolutionary Criticism*, London: New Left Books.

Easthope, Anthony (1987) A kiss of the pink, in *Plural*, Winter 2.

Hall, Stuart *et al.* (eds) (1980) *Culture Media Language*, London: Hutchinson.

Hornby, Nick (1992) *Fever Pitch*, London: Gollancz.

Lovell, Terry (1980) *Pictures of Reality*, London: BFI.

Lovell, Terry (1981) Ideology and Coronation Street, in *Coronation Street*, London: BFI.

Marcuse, Herbert (1955) *Eros and Civilisation*, USA: Beacon.

Mercer, Colin (1981) Pleasure, in *Popular Culture* (Course U203), Milton Keynes: Open University.

Morse, Margaret (1983) Sport on television: replay and display, *Regarding Television* (ed. E. Ann Kaplan), USA: AFI.

Mulvey, Laura (1975) Visual pleasure and narrative cinema, in *Screen* 16(3), London: SEFT.

Thompson, Grahame (1983) The carnival and the calculable, in *Formations of Pleasure*, London: Routledge.

Wenner, Lawrence A. (1989) *Media, Sports and Society*, Newbury Park, CA: Sage.

Whannel, Garry (1992) *Fields in Vision: Television Sport and Cultural Transformation*, London: Routledge.

Part 2

Sport, cultural politics and political culture since 1983

5 Pleasures, commodities and spaces

'Politics,' says Drake. 'You can't eat them, you can't sell them and you can't sleep with them.'

(from *The Honourable Schoolboy*, John Le Carré, 1977: 252)

In re-reading *Blowing the Whistle*, it is apparent that a gap had opened up, in which politics tended to drift away from other elements of the social and cultural world. Politics as here constructed seemed to have little to do with pleasure, with consuming, or with inhabiting space. Insufficient attention was paid to the pleasures of sport, to the ways in which it is consumed, or to the places in which it is consumed. In order for sport to be consumed, of course it has to be produced, and produced in commodity forms. This chapter explores the way the pleasures, commodities and spaces of sport interrelate. I once stood at the top of an Olympics ski-jump with two colleagues. We stared down at the terrifyingly steep descent, at the slight upturn at the end, and beyond that at what appeared to be a tiny landing area, surrounded by spectator terracing and sponsors banners. One of my colleagues suggested that if an anthropologist came down from Mars, she would want to know what terrible crime the ski-jumpers had committed, that they had to be subjected to such a terrible ordeal. The story reminds us of the need for a degree of critical distance, of estrangement. In order to fully understand cultural practices, they need to be made strange. We need to alter our perspective to avoid merely taking things for granted.

An American runner in the 1960s, Jim Ryun, was reported to train until he was physically sick, and then to continue the process two or three times more. Intensive training regimes, accustomed to habituating the body to pain, to enhancing the ability to go through the pain barrier, became common in the 1960s, and by the 1970s were being transferred to the exercise regimes of ordinary people through such aphorisms as 'feel the burn', and 'if it ain't hurtin', it ain't workin'. As Jean-Marie Brohm (1978) has analysed, there is a culture of systematic Taylorisation of the human body; and it is a culture which is, in some ways, pathological. The collapse of Eastern communism, and opening up of secret archives, provided plenty of evidence for methodical use of performance enhancing drugs in the GDR and other states. A simple perusal of the statistics of athletic performance, when correlated with the gradual imposition of a more rigorous regime of random drug testing, would appear to confirm suspicions that the routinised use of drugs was by no means unique to the communist bloc. Lack of confidence in the ability of governments, and national and international federations, to implement drug testing procedures with adequate rigour led eventually to the establishment of a new global body, the World Anti Drug Agency (WADA), which is not finding the task a straightforward one.

A heavyweight boxing champion, George Foreman, last active in the mid 1970s, returned to boxing in his mid forties, 20 years later. Boxing in itself is a very strange activity, but for it to be possible, in this most physically demanding of contests, in which mistakes are instantly and literally punished, for a man in his forties to compete at the highest level raises questions about standards. Meanwhile a fellow professional, Mike Tyson, resorted to biting off the ear of an opponent. It would be hard to explain the sporting dimension of all of this to our anthropologist from Mars. Foreman, though, was able to re-establish his public profile, to have the sense to retire a second time, and to use his new visibility to promote a cooking device, the 'lean mean grilling machine'. It is an interesting symptom of the ubiquity of promotional culture that now he may well be better known for his grilling than his boxing.

Recent developments in so-called extreme sports, in 'Iron-Man' events, in ultra distance competition, push sporting practice well beyond the development of healthy bodies, and into the sado-masochistic. Even the casual and informal cultures of physical exercise, such as frisbee, and beach volleyball, have a remorseless tendency to generate elite levels, and modes of competition. Indeed the world of sport generally is easily parodied, and can be rendered as absurd. Take cricket: an outdoor sport that cannot be played during rain, being a national sport in a country known for its unpredictable climate. Or darts – a 'sport' played largely by fat men with beer bellies. Or golf – a game in which the best player in the world, Tiger Woods, would probably not be easily admitted into membership of many clubs if he were not famous. Or Formula One motor racing – a series of events in which cars 'race', yet rarely pass each other; or rugby – a combination of high speed running, repressed sexuality and assault and battery. Or synchronised swimming – I rest my case.

Viewed from this perspective it is surprising that any of it can be taken seriously, and yet of course it is. So understanding how, for those who are participants and/or spectators, the attractions of sport are established, constructed and consumed is a necessary element of analysis. Pleasures are rarely simple – combining as they do the social and the psychological, the collective and the individual, the public and the private. As well as taking an estranged, distanced look, it is, paradoxically, also necessary to get close. Some of my own writing in the past has been criticised on two accounts. First, that while constantly acknowledging the pleasures of sport, it has rarely discussed or analysed them; second, that there is an absence of the personal and experiential. This book includes a substantial recounting of sport-related experiences, where this experiential material helps to reveal a mode of thinking or a form of analysis.

But a few principles need to be reasserted here. Sport is not a single static or unitary object, and generalisation, whilst inevitable, can be perilous; it is not a universalised set of practices, but always, in any specific case, has a distinct character, growing out of the particular histories, rituals, people and economic circumstances that have interacted; it does, in both its participatory and spectatorial modes, provide a whole set of complex pleasures, strange and baffling though they may be to the many people for whom sport itself is a strange irrelevance. Until the nineteenth century, 'sport' in British dictionaries and encyclopaedias generally referred to the field sports of hunting, shooting and fishing. Sport at all levels of society from the aristocracy to the popular classes featured cruelty to animals – bull- and bear-baiting, badger-baiting, cock-fighting and dog-tossing. Movements to outlaw such activities have gradually rendered them residual, marginal or specifically illegal, yet just because cultures are residual does not mean that they have lost their cultural significances.

David Whitson gave an eloquent account of the gradual marginalisation of shinty, a sport struggling to hold on to an audience who increasingly turned to more 'modern' and 'urban' sports such as football and rugby (Whitson 1983). Residual cultural practices, though, do not necessarily disappear, but can often remain, residual and marginalised, but still rich fields of localised cultural significance. I watched a shinty match on Skye (not the satellite television channel, but the Scottish island) in the 1970s. It was early evening, and the odd hundred or so spectators spent much of the time swatting midges – the small insects that rise in their thousands in Scottish river valleys at dusk. The hard ball, moving at some speed, hit a player on the forehead with a loud crack. No one was very concerned and the player carried on as if nothing had happened – a large egg-shaped lump gradually developing above his eye. Clearly he was not an expensively acquired and highly valued player, who, at the elite levels of present-day football, might have been surrounded by attentive trainers and paramedics. The casual milieu and macho masculine ethos would have abhorred such a fuss. In such settings, sport assumes a very different character than in its mediated forms. Karl Spracklen provides a rich account of the tough masculine ethos of rugby, quoting one player as saying 'When you're putting yer body on t'line fer beer tokens you've go'a wonder why' and another as saying 'I wouldn't die for my team, but I would seriously consider going into a long term coma for it' (Spracklen 1995, 1996). The embedded and culturally specific flavour of such utterances is a long distance from the corporate-speak with which rugby at its top levels is now marketed.

Emergent sports that become commercialised, systematised and marketed, such as beach volleyball, nevertheless still continue to exist in casualised and simplified forms. Beach volleyball has acquired an organised and competitive form but is still played, for fun, on the beach. In other words the sport has been characterised by a remorseless transformation of casual leisure into serious leisure, but also by a retention of the values of casual, informal and spontaneous play and indeed by forms of resistance to commercial incorporation. The collection *Lifestyle Sport*, edited by Belinda Wheaton (2004), explores these issues in fascinating detail. One of the hardest tasks for any analysis of sport is to retain a recognition of the different and distinct levels and cultural contexts, not just of different sports but also of the same sports in different settings. Indeed it is precisely the cultural specificities of actual sporting practices that provide the character, the flavour and texture of the experience of sport. The very specific nuances provided by the setting, the milieu, the distinctive rituals, habits, manners and forms of slang of participants and spectators constitute the embedded and localised meanings. One reason that cultural critics of the sports business are hostile to the processes of commercialisation is that it is this very embedded, localised richness that tends to disappear in the more homogenous mediated forms that dominate 'sport' today.

In any sporting event there are complex cultural elements at work, sometimes combining in harmony, sometimes existing in tension. Baseball and football both have historically distinctive male working-class roots. Both are changing and have been changed by the forces of television, sponsorship and advertising, yet both retain a great deal of the character they have always had. Lived experience and mediated form, spontaneity and formal ritual, localised practices and global images all rub up against each other. The internal geography of stadia, their external location, their immediate environment, the symbolic meanings which are condensed onto them, the rituals and habits of those who watch sport within them; all are part of a cultural interaction. In Boca Juniors stadium in Buenos Aires, in Yankee Stadium in New York, in Ibrox Park in Glasgow, working-class masculinity and commodified sport collide, fuelling a process that cannot simply be reduced to the triumph of the latter over the former. Nor is it simply a matter of suggesting that participation is better than spectatorship; or informal better than formal. In Rio de Janeiro, in the world's largest stadium, spectacular football occasions take place before huge audiences. Even the stadium tour has been transformed into the Maracana Experience in which you are able to walk down the tunnel, with lasers, dry ice and ever louder sounds of crowd noise, chanting, singing, drums and samba from all sides until you emerge up the steps to see the green field and the vast concrete bowl. A few miles away, on Copacabana Beach, every day from morning till around midnight groups of people play football bare foot, in the sand, yet with proper goal posts. The two places are a few miles apart geographically, a million miles apart sociologically, and yet intimately connected culturally. Understanding the cultures of sport, and thereby considering politics, is not a matter of determining that the latter experiences are in any sense more real, or more authentic, but rather trying to understand the two forms and the ways in which they interact. It is useful, therefore, to start by looking at the complex pleasures of sport. Class specificity provides a way of highlighting the need for thick description, to understand the situated and embedded nature of the pleasures of sport, as in this oft-quoted description:

> For a shilling, Bruddersford United turned you into a critic, happy in your judgement of fine points, ready in a second to estimate the worth of a well-judged pass, a run down the touch line, a lightning shot, a clearance kick by

back or goalkeeper; it turned you into a partisan, holding your breath when the ball came sailing into your own goalmouth, ecstatic when your forwards raced away towards the opposite goal, elated, downcast, bitter, triumphant by turns at the fortunes of your side, watching a ball shape Illiads and Odysseys for you; and what is more it turned you into a member of a new community, all brothers together for an hour and a half, for not only had you escaped from the clanking machinery of this lesser life, from wages, rent, dole, sick pay, insurance cards, nagging wives, ailing children, bad bosses, idle workmen, but you had escaped with most of your mates and your neighbours, with half the town and there you were, cheering together, thumping one another on the shoulders, swapping judgements like lords of the earth, having pushed your way through a turnstile into another and altogether more splendid kind of life, hurtling with Conflict and yet passionate and beautiful in its Art. Moreover, it offered you more than a shilling's worth of material for talk during the rest of the week. A man who had missed the last home match of t'United had to enter social life on tiptoe in Bruddersford.

(J.B. Priestley, *The Good Companions*, 1929: 5–6)

Priestley provides here a rather eloquent picture of the nature of a particular form of popular working-class masculine pleasure. It hints at the richness, the subtlety and variety of the pleasures of sport spectating. It reveals the ways in which football and sporting knowledge function as a form of alternative male cultural capital easing the processes of bonding and homosocial exchange. It also reveals the exclusion of the feminine and the ways in which sport often exists precisely as a world apart. It should be said, too, that Priestley's own sensibilities, in which the ball is imagined as shaping 'Illiads and Odysseys', are conceivably atypical of working-class football as experienced, to say the least.

The pleasures described by Priestley are to a large degree associated with masculine sociability, but for those who appreciate and consume its subtleties, sport also has a rare ability to offer pleasures that are unexpected, extraordinary, and amazing. They produce, for a fleeting moment, that disruptive and disorienting mode of pleasure that the French refer to as *jouissance*.[32] I once saw a German football match between Bayer Leverkusen and Werder Bremen. About 30 minutes in, Bremen were awarded a free kick, to be taken by Mario Basler, nicknamed Super-Mario by the fans. Basler took his time, chose his spot and curved the ball around the right side of the wall into the top right-hand corner of the net. Due to some technicality, undetectable from where we were sitting, the goal was disallowed, and the kick ordered to be retaken. The Bremen players fussed around the referee, yelling and gesticulating impotently. Leverkusen's players tried to pull them away. Scuffles broke out. The small group of Bremen fans were incensed, whilst the majority of the crowd chuckled, yelled, and whistled. It took some time for order to be restored. Only Basler remained aloof, standing, watching the mayhem with a detached amusement – a half smile on his lips. Eventually the referee gave the signal for the kick to be retaken. Basler stepped up, surveyed the goalmouth for a moment, and then bent the ball around

the *left* side of the wall into the top *left* corner of the goal. Such anecdotes of popular memory not only have a poetic value, being a form of 'emotion recollected
in tranquillity', but serve both to bind and separate audiences. Most football fans
will recognise the joy of the moment I have described, most non-sport fans find
it somewhat incomprehensible and pointless. It is, I think, only by trying to
understand the interlocking nature of the pleasure, the unity and the difference,
that we can start to unlock the social dimensions of the pleasures of sport.

During Euro 96 one of the supporting events was a set of 5-a-side football
tournaments, sponsored by Coca-Cola. These took place on a large number of
pitches on Clapham Common. The centrepiece 'stadium' where the finals took
place was a mock-up version of Wembley Stadium, complete with Twin Towers.
It could have been a rather sad and lame postmodern camp joke, but in fact it
was suggestive of a sense of fun and wit. It managed to provide the final games
with a sense of occasion while not over-burdening them with too grave a sense of
seriousness. It was an instance of popular festivity managing to survive on the
periphery of global spectacle.

In 2003, Paris was hit by a heat wave that became referred to as *la canicule* –
literally 'searing heat'. The temperature remained above 40 degrees C (104
degrees F) for over two weeks. Thousands died from the effects. In the midst of
this, a few dozen Englishmen and women abroad crammed into an English-style
bar, The Frog and Rosbif, to watch the FA Community Shield Game between
Arsenal and Manchester United. It marked a peculiar and bizarre form of commitment, to spend time in this hothouse of a pub, in the middle of an otherwise
hot and sleepy Parisian August Sunday, especially as few of those there were fans
of either club, and the match itself was of no competitive significance. It was
characteristic of a post-fan sensibility in which the sheer difficulty, eccentricity,
or general zaniness of the act of spectatorship provides part of the pleasure. The
same sensibility is detectable in the name 'barmy army' adopted by a large group
who follow English cricket abroad, in the proclaiming that 'we're all mad, us',
and in the lengthy and enjoyable but obsessive retelling of travellers' tales
involving endless problems of travel and accommodation.[33]

Although the focus of this book has been on the spectacle of modern sport
there is also an undeniable experiential pleasure of participation. Some have
chosen to counterpose this supposedly genuine, real and rich experience with the
false needs generated by commercialised and commodified spectatorship. I don't
go along with this; in fact, if you want the truth, I think it is rubbish. I am all for
people playing sport, and I am also in favour of people, if they so choose, painting, writing novels, making films and playing music. To suggest that such people
might somehow be better off not going to sports stadia, art galleries, concerts and
cinemas, or reading books, would simply be foolish. It misunderstands the nature
and richness of cultural play. While participating and spectating are distinct and
different social practices, they also have a relation, in which each informs and
frames the other.

I have at various times got huge pleasure from activities such as swimming in
the Pacific, running in the Algarve, playing golf in Scotland, football on Clapham

Figure 5.1 'Welcome to Wembley'.

Figure 5.2 Wembley in cardboard on Clapham Common, 1996.

This is an interesting instance of sponsorship at the lower end of a sport. The Coca-Cola name was omnipresent at this multiple category multinational 5-a-side festival, but the event provided a lot of fun and exemplified the festive possibilities lurking beneath the dominant spectacle of mega-events

Common and petanque in Brittany. Once I almost got taken down a bobsleigh run in Canada, but the rides were cancelled before my anticipatory terror could be put to the test. I have also enjoyed being a spectator, often because of the particularity of the circumstances – watching athletics in Birmingham, tennis in New York, shinty in the Scottish Western Isles, baseball in Chicago and Lance Armstrong winning the 2003 Tour de France in Paris. I pick these examples to suggest that the cultural experiences involved in consuming sport may be commercialised and commodified but they always also involve other forms of experience and exchange – to do with shared experience, with popular memory, with a sense of place and space, a sense of cultural tradition, and an awareness of and openness to the unpredictability of sport events. As I argued, in the paper from *Innovations* reprinted in this

Figure 5.3 Villa Park, Birmingham, UK.

Figure 5.4 Yankee Stadium, New York.

collection, these things are always on the point of being commodified but there is still a process that, if only briefly and temporarily, eludes commodification.[34]

The spaces and places of sport come to have a strong attraction. I am not alone in enjoying visiting famous stadia, even if the event is not spectacular, indeed even if there is no event. Seeing Real Madrid play, seated in the Tribuna Preferencia (so exotic sounding a name to our British ears, compared to the North Bank), next to a man who exuded a pleasant aroma of brandy and whose cigar took the whole of the first half to consume, was unforgettable even if the match

Figure 5.5 Maracana Stadium, Rio de Janeiro.

Figure 5.6 Estadi Olimpic de Montjuic, Barcelona.

The drama of a big crowd and a big occasion are undeniable, especially when, as with our visit to Yankee Stadium in 1999, a record score is attained. But the magic resonances of place exist even in the absence of a live event, when memories of the Barcelona Olympic Games of 1992 or the aesthetic joy of the best Brazilian performances can be evoked.

itself was dispiritingly one-sided and dull. Visits to the Barcelona Museum, the Maracana Experience, and the museum at Boca Juniors stadium, situated in a rough part of Buenos Aires, have all been memorable. Actually the great irony is that stadium visiting has become an alternative mode of consumption – much cheaper when there is no sport event on. This in turn suggests much about the fetishisation of space, and the commodification of place.[35] The magic of sport can be a potent broth on those rare moments when the importance of the occasion, the unpredictability of the event and the extravagance of the performance all come together. The clinging on to such moments through momento, anecdote, popular memory, ritual and sacred site is a thinner, but still appetising, gruel.

Commercialisation and commodification

'What do you want, Mr. Westerby?'
'A deal.'
'Nobody wants a deal. They want a commodity. The deal obtains for them the commodity. What do you want?'
(dialogue from *The Honourable Schoolboy*, John Le Carré, 1977: 521)

Follow the money …
(advice from 'Deep Throat', in *All The President's Men*, 1976)

Sport was never purely amateur, never simply for fun, but the process by which, during the last three decades, sport has been thoroughly penetrated by capital has been dramatic and transformative. The concept of the commercialisation of sport was a key element in early critiques of sport. Such critiques were prescient in that the scale of commercialisation of sport has become so much greater in the last three decades. This process was driven initially, during the 1960s, by television, then, from the 1970s, by advertising and sponsorship and in the last decade also by merchandising. John Horne, in *Sport in Consumer Culture* (2006), outlines the social and economic processes that have contributed to the rising economic force of the merchandising element in the sports business. The commercialisation of sport is not entirely new, of course, indeed organised and regular commercialised sport was well established, in England at least, by the end of the nineteenth century. However, it was the combination of the growth of jet travel, television coverage and commercial sponsorship that triggered a transformation of sport in the 1960s. Television, sponsorship, advertising and merchandising are still, together and separately, the dynamic force underpinning the commercialisation of sport.

One feature of any capitalist system is the search for new areas that capital can invade, and fresh aspects of social practice that can be monetised. The gradual eclipse of amateur sport by professionalisation is a consequence of this process, which does not simply involve the commercialisation of sport, but also its commodification. The dynamic processes of capitalism constantly find new ways of transforming sporting practices into sets of commodities that can be exchanged and can generate profit. The rights to sporting events can be sold to television, the perimeters of grounds to advertisers, space on shirts to sponsors, replica shirts to fans. The expansion in the scale of sports merchandising is one of the most visible and dramatic parts of this process. These processes are not restricted to the elite and spectacular levels of sport – take a look around your local gym, sport centre, or sport club for evidence. Their impact on the practices of sport have been profound. Ethics are distorted, morals compromised, and politics twisted. Whistles are blown but ears are plugged.

Once the rights to major events became lucrative television commodities, the sporting entrepreneurs and their allies in sport governing bodies embarked on a ceaseless search for new events and new competitive formulas for profit genera-tion. The impact of this can be seen in the over-stuffed calendars of tennis, golf and football. Top footballers and tennis players in particular can suffer from burn-out produced by the lack of adequate rest periods. The relatively poor performances in the 2002 World Cup of nations depending on players in European leagues was striking. The emergence of competing governing bodies and multiplication of weight divisions has led to so many 'World Title' fights that boxing has lost much of its remaining credibility. Both rugby league and rugby union have become transformed by the ethos of the market. They adopted over-optimistic expectations of revenue, new forms of competition were established, new and in some cases ludicrous names imposed, and in the case of rugby league, the whole sport shifted, in the UK, from winter to summer.[36] The belief, unfortu-nately widespread amongst the new class of brokers, promoters and consultants who infest sport, that any given sport just needs the right marketing in order to mimic the financial successes of football, is manifestly absurd, and yet continues to impress governing bodies.

The image of the Brazilian football team is in many ways a marketeer's dream. The most successful nation in the World Cup, they also, usually, offer an extrav-agant and appealing flair in their style of play, and can be readily associated in advertising and promotion with all the colourful exotica of carnival, complete with samba soundtrack. Little wonder, then, that the Brazilian Football Federation entered into a lucrative contract with Nike that has put Brazilian shirts on the backs of men, and women too, around the world. The failure of Brazil to win the 1998 World Cup came after a curious incident in which star player Ronaldo suffered a mystery illness, some said a fit, during the night before the final. Withdrawn from the team for the final, and then reinstated, he played like a sleepwalker, yet strangely remained un-substituted. His malaise in turn affected the whole team, who were clearly out of touch and allowed host nation France an easy victory. Rumours abounded – it was unclear what forces had led to the reinstatement of Ronaldo, or precisely who took the key decision. The com-pany denied suggestions that the Nike contract specified that he must play, and no evidence to the contrary has emerged. As to the mystery illness, speculation was rife as to whether it was caused by nerves, a virus or even poisoning. We may never know the full story, but the whole episode drew attention to the impact of the marketing imperative. The itinerary of top teams, whether it be Brazil, Real

Madrid or Manchester United, is now more to do with opening up new markets than it is with rational pre-season preparation.

One sport that has made a huge success of promotion is Formula One motor racing, one of the major television sports. The man behind the success is Bernie Ecclestone. In 1970 he purchased an interest in Motor Racing Developments, the Brabham team giving him a place in FOCA, the car constructors association (Beck-Burridge and Walton 2001). FOCA began using Ecclestone's company as the commercial intermediary. With Ecclestone's backing, Max Mosley became head of FIA, the governing body, and promptly began dealing directly with Ecclestone's company, effectively reducing FOCA's role. Ecclestone's company sold the television rights, paying a proportion on to the constructors, the track owners/promoters and FIA. Ecclestone's company, to all intents, appeared implicitly to 'own' Formula One. In 2001, Ecclestone had sold a further 25 per cent of his Formula One business, SLEC, to Kirch, the German Media Group, for a sum which may have been as much as £1000 million. He was now third in the overall UK Rich List, with a fortune estimated at £3 billion (Beck-Burridge and Walton 2001). Ecclestone has developed, in recent years, a great skill at selling off parts of his enterprise for considerable sums, whilst remaining in effective control. In 1997 the Labour Government announced that Formula One would be exempt from the proposed ban on tobacco sponsorship. When it emerged that Ecclestone had made a £1 million donation to the Labour Party before the election, the resultant furore caused the Labour Party to return the donation. Tobacco sponsorship of Formula One was eventually outlawed by the European Union in 2005.

In the UK, the sport had always been televised by the BBC, so it was a shock when, in 1997, Ecclestone sold the UK rights to Formula One to ITV, for five years, for £65 million. This is roughly equivalent to £650,000 per Grand Prix, around £300,000 per hour just for the rights. As two hours of television on ITV contains 12 minutes of advertising, this would mean charging £50,000 per minute for advertising just to cover the cost of acquiring the rights. Given Grand Prix audiences of around three to five million this is not easy, although ITV attempted to increase the revenue potential by giving fuller coverage to the two days of qualifying. ITV coverage does also give sponsors the opportunity to reinforce their sponsorship with television advertising. The attempt by Formula One motor racing to develop its American market went disastrously wrong in 2005 at Indianapolis. An extraordinary row developed after several teams were handicapped by having the wrong sets of tyres. Whatever the rights and wrongs of a complicated internal wrangle, it was clear that the fans were not the top priority, a fact all too clear to the American fans streaming away from the non-event. Many of them took the opportunity to express in strong terms to television cameras their disgust and the minimal chance that they would ever go to see a Formula One event again. Without income from television, sponsorship and advertising, of course, Formula One motor racing, with its massive technical expenses, would not exist. The economic power of advertising should not be underestimated. A recent estimate put global spending at US$435 billion (Jackson, Andrews and Scherer 2005: 4). Within sport, as Jackson and Andrews (2005) discuss in *Sport, Culture and Advertising*, advertising has both an economic and a cultural impact. Advertising banners fill a substantial amount of the visual space of any television broadcast of sport, yet we are so habituated that its presence is now totally naturalised. Only Wimbledon tennis and the Olympic Games remain unsullied.

The climate in which marketeers, promoters and advertisers command such cultural power is one in which the very richness of language is itself being diluted. On November 8, 2002, McDonald's announced that they had signed a marketing deal with tennis stars, Serena and Venus Williams – I'm sorry, I mean the Williams sisters had been invited to join 'the McDonald's family'. 'We are thrilled to welcome Serena and Venus to the McDonald's family,' said Bill Lamar, senior vice president and chief marketing officer for McDonald's USA. 'The Williams sisters are two vibrant, dynamic personalities adept at scoring points on the tennis court. We're confident they'll be tremendous assets in "netting" positive results for our Dollar Menu.' 'Venus and Serena are great tennis players known for their style, their energy and their enthusiasm,' added Marlena Peleo-Lazar, McDonald's USA vice president and chief creative officer. 'We're excited to be working with two of the most sought-after people in sports.' In addition to starring roles in McDonald's TV advertising, the Williams sisters' three-year agreement includes public appearances for many of McDonald's philanthropic efforts including those for Ronald McDonald House Charities®. 'We're both huge fans of McDonald's, and we both love kids,' said Venus Williams. 'It's really exciting to be working with McDonald's and the Dollar Menu campaign. And what's so special is that we share McDonald's passion of giving back to the community.' Serena added: 'We grew up with McDonald's. We're delighted to team up with them, on both their advertising and the important community work to benefit kids.' The hamburgers may be digestible but the language is not, and the corrosive insincerity of these promotional banalities starts to rob words of their meaning.

Follow the money

The main sources of income for top-level sport are television rights payments, sponsorship and advertising, merchandising and gate receipts. American Football, basketball, baseball and ice hockey make massive sums in television rights alone. On a global scale, though, football earns far more than most other sports, apart from the technology-intensive Formula One motor sport. Some of this money goes to financing ground improvements, a lot on the purchasing of players but the major share goes to the wages of star players. How star players spend their money is beyond the scope of this analysis, although it is worth noting in passing that a new magazine, *Icon*, aimed at super rich footballers, and not available in the shops, has just been launched. It featured, in its first issue, an item on helicopter shopping, which left those of us who do not earn £50,000 a week wondering whether this referred to shopping *for* helicopters or shopping *by* helicopter.

The sport now has an extremely steep pyramid of earnings. A small elite in the Premier League earn more than £40,000 a week, whilst the average League Two player (that is, in effect three divisions below the top level) earns just £38,000 a year, still more than most university lecturers, teachers or nurses. This amounts to a bit less than £1,000 a game, in which around 30 players will be involved, including substitutes. This means a wage bill of around £30,000 per game. Around 3,000 people watch games at this lowly level. So notionally, the first £10 of the cost of admission goes to cover the salaries of players; a point that spectators probably ponder when exercising their right of abuse. At the elite level the combined weekly wage of the 22 players could easily top £500,000 and gate receipts of more than £1 million per match are common. The admission price of football during the last 20 years has risen much faster than that for comparable forms of public entertainment such as the cinema. In a period in which the income from television has risen enormously, rather than reward loyal fans with lower prices, clubs have chosen to increase admission prices way above the inflation rate.

The concept of the commodity form presupposes the construction of an object or service which can be traded, through the abstract system of equivalence of money, in order that surplus value may be extracted in the form of profit. The term 'commodity' has come to be used, too often, as an over-simplified label and requires a degree of deconstruction in order that it continue to be productive. Who buys sport? The cash-nexus intervenes in numerous ways. People buy tickets, season tickets, executive boxes and hospitality packages. They also purchase television sets, digital boxes and satellite decoders; and may rent access to dedicated sport channels. They may buy newspapers for the sport sections, or dedicated sports magazines. Some also purchase sport merchandise; most notably replica shirts. This is not the only source of revenue for sport, of course. Television companies pay huge sums to acquire rights. Sponsors and advertisers pay, but sometimes they are buying from a sports club or stadium owner, sometimes from a club, and sometimes from a governing body. There has risen a whole new tier of expertise – sport agents, sponsorship brokers, event managers, public relations consultants – who also make money from sport; albeit in and through another set of economic relations.

If the customer appears in diverse forms, so too does the vendor. Who is 'selling' sport? Sport clubs and stadium owners sell admission, at a variety of price levels. Catering is often franchised, with clubs and/or stadia taking a cut. Merchandising may be in the hands of a club, a governing body or a licensed retailer. Television companies are both buying and selling sport. Commentators and experts sell their expertise to television, who purchase it to enhance the value and audience appeal of their product. Sponsors and advertisers buy sport in order to boost sales, and in doing so are investing in image association.

Clearly, then, there is not one simple 'commodity' here but rather a whole set of overlapping commodities, embedded in a diverse but linked set of economic relations. Equally, we are not dealing with a simple unitary commodified object, but rather a complex set of objects, practices, processes and symbolic forms, which all too easily become condensed together in the category 'sport'. We are never simply dealing with monetary capital, but also with cultural capital, with symbolic value, with icons, with stars, with narratives and with discourses.

Signification has its own history, sedimented common sense, popular memories, cultural sensibilities, structures of feeling. Adherence to and involvement in the processes of sports spectatorship have their own historically shaped and formed sensibilities, in which the shared memories, values and commitments continue to form and re-form the experience of 'consuming' sport. When people purchase 'sport', what are they purchasing? At the level of basic economics, people buy entrance to a stadium, or subscribe to a sports channel, in order to view a spectacle.

They do not, however, generally acquire a commodity which can be traded, sold on. They do acquire a form of sporting cultural capital, and they also undergo an experience; of excitement, involvement, passion, emotional peaks and troughs. Welsh comedian, poet and rugby fan Max Boyce's poem which features the line 'I know, cos I was *there*' expresses the importance of the situated experience of the unpredictable live event. These experiences may be intricately linked to a commodity, but are not themselves reducible to a commodity form. They may, of course, seek to embed the memory, the traces of the experience, in the form of merchandise – souvenir programmes, replica shirts, and posters – but these commodities are not the experience, but rather indices that mark and identify the memory of the 'being-there-ness' of experience.

Why do television companies buy rights? Why 'do' sport? The most obvious answer is of course that they wish to win audiences, although apart from a few major events, sport is not an especially prominent means of winning audiences. In the case of companies who make their own revenue from selling advertising, it may seem that the sporting commodity is simply 'sold on'. However, as Dallas Smythe pointed out, advertisers are not buying the programmes, they are buying audiences – in short they are buying us.[37] The programmes, from this perspective, are not the commodity, but simply the means of producing the commodity of audiences. We, the viewers, are the commodity which advertisers purchase. This provocative refocusing of analysis offered by Smythe gives us much purchase on an advertising-based television channel, but does not account effectively for public service broadcasting or subscription television. Clearly then, in analysing television sport, we are not dealing with one simple commodity or one simple set of economic relations. Public service broadcasting, dependent on public finance, is typically assessed not on a programme-by-programme basis, but on its whole service. This has usually involved the requirement to provide a range of programming for a range of audiences, including sport fans, and endeavouring to ensure that relatively minority audiences are not ignored merely because their lack of spending power makes them an unattractive niche market for advertising. In opting to pay for, or as in a licence-based system such as that of the UK, being required to pay for, a whole service, we enter into a different relationship. As consumers, we are buying a whole service, and it is this whole service that constitutes the commodity. Conversely, with subscription channels, a niche market has been developed, and those who select to subscribe are purchasing the channel. Audience evidence on Sky Sports suggests strongly that football is the element that drives the market, with audiences for most other sport events considerably lower.

Smythe's argument gives us some purchase on sponsors and advertisers who are buying access to audiences; but in order to capitalise on their access to us, they seek to associate their products with the connotative resonances of sport events, sometimes in quite complex ways. It is no coincidence that those least nutritious products, Coca-Cola and McDonald's, have been amongst the most keen to associate with the youthful and healthy images that sport facilitates. The economic relations through which the new professionals of the sports world – sport agents, sponsorship brokers, event managers, and public relations consultants – intervene in sport adds another dimension. Their income is usually based on receiving percentages, of the revenue they can generate for their client, or of the size of the rights payments they negotiate. On a simple level, they are selling their negotiating skills. This skill involves the inflation of value, or to put it another way, the ability to increase surplus value. In an era in which symbolic value, as Baudrillard has argued, has eclipsed use value, such skills can gain very large rewards (Baudrillard 1972).

All these forms of economic relation depend ultimately upon the performativity of sport – the spectacle is initially not an object but a process. Indeed, it is an unpredictable and unscripted process, and therein precisely lies its specific appeal. The capitalisation of sport involves exactly the process of transforming this process into commodity forms. This, however, is not a single simple or unitary process, but a complex layering of economic relations, which do not neatly work together. At the cultural level, the tensions and contradictions are even more apparent.

Take football spectatorship, which can now occur in a variety of forms – at the stadia, at home, in a bar, or in a city square.[38] Each cultural context has its own practices and conventions. In stadia tensions can arise between the predominant segmented and ordered all-seated geography and the historically shaped desire of fans for fluidity, carnival and disorder, all of which suggest standing. Stewards are instructed to ensure that fans remain seated. The home can be a site of gender and generational tensions over control of the switch, and sport in particular tends to polarise gendered viewing habits. The viewing context of bar and city square, ironically, has reproduced many of the historically shaped rituals of fandom, now rendered difficult within stadia. Bar and city centre, as well as reproducing, in transformed form, a residual and threatened set of spectatorship practices, also apparently subvert the commodification of television, in that they can enable the viewing of subscription channels. Of course, in a bar, we are paying for it through alcohol, but, we feel, we just might have consumed those drinks anyway.

To sum up, then, I am suggesting that while commodification is of central value in analysing sport and culture, if we are to continue to build on existing work, we need to avoid the tendency towards one-dimensionality, by paying close attention to the multiple levels in which it occurs, to the unevenness, the lack of fit, the discontinuities, the tensions, the contradictions, and perhaps to remember that, at the heart of the process, lies a set of relations between the performative spectacle and the gaze of the spectator which can never be totally subsumed by commodity, and retains on occasion the ability to offer the sublime and transcendent moment (see Whannel 1994b).

At the same time, of course, we need to continue to register the ways in which economic relations also shape the political process. Cricket contact with Zimbabwe has continued despite the unease and anger many both inside and outside cricket have felt and expressed, partly because the commercial arrangements and contracts framing sporting tours, and the potential costs of compensation, have been used to prevent the adopting of a principled stand. We need to try and force the authorities to investigate, rather than cover up, issues associated with the use of performance-enhancing drugs; with kick-backs and bungs in football; and with the malevolent influence of gambling on the manipulation of sports performance.

A writer for *Sports Illustrated* famously pronounced that when the Brooklyn Dodgers left for Los Angeles in 1958 'we lost our innocence forever'. For me, two events above all mark the colonisation of sport by corporate capital. The first was highly publicised and visible, the second less momentous but deeply personal. The first concerns athletics. In many sports the transformations were rapid, dramatic and painful. Undercover payments to top stars had been common in athletics since the 1950s, but the sport, centrepiece of the Olympics, retained its amateur facade. The rapid escalation of television rights payments and sponsorship revenue during the 1970s made it impossible to sustain this position, and means had to be found of openly rewarding top athletes. Trust funds, permit meetings, prize money and agents all arrived in quick succession. An abortive series of high profile races between Sebastian Coe and Steve Ovett planned for 1982 failed to happen. ITV acquired the rights to British athletics from 1985 and centred their promotional efforts around a much hyped but total mis-match between American 1500m runner Mary Decker, and the South African Zola Budd, whose collision with Decker in the 1984 Olympics probably robbed Decker of a medal. The build-up to the race was more like that of a prize fight, did little to enhance the credibility of the sport, and, because, as predicted, Decker won easily, was not even good theatre.[39]

To understand the second occurrence, I need to remind you that growing up as a Fulham supporter, I spent much of the 1960s following the team. In this period they managed regularly to avoid relegation from the First Division, often with a theatrical and dramatic flair for the last-minute escape. They never came close to winning anything, although they did get to the FA Cup Semi Final twice, in 1958 and 1962, finally reaching the Final in 1975, when they lost to West Ham United. As a boy, I had always wanted to run on to the pitch and then cheer the victorious team as they celebrated. The nearest I got to this was at Northampton in 1966, when, along with hundreds of others, I ran across the pitch, ecstatically celebrating a 4–2 win, capping a glorious run of games in which Fulham gained 21 out of a possible 24 points to avoid relegation. It was not, however, a trophy winning moment, and the team did not feel that this was an occasion for victory waving.

During the 1970s, Fulham did finally fall out of the First Division, and then dropped to the Third. In my twenties, I moved away from the area, drifted away from my close involvement in following Fulham, although I continued to regard myself as a fan. In 1982 Fulham needed a point against Lincoln to clinch promotion from the Third Division – not an earth shattering moment in the broader scheme of things, but nevertheless, a trophy. My boyhood desire to be part of the shared jubilation of fan and team resurfacing, at the conclusion of the match I managed to heave my no longer slight frame over the fence, one of the older people so to do, and amble, rather than dash, across the turf (I am restraining, just, the temptation to call it the sacred turf). We assembled in front of the Cottage, and waited to cheer our heroes. After a while some figures emerged – a few of the team, along with officials – but the most prominent object was a very large cardboard cheque, promised by a bank as a reward for winning the Championship. My euphoria collapsed, my enthusiasm for cheering a cheque from the sponsors being minimal, and I trudged home with a heavy heart and a deep feeling of having been robbed.[40]

Spaces, places and mega events

> The official feast asserted all that was stable, unchanging, perennial: the existing hierarchy, the existing religious, political and moral values, norms and prohibitions. It was the triumph of a truth already established, the predominant truth that was put forward as eternal and indisputable. That is why the tone of the official feast was monolithically serious and why the element of laughter was alien to it.
>
> (Bakhtin 1968: 9)

> That's it baby, if you've got it, flaunt it, flaunt it!
>
> Broadway producer, Max Bialystock, played by Zero Mostel, in Mel Brooks' film *The Producers* (1968), yelling from his window to a gold Rolls Royce at street level

Like the official feast described here by Bakhtin, the rituals of the World Cup and the Olympic Games celebrate the triumph of a truth already established and, like the official feast, major sport events and their Opening Ceremonies are monolithically serious. If television is the means by which sport became commercialised then major events are at the heart of television's world of sport, helping to win viewers and promote the channel, whilst opening up the route to a global market. In the battles to stage major events much is now made of the concept of legacy, and yet there is little sign of the benefits of such legacy from previous major events. Many of the sites of major events – Olympics, World Cups and World Fairs – have become sad, dispiriting and decaying – unloved, unwanted and without purpose. These are the real badlands of modernity. Constructed in a moment of rampant civic boosterism, in which there is, typically, a sudden convergence of interest from councillors, architects and town planners, building contractors, and sports administrators, they have rarely fulfilled the promise of long-term planning gain. The element of laughter is alien to these decaying 'legacies', apart, perhaps, from the hollow laughter of those city taxpayers who pick up the tab for decades to follow.[41]

Ever since the commercial success of the 1984 Olympic Games and the esca-lating intensity of the bidding race, in 1986, to stage the 1992 Games, the Olympic bidding process has produced allegations of inducement, bribery and cor-ruption, some of which proved to be true, to the extent that IOC members had to be dismissed or persuaded to resign. Despite the new rules designed to reduce the likelihood of such occurrences, huge sums are invested by the bidding cities, all of which helps provide the IOC with a vast cost-free publicity machine. In the process, all cities lay an emphasis on legacy, on attempting to convince a sceptical public of the permanent value of expensive infra-structural investment.

The 'Great Stadium' of the 1908 Olympics in London survived as White City, a venue for greyhound racing and athletics, into the 1970s and was eventually demolished with no trace and no proper commemoration of its historic role. The White City was not simply demolished, but obliterated from history – there is no visible sign, memorial or plaque to indicate that here an Olympic Games was staged. The huge pavilions of the Paris World Fairs (the Grand Palais and the Petit Palais) built for the 1900 Exposition Universelle, and Palais de Chaillot and the Palais de Tokyo built in 1937 for the Exposition Universelle, were for some years rather sad hulks, and no one quite knew how to breathe new life into them. Eventually municipal funding and commitment gave the Palais de Chaillot and the Palais de Tokyo a new life as museums and extensive renovation work is being carried out on the Grand Palais and the Petit Palais as I write.

The greater Wembley site of the 1923 Empire Exhibition is similarly full of giant sheds and pavilions that, after the Exhibition, never found a higher purpose than light industry, and storage. Wembley Stadium, originally named the Empire Stadium, was built for the British Empire Exhibition of 1923, finished in 1922 and used for the Cup Final for the first time in 1923. Mythologised as the home of English football with its iconic twin towers, it was never a great stadium to watch football, with its shallow raked terraces and immense gulf between specta-tors and pitch. The lack of atmosphere made it a non-intimidating venue for foreign countries and, observing England's national side consistently playing more relaxed and flowing football at other domestic venues, one wonders at the tense and deadening impact it may have had on their performances.

However, the redevelopment of Wembley has been a long and twisted tale, even though a fine looking stadium has now risen above its surroundings. It is a tale of conflicting aims and objectives, the divergent interests of state, owners, investors, governing bodies and entrepreneurs. The Football Association wanted a new showcase for football. Chelsea chairman Ken Bates urged on them an adaption of his own model of combining a stadium with hotel, restaurant and retail facilities. This scheme, the commercial value of which to Chelsea is still unclear, would have added massively to the cost of construction, but was intended to provide a greater revenue stream. The more nostalgic both within and outside the FA wanted the costly preservation of the twin towers in any new scheme. The more pragmatic sought the best return on their investment. The Government, while still undecided about committing to an Olympic bid, pressed for a stadium suitable for athletics, whilst also promoting the construction of a

Figure 5.7 Wembley Stadium, London. The old Wembley stadium enabled the 'being-there-ness' of the big occasion, but was not a great place to watch football. The impressive new football stadium that has replaced it probably has a more promising future than that faced by the 2012 London Olympic Stadium, once the Five Ring Circus leaves town

dedicated athletics stadium at Pickett's Lock, North London, to stage the 2005 World Athletic Championship. As with the Bates scheme, this would cost much more than a simple football stadium.

The underlying problem is that to stage an Olympic Games you need a stadium of a minimum capacity of 80,000 capable of staging athletics. However, such a stadium is of no long-term value for athletics, which is simply not a popular enough sport to draw crowds of that size for any event other than an Olympics. Conversely, oval arenas with running tracks are very unpopular with football fans, who feel they lack atmosphere and place the fans too far from the action. The option of building a big stadium that can be scaled down subsequently has become a popular one with architects. However, that was not appropriate for Wembley, as the FA wanted a large capacity stadium. A bizarre hybrid scheme that would have allowed for the conversion of the stadium to accommodate an athletics track on a temporary basis was dropped only after it became clear that, not only would this be prohibitively expensive, but also it would take several months to convert with resultant loss of revenue.

In the meantime Government policy became unclear, with Minister Chris Smith and other Government spokesmen appearing to be taking different positions. The Pickett's Lock scheme collapsed, and the FA turned their back on the athletics option, leaving the putative London Olympic bid no option but to plan a new athletics stadium. The new Wembley Stadium has a reasonable chance of success, as it can expect, in addition to England internationals, the

FA Cup Semi Finals and Finals, and the Football League play-off games, also to stage rock concerts, and periodic European football finals. The road to viability may well be rocky, because, as this book was completed, the construction company, already accumulating debt due to completion delay for which they have to assume liability, were contemplating legal action on the grounds that the original brief had been changed.

The bigger issue will concern the after-life of the London Olympic stadium of 2012. The laughable suggestion that Leyton Orient, a club whose entire loyal support could fit into a reasonable size cinema, should move in is, one supposes, a non-starter. Providing a new home for Tottenham or West Ham seemed more practical, but West Ham have now rejected the possibility on economic grounds, and Tottenham seem disinterested. Without a keynote tenant, with the new Wembley occupying the ground for major events, and the possibility of a revamped Millennium Dome mopping up the mid-range events, it could otherwise struggle to find a long-term role. So often in the past mega events have begun with architects' blue-prints and models and fine promises of legacy, only to yield white elephants, empty shells and rusty relics.

From architects' plans to wreckers' balls?

It is pointless simply to embark on a national self-flagellation, as some commentators have done, and bewail the supposed unique inability of England to organise such matters, because the problem of legacy is common to the construction of grandiose facilities for one-off events.

When Paris was awarded the 1924 Olympic Games, the architect imagined 'the most beautiful stadium in the world'.[42] In the event, the government dithered over the estimated cost of 20 million francs, and the Comité Olympique Français were forced to make a contract with the Racing Club for their stadium (Gravelaine 1997: 13). This venue began life in 1907 as le Stade du Matin, but by the time of the 1924 Olympics it had become the Stade de Colombes.[43] The first Olympic village was built for the 1924 Games, near Colombes. It was conceptualised as an innovative construction that would be built to last and used after the Games for sporting activities.[44] A commentator at the time described it: 'It was a true village, and a beautiful village, with all modern comforts installed.'[45] On a recent research visit to the area, I could find no trace of the village.

In 1928, the stadium was renamed again, after Yves du Manoir, a rugby player who played more than 100 games for RCF between 1923 and 1927. In 1928, he died at the age of 23 and they named the stadium after him.[46] The stadium, which held around 60,000 people, was used for games in the 1938 World Cup, including the final, and for French international rugby games until the construction of the new Parc Des Princes in 1972. *The Guardian* (4/1/04) recently described it as the equivalent of Wembley, Twickenham, and White Hart Lane, combined with a touch of Madison Square Garden, as boxing was also staged there. Despite the demolition of most of the covered area, it remained home to

Racing Club de France but entered a long period of decline from 1972 until 2004, when it was decided to raise 250 million euros to redevelop it.

The local council raised six million euros to fund a feasibility study. Simon Guillam, marketing consultant to the English rugby federation, advised basing plans on the redesign of Barcelona's Olympic stadium, bringing in music concerts, cultural events and commercial activities, as well as shopping, in order to keep visitors coming and spending for the whole day. Largely privately financed, the redevelopment was to have a 20,000-seat stadium and the intention was to revive the fortunes of Sporting Club de France, open the complex in time for the 2007 Rugby World Cup and use it to promote the Paris Olympic bid (*The Guardian* 4/1/04). The optimistic hope that the new modern complex would be a key element in Paris's staging of the 2012 Games was of course rudely shattered in July 2005 when the 2012 Olympic Games were awarded to London, and it is not yet clear whether or how the plans will be revised. Meanwhile the stadium is currently a sorry sight, half fenced off with corrugated iron, although it is surrounded by fairly well used pitches. Many of the issues related to major stadia are present in this story – the use of major events to trigger public investment, the relationship between architects and builders, municipal authorities and sports administrators, the tendency for stadia developed in relation to major events to go into decline where no clear strategy or finance for redevelopment is available, and the importance of constructing spectators as consumers in current development strategies.

The project for a grand stadium in Paris was under discussion for many decades, during which debate raged about what kind of stadium was required, for what purpose, and who would pay for it. There were plans for a stadium holding 116,000 for the 1937 Exposition Internationale that did not come to fruition. An abortive attempt was made to develop a stadium at Vincennes. Eventually an opportunity presented itself in 1965 with the construction of the Périphérique, the Paris ring road, which was going to involve the destruction of an old velodrome in the Bois de Boulogne. The decision was taken to replace an old stadium with a new modern stadium, Le Parc Des Princes, on top of Le Périphérique, which would pass under it in a tunnel. The Parc Des Princes stadium, which Gravelaine calls remarkable for its era, however, only had 49,000 seats and offered rudimentary comfort, which, Gravelaine comments, was doubtless sufficient to satisfy the supporters, but not to appeal to the family customers that the Stade de France would subsequently attract (Gravelaine 1997: 17).

The much-praised Stade de France, constructed for the 1998 World Cup, was the result of an architectural competition. From the 1960s Paris had undergone a series of architectural upheavals – the removal of the food markets, Les Halles, and construction on the site of a giant underground shopping mall; the building of the Pompidou Centre, and the Montparnasse Tower, followed by a series of *grands projets* fostered by President Mitterrand, culminating in the opening of the enormous Bibliothèque Nationale on the Seine. But the era of *grands projets* was coming to an end. There was a feeling that the construction of a new stadium could be the last grand project of the century – 'Après la très Grande Bibliothèque, le Grand Stade!' commented Francis Rambert (1995: 14).

The Stade de France, an elegant design, perfect for football, with good transport access and a clever separation of vehicles and people on different levels, was popular with spectators. It was also, by current standards, relatively cheap, comparing favourably with the expensive redevelopment of Wembley. However, the commercial strategy for its future was weakened by the lack of a keystone tenant, football club Paris St Germain electing to stay at the cheaper and more compact Parc Des Princes. At present the Stade de France stages football internationals, athletics and other sport events, and a motley collection of festivals and concerts. Without major regular club football, it is not easy to make the finances work well. London's proposed Olympic stadium is likely to have the same problem unless Tottenham or West Ham can be persuaded to relocate after 2012.

The Soviet Union constructed in the 1930s a large park-based exhibition site, VDNH (the acronym stood for Exhibition of National Economic Achievements, but became known colloquially as Vaydenah). Complete with grand pavilions, and spectacular fountains with golden statues, it was opened in 1939. By the 1990s the pavilions were filled with stalls selling cheap electronic goods, and cheap and tawdry merchandising swamped the grandeur. The 1936 Berlin stadium was constructed in 1935, partly destroyed during the war, and rebuilt in 1948. Owned by the city, Hertha Berlin now play there. Despite the partial reconstruction, the oppressive authoritarian architecture of the Berlin Olympic stadium is doomed forever to symbolise Nazi tyranny. Hertha Berlin are a rather undistinguished side, whose small support must feel cowered within this unfortunate monument to a terrible past. In the year of the Berlin Olympics, 1936, London's Crystal Palace burned down. The great glasshouse centrepiece of the 1851 Great Exhibition, it had been demolished and rebuilt in an area of south London that became known as Crystal Palace. The site of the fire is still a flat debris-strewn and desolate plain at the top of Crystal Palace park and, again, no one knows quite what do to about it. Further down the hill, sports facilities, once considered state of the art, a swimming pool, recreation centre, and athletics stadium are suffering from neglect and decay. The Brussels World Fair site of 1958 was decaying and tawdry for decades – the vast structure of the Atomium patently a highly visible embarrassment that no one knew quite what to do with. Only recently has the site been refurbished.

London's Millennium Dome surpassed these tales of sad decay and succeeded in becoming an embarrassment even before it opened. It was all too clear that there was no clear vision as to what it should contain, and in the end it housed a dispiriting, meretricious and sponsorship heavy set of 'attractions' whose subtext celebrated 'New Labour' and the Third Way. The Millennium Dome provides another example of legacy as embarrassment. The founding fault was the placing of form ahead of function. The Government chose to have a dome in advance of any serious thought about what it should contain, so it was no surprise that content became such a vexed issue – there was no rationale for it to be a dome in the first place. Conceived by the Conservative Government, it was inherited by Labour who almost abandoned the project, only for Blair to argue, from a minority position in cabinet, to proceed. A hapless and leaderless potage of 'experts' from design, marketing, show business and the arts patently failed to come up with any clear direction or consensus. Charged with finding commercial sponsorship, the contents of the Dome were from the start in hock to its commercial supporters. Ironically the Dome succeeded only in being a flabby monument to a baggy concept – the Third Way. The dispiriting and unexciting exhibits seemed so often to have a hidden subtext – the old grey public culture was being replaced by a bright pastel friendly commercially driven world of individual choice and consumption. The most depressing feature of the whole project was the massive denial of the symbolic strengths of the public culture established by the 1945 Labour Government and celebrated in the Festival of Britain in 1951.[47]

The opening night of the Dome, on Millennium Eve, was an unmitigated disaster, with long queues of very angry VIPs waiting to be ferried in, and then being handed a lukewarm glass of champagne. The subsequent year only succeeded in pulling six million visitors; actually quite respectable but less than half the number budgeted for. The mothballed building continued for some years to be a charge on the public purse, while a deal with a private tenant or purchaser was sought, before plans were announced in 2006 for its redevelopment as a multi-facility leisure site, and its renaming after sponsors O_2. Given the fiascos of Pickett's Lock, Wembley in its early stages and the Dome throughout, the success of the London bid seems even more surprising and even more of a triumph for its bid team.

Indeed the afterlife of mega event venues has rarely been happy. The 1972 Munich Olympic stadium, marred rather than enhanced by an extraordinary transparent roof, far too flimsy and delicate in appearance to blend in with the solidity of the rest of the stadium, is fated to be remembered always in relation to the seizing of Israeli hostages by Palestinian terrorists, and the subsequent farcical shoot-out. Montreal's stadium in 1976, famously, went so much over budget that the citizens of Montreal only finished paying for it in 2006, a well-known fact that eclipses in the memory of many any clear idea of what the stadium actually looked like. The dangers of an expensive building project with public funding for a high profile event with an immoveable deadline should be all too evident. The Lenin stadium in Moscow, used for the 1980 Olympics, has a certain majesty about it, but is visibly suffering from years of under-investment in maintenance.

The rigid cost control of the privately funded Los Angeles Olympics of 1984 ensured minimal investment in new facilities and a re-use of the 1932 stadium, showing that the Olympic Games do not have to require massive investment in new facilities of questionable long-term value. Seoul, by contrast, spent huge sums of public money on lavish brand new facilities. There is a value in municipal involvement, allied to continued investment and a long-term strategy. Rome's Olympic stadium was built in 1952 in preparation for the 1960 Olympics and is still used for athletics, international football and by Lazio and Roma. Barcelona is constantly held up as the model example of Olympic-led regeneration of a city, and it is true that the re-imaging of the city has had a significant impact on tourism. It is worth remembering that, like Los Angeles, they chose, wisely, to reinvigorate an old stadium from the 1930s rather than invest excessively in an elaborate new status symbol. Of mega event sites, only the 1896

Athens stadium survives with a real dignity and grace – the beautiful white marble stadium remains a monument – not transformed into anything, but simply there and offering onlookers a glimpse of the marvellous. Far from leaving a legacy, much mega event architecture bequeaths an embarrassment. It is worth pondering why there is such a lack of reverence for the sites of history in a sporting environment obsessed with golden moments and records of triumphs.

It is odd to recall that it is only the last four Olympic Games that have been the subject of intense and vastly expensive bidding races. From 1968 to 1984 the supposed purity of the Olympic Ideal had to contend with political gestures such as the Black Power salute in 1968; terrorism in 1972; and political boycotts in 1976, 1980 and 1984. Only Tehran and Los Angeles were in contention to stage the 1984 Olympics. However, the commercial success of Los Angeles, and the changing state of global politics, encouraged much more enthusiastic attempts to win the Olympics. In the watershed year of 1986, six bidding cities spent an average of ten million dollars each in the race to be awarded the 1992 Games, eventually won by Barcelona. The International Olympic Committee encouraged the process of hotly contested bidding races, and the intense lobbying involved. Staging the Games, indeed merely bidding to stage the Games, provides a means of boosting a whole range of city regeneration strategies, and with such large sums involved, it is not surprising that suspicions of corruption should be present. However, suspicion of bribery by bidding cities hardened into prima facie evidence during the 1990s, eventually forcing the resignation of several IOC members.

In 1998 a local television station in Salt Lake City produced the first documented case of corruption in the bidding process. In *Inside the Olympic Industry* Helen Lenskyj argued that this was not merely an isolated case, and draws attention to consistent patterns of relationship between bid committees and IOC members (Lenskyj 2000). Lenskyj reviewed the reports of the IOC Ad Hoc Commission, the Salt Lake Board of Ethics Report, the USOC Special Bid Oversight Commission Report and the Report of the Independent Examiner for the Sydney Olympic Committee and concludes that they constituted a persuasive case that the rules regarding gifts, hospitality and services were being breached and that some IOC members and their relatives were receiving extensive benefits from bid committees (Lenskyj 2000).

The focal point of the Olympic Games has shifted from national prowess to urban regeneration. The much-publicised battle of the medal table that was such a feature of the period of cold war symbolic contestation between East and West was always a complete artifice. The apparent domination of the USA and the Soviet Union disappeared if one took population size into account. Dividing medals won by population produced a different picture, in which Cuba, the German Democratic Republic and other Soviet satellite countries, and the Scandinavian countries typically performed the best, with the supposed sporting great powers way down the list. Dividing gold medals won at the Sydney 2000 Olympic Games by population (in millions) gives the following result:

1	Bahamas	3.33
2	Cuba	0.97
3	Norway	0.87
4	Australia	0.80
5	Hungary	0.79
6	Estonia	0.74
7	Netherlands	0.73
8	Bulgaria	0.66
9	Lithuania	0.55
10	Romania	0.49

(source: www.nationmaster.com, derived from IOC figures)

The concept that one can buy gold medals through investment, currently so influential in British sport governing bodies, is also open to doubt. Making a rough estimate based on spending on sport, medal success and population, Germany's medals at the 2000 Olympic Games may have cost twice those of France and five times as much as those of Poland. The evidence that investment in elite sport brings proportionate medal success is less than convincing, but the unique aura of the Olympic Games constitutes a powerful allure for politicians in search of a feelgood factor.

The Olympic Games has been remarkably successful in utilising public investment in infrastructure, commercial revenue from television and sponsorship, and public enthusiasm in the form of volunteer labour. Every July, in the build-up to 2008, Beijing stages an Olympic Cultural festival to celebrate having been awarded the Olympic Games. The festival features pop concerts, art exhibitions, Olympic souvenir markets, a festival of sport films, and a contest to select an Olympic song. Efforts have begun to recruit 100,000 volunteers for the Games.[48] The slogan is One World, One Dream, a utopian figure that masks the numerous opportunities for corporate promotion and enrichment that the Games provide. Olympic imagery, rich in signification is also now available commercially. In 1995 the IOC established the Olympic Television Archive Bureau (OTAB), a repository of over 20,000 hours of film and television footage of the Olympics. Clients can purchase historic footage for use in advertising (Jackson, Andrews and Scherer 2005: 6). Mega events are now on the agenda of every major city in the world. They are part of a city's development strategy, linking infrastructural development, job creation, enhanced visibility and increased tourism. Yet the evidence for the benefits of staging mega events to such strategies is at best patchy.

The staging of such events combines both public and corporate conspicuous consumption. In the late nineteenth century, Veblen, in *The Theory of the Leisure Class* (1912), outlined the way the affluent class in America took to advertising their affluence through forms of conspicuous consumption – the acquisition of grand houses, with liveried servants and elaborate banquets. Subsequently, the yacht, the expensive car and the executive jet became symbolic advertisements for wealth and power. In the 1960s, Galbraith's *The Affluent Society* (1958) identified the spectacle of inequality through which a rich and successful class utilised ostentation as the advertisement of success, opening a gap between private wealth and public squalor. In *The Status Seekers* (1960), Vance Packard portrayed a rather different mode of status in which hard work and the badges of success (the corner office, the key to the executive washroom) became significant markers of status. Nowadays, the ticket for the corporate day out, the seat in the executive box and the helicopter ride to the racing have become signifiers of corporate status. Between 20 and 25 per cent of tickets for some major events now go to administrators, sponsors and to corporate hospitality. In *Mega-Events and Modernity* (2000) Maurice Roche analyses the ways in which mega events provide means of public and corporate display. Such events have now become iconic means for cities to proclaim, with a macho swagger, their success, their dynamism, and their virility. The guiding principle is, 'if you've got it, flaunt it'. Underpinning this, of course, are the careful profit and loss calculations of municipal accountants, the lobbying of property developers, and the manoeuvring of the new brokers of the international sport business.

6 Nations, identities, celebrities and bodies

> Great Britain is a degenerate country, riddled with complexes because of its loss of power, inhabited by fox-hunters in ludicrous costumes, and hypocritical lefties who send their spoiled children to private schools. The British have bad health-care, bad teeth and bad skin, which they regularly burn on southern beaches because they find suntan lotion unsporty. Their food is inedible, and their beer tepid and tasteless.
>
> (Item in *Frankfurter Allgemeine Zeitung*, June 2002)[49]

Sport, arguably, has its greatest social and political impact in relation to the processes by which individual and national identities are constructed. The majority of the top sporting events are associated directly or indirectly with national contestation. The representations of sport reproduce national stereotypes of others, whilst offering celebratory, patriotic and often xenophobic ideas of who 'we' are. This is complex, because some are or feel or choose to be excluded; some are internationalist by inclination or multinational by background; localist and regionalist sympathies divide nations; and national identities are always constructed from a complex combination of elements. Sport has also become a significant representational source for images of fit, sexualised bodies. It is noteworthy that a current slang phrase for sexually attractive is 'she looks fit'. So the representation of sport is an element in our senses of who we are, who other people are, and what sort of identities constitute our countries and nations and other people's countries and nations.

Some years ago it was decided that the Ryder Cup competition between the United Kingdom and the USA had become hopelessly one-sided and it could become more competitive if it was Europe vs the USA. There were two interesting side effects of this change. The first was that it added a new event to the relatively small set of popular cultural practices that can contribute to an emergent sense of European identity. The second is that, in the new, more competitive environment of the competition, elements amongst the Ryder Cup spectators have become gradually more strident, partisan and aggressive, eroding the conventions of respect and courtesy common at golf events more generally.

This shift was also visible amongst the USA team and their associates who ran across the green celebrating a victory, before the European golfer had had an opportunity to hole out.

Yet, of the corporate ritual occasions that hail us, major national sport events are still one of the more effective. To hear crowds sing at international matches at Twickenham, the Stade de France, or Hampden Park, to see the 'tifosi' cheering Ferrari, to witness the blizzard of confetti that greeted Argentina's 1978 World Cup win, is to experience a fierce and tribal patriotism not generally manifest in many other contexts. National identities, then, are powerful forces. However, in postmodern culture, the heightened elements of self-reflexivity, irony and pastiche means that the elements of national signification can sometimes, in the popular mode, collapse back into parodic playfulness, which, given the damage that intense nationalism can produce, may not be altogether a bad thing.

As the quotation at the start of this chapter suggests, the stereotypes others have of us often appear slightly ludicrous and often outdated. The stereotypes we have of others, by contrast, while recognisably exaggerated and parodic, are, it seems to me, more likely to be perceived as representing a degree of veracity. Like any victim, we can perceive modes of unfair treatment not apparent to the perpetrator; but are likely to be blind to our own stereotyping of others. The construction and articulation of national identities is, though, a complex cultural process. The nation itself is not a neat fixed object. Few nations have existed with relatively unchanging frontiers for centuries; the vast majority have been subject to shifting boundaries, have been victims or perpetrators of conquest and colonisation, and have been subject to internal contestation between competing groups. The identities that coalesce around notions of nationhood appear to have, indeed characteristically lay claim to, a solidity and a history rooted in the soil. Yet such national mythologies are the site of struggle and contestation and are constantly reshaped and reformed.

The word 'mythology' is apt in denoting a process of constructing national narratives – stories that organise, explain and clarify the ways in which people can live their relation to a broader collectivity. Some of the components of this process in England[50] – the Dunkirk spirit, Churchillian resoluteness – are to do with recent history and notions of national character. Some – the imagined rural idyll of church, village green, cricket, beer in ancient pubs and ducks on the pond – are to do with landscape and architecture and an idealised pastoral image of organic community. Some – Boadicea, Henry V's Agincourt speech, Drake, Raleigh and Nelson – are embedded elements in a half-remembered popular history. Some – Shakespeare, Dickens, Jane Austen, Wordsworth, Constable, Turner – are to do with selective tradition, and the construction of cultural hierarchies. Together they become part of a national narrative that is not narrated in explicit form and yet is understood, comprehended and is part of a popular common sense. The structuring of this national imaginary is masked, and only if one considers how a different social-political environment might have woven different figures more prominently into the national tapestry (Wat Tyler, Robin Hood, the Levellers, Mary Wollstonecraft, Shelley, William Blake, Annie Besant) does the process of hierarchisation become more apparent.

The mythologies of national cohesion, the mapping of territory, the invention of tradition and ritual all contribute to the production of, in Anderson's term, 'imagined communities' (Anderson 1983). Ritual and tradition, of course, play a particularly prominent role in English society. Those who try to describe our national cultural life often resort to lists in which sport events such as Derby Day, the Boat Race, the Cup Final, Test Matches, the Grand National feature along-side other corporate national occasions – the State Opening of Parliament, royal weddings, trooping the colour. Ritual, in its apparent timelessness and cyclical recurrence, lends a solidity, a sense of permanence, to the constructions of national identity.

Yet apparently ageless rituals all had their moment of invention and have since been subject to reconstruction in adjustment with the changing times (see Hobsbawm and Ranger 1983). Take for example the crisis within the British state over how to mark the death of Princess Diana: the subsequent uneasy nego-tiations between monarchy and government about the mode of presentation necessary to assume leadership of the public mood; and the challenge to that leadership by the Earl Spencer, who temporarily voiced a popular mood of dis-content with the monarchy's failure to echo and embody public sentiment. Another example can be found in the state and the BBC's endless reworking of scenarios to cope with the death of the Queen Mother, in which the twin dan-gers of over-reacting and under-reacting loomed. More recently, and apparently with the benefit of a modernised public image input into the aristocratic and ultra-conservative world of the Court, the Jubilee Year managed to reinvent and reinvigorate the monarchy, temporarily stemming a small but growing republican sentiment amongst the public.

Constructions of national identity, then, have no fixity – they need con-stantly to reinscribe both their object – the nation – and their audience – the citizens. An instance was the debate triggered by Andrew Wilson, Scottish Nationalist Party (SNP) finance spokesman, who suggested that Scots ought to break with the tradition of cheering on the opponents of 'the auld enemy' and support England instead. A *Guardian* piece on the subject referred to increased sales of Argentinian wine and the appearance of lime green Nigerian shirts in Scotland as indices of support for England's opponents in the 2002 World Cup (*The Guardian* 14/6/02). The piece suggests that 'it's not easy to find many Scots openly supporting England in the World Cup'. One Englishman, working in Scotland, is quoted as saying: 'We would support the Jocks in the World Cup, maybe grudgingly, but we would support them. I thought they would have returned the favour. What's their problem?' There is an interesting incompre-hension expressed in this quotation, rooted in a denial of the relations of dominance and subordinance that have structured British history. Some Americans have in recent years expressed a rather similar lack of comprehension of anti-American sentiment in other parts of the world.

The Guardian speculated as to whether the supposed anti-Englishness of the Scots is 'simply playful small country big country rivalry – or a case of dour and heartfelt Anglophobia'. Sociologist David McCrone is quoted as characterising it as having an element of tongue-in-cheek irony. McCrone's research suggests 83 per cent of Scots have no antipathy to England, while a *Scotsman* survey reported that 29 per cent of Scots would be supporting England, 18 per cent favoured their opponents and the majority (53 per cent) had no preference. In other words it is somewhat of a non-story (*The Guardian* 14/6/02). It does however illustrate both the constant process of hailing subjects to a national identity, and also the ways in which social actors resist such calls.

Such constructions do not exist in isolation, but rather in the context of a discursive field in which the identities of other nations are also articulated. Englishness exists in relation to two distinct cultural and geopolitical formations. The first constitutes its relation of dominance over the subordinate Celtic nations of the United Kingdom; the second constitutes its distanced relation with continental Europe – indeed in English public discourse the term 'Europe' most typically denotes somewhere else (the mainland) and not where 'we' are (see Whannel 1997). Englishness and Britishness are always articulated in relation to their others – Europe, North America, the 'non-white', but above all foreigners. 'Johnny Foreigner' is a characteristic figure here. *Daily Mail* readers may invoke him straight, *Guardian* readers with deep irony, yet both will recognise the implied other – the rest of the world – that does things differently. To the English sensibility, it is not the past that is a different country, it is the rest of the world. It is on the terrain of national identities that the complex and contradictory tensions around concepts of familiar and strange, self and other, domestic and foreign, are worked through. It is through discourses of national identity that the imagined similarities and differences between 'us' and 'them' are explored. I want to illustrate this by looking at Anglo-German relations as constructed in popular press representation, with specific reference to England vs Germany football. In particular I will focus on the construction of mythologised figures – the 'beach towel' and the 'oompah band' – and the ways in which they fit into more generalised discourse about 'German-ness' and 'Englishness'.

On beach towels and brass bands: England and Germany

Conflict is a significant feature of representations of Germany in the English media. Even before the Second World War, the legacy of the First World War propaganda had a big influence on popular cultural representations of Germany. Lines from First World War songs – 'Kaiser Bill is feeling ill, the crown prince he's gone barmy', 'We'll hang out the washing on the Siegfried line', 'Belgium put the Kibosh on the Kaiser' – probably lingered in the public imagination. A whole series of atrocity stories, designed to inflame public sentiment against Germany, were released, and only after the war did it emerge that the vast majority were utterly without foundation. Philip Knightley, in his history of propaganda, *The First Casualty*, asserts that 'More deliberate lies were told than in any other period of history' (see Knightley 1975). Ironically, the adverse reaction as the propaganda lies were exposed probably contributed to a tendency to under-report the Nazi atrocities of the Second World War.

The impact and the legacy of the Second World War produced a whole range of representation which rendered the Germans more as comic than as menacing. Radio show *ITMA* utilised the comic German accent in the character of Funf. Rewritten lyrics were popular – 'Hitler has only got one ball' to the tune of Colonel Bogey, for example. A new generation of post-war comedians, marked by the war experience, etched it into their comedy. *The Goon Show*, written by Spike Milligan, was full of military figures, and service references, and Germans appeared as figures of fun – authoritarian and humourless.[51] If Funf and Milligan's German characters were comically ineffectual, the use of the German accent, and German involvement to denote a sinister menace, is a prevalent device in a whole range of films, such as *The Third Man*, *The Thirty Nine Steps* and *Dr Strangelove*. One legacy of the Nazi regime in English popular culture has been the suturing of the German accent to two apparently contradictory elements – the comic and the menacing.

In the course of post-war reconstruction, and the mythologising of the German 'economic miracle' (see Kettenacker 1997), a new stereotypical element – German efficiency – came to be grafted on to this amalgam. The long running BBC comedy series about the Home Guard during the Second World War, *Dad's Army*, in a rare episode in which German characters appeared, contrasted English loveable eccentricity against humourless efficiency combined with sinister menace. In the BBC series *'Allo 'Allo*, set in a small French town during wartime, national identity is denoted by accent. Everyone, English, French and German, become figures of fun. However, there is an interesting distinction between the fat German colonel, who is basically relatively friendly and not a real Nazi, and the thin menacing Herr Flick of the Gestapo. A broader demarcation of stereotype is suggested here, in which there are fat Germans (jolly, thigh slapping, with bratwurst and steins of ale) and thin Germans (humourless, efficient and sinister). In the last 20 years, the image of German efficiency has become marketable – *Vorsprung durch Technic*, as they say in Germany. Is there here a set of clues to our contradictory constructions of German-ness? On the one hand a whole set of fears – the Nazi legacy, German expansionism, Germany's post-war economic miracle, German efficiency – are all condensed onto the thin, efficient, humourless and sinister. On the other hand, a fat figure of fun suggests a recognition of similarities, at least in terms of working-class masculinity – German men, like British men, rooted in a culture of beery vulgarity.

It is important to recognise that images of national identity do not speak to a unified national subjectivity. Many analyses stress the prominence of sport in the process by which people are hailed by constructions of national identity, but the following of football is highly gender specific; even though a greater percentage of women may temporarily be hailed by patriotic identification during the period of a World Cup. Conversely, the media focus on Tim Henman's chances of becoming the first English player to win Wimbledon since Fred Perry may well have hailed more women than men. Royal occasions mobilise the appearance of a strong public support effectively, but the consensual mode of address of newspapers doesn't entirely mask the not insignificant proportion of the nation who remain unmoved or antipathetic. I have already referred to ambivalence or distance from an English-dominated British national address amongst members of the subordinate Celtic nations within the UK. Black-British and Asian-British citizens may have similar ambiguities in relation to patriotic positionality.[52] So any textual analysis needs to recognise limitations, in that subject-positions within the text do not have a neat correspondence with the positionality of actual acting subjects. Class, race, gender, generation, and ethnic distinctions; family histories; and forms of media consumption all intervene. Nevertheless, it is reasonable to assume that certain mythologies have the cogency that their structured regularity and cyclical recurrence would suggest.

Press coverage of sport, as many studies have pointed out, makes considerable use of the imagery of conflict and war, utilising metaphors from gladiatorial combat, bull-fighting, boxing and battles. English press coverage of England vs Germany encounters has been haunted by the Second World War – references to it constantly force themselves to the surface in a significant instance of the return of the repressed. Before the 1966 World Cup Final one paper commented that if Germany beat us at our national game we should remember that we had twice beaten them at theirs. During the 1990 World Cup a *Sun* headline proclaimed 'We beat them in 45, we beat them in 66, now the battle of 90'. Most dramatically, and controversially, during Euro 96, the *Daily Mirror* ran a headline 'ACHTUNG! SURRENDER: For You Fritz, Ze EURO 96 Championship is Over'. This last instance appeared sufficiently out of tune with the dominant public mood that the *Daily Mirror*, under pressure from the public and other papers, was forced to capitulate with a mock apology.

Joseph Maguire has pointed out that European integration at a political level is outpacing European integration at an emotional level. In his analysis of anti-Europeanism in the English press, he sketches out a context for the Euro 96 coverage in which the mad cow crisis was at its peak; a European political summit meeting was taking place in Florence to discuss the problem; there was continuing speculation regarding England's attitude towards the proposed single currency; John Major's position as Prime Minister was precarious; and a General Election was imminent (Maguire and Poulton 1999; Maguire *et al.* 1999a, 1999b). With the broader context of deep-seated English concerns regarding national decline and rapid social change, Maguire suggests that an anti-Europeanism in the English press developed around two interwoven themes: nostalgia and ethnic assertiveness/defensiveness. The broadsheets, despite deploring the tabloid use of war imagery and militaristic metaphors, enjoyed the utilisation of similar images themselves, albeit through a more sophisticated and less confrontational style.

Maguire suggests there was a longing for some mythical golden age, which was both reflected in and, in turn, fuelled by the media. English media coverage of Euro 96 served more to 'divide' than to 'unite' the nations of Europe, especially in relation to Germany. By contrast German press coverage was marked by a distinct disinterest in nostalgic or other historical references of their own and dismay at the English press evocation of past hostilities between the two nations

(Maguire and Poulton 1999; Maguire *et al.* 1999a, 1999b). While broadly accepting this characterisation of the coverage, I want to suggest that, at least in the 2001 coverage, it is possible to detect ambiguities and contradictions.

I think there are three reasons to advance this hypothesis. First, constructions of national identities are concerned to mark similarities as well as differences; and mark positives as well as negatives. Such constructions can highlight desirable qualities of other-ness, that by implication, Englishness lacks and could do with a bit more of. Take, for example, the appeal to a bohemian hedonism in the alcohol adverts that adopt the slogan 'there's Latin spirit in everyone'. In this light, references to German efficiency can have an ambiguous quality – efficiency is something that might improve Englishness. Second, post-modern irony is a significant feature of popular entertainment, and the tabloid press plays with and parodies its own conventions. The recent debate in the broadsheets about the undesirable nature of the supposed hatred of Germany in society, whilst making a worthwhile and valid point, didn't really consider the parodic playfulness of some tabloid journalism. *The Sun's* sending a Page 3 oom-pah band to Germany was a means of drumming up a story out of nothing, a pretext (not that *The Sun* really needs one) for objectified and sexualised glam-our pictures, and a way of including the newspaper itself at the centre of the story. It did however also have a playful quality, and it could be dangerous to read this as an index of popular hostility to German-ness. It constituted a teasing provocation, and it is worth noting that, in everyday exchange, teasing implies a degree of closeness – one doesn't tease strangers until one feels at ease with them. Third, tabloid humour contains aspects of male banter, one of the ways in which masculine solidarity is forged (see Easthope 1990). Tabloid humour is often crude, vulgar and rooted in stereotypical portrayal, but nevertheless it may be that it works best where two cultures (in this case German and English football cultures) clearly have similarities as well as differences. The tabloid press build-up to the match, while marking differences, is also implicitly underscoring similarities.

In September 2001, England beat Germany 5–1 in Munich, a sensational result no one predicted.[53] In the English press coverage of the build-up to the most recent England vs Germany match, I was struck by two motifs. The first motif was the beach towel, most strikingly in the *Daily Star* headline, 'you can stick your beach towels up your ****'. This drew attention to our strange relation to the supposed German efficiency. The second was a battle of the bands. England's hotel was supposedly subject to noise from a German 'oompah' band. Seeking to wring more out of this story, the *Sun* newspaper sent its own band – a group of Page 3 girls, whose music accomplishments were not put to the test, but whose photogenic properties helped flesh out *The Sun's* build-up coverage. Interestingly, this brass band motif appeared to draw attention, not to the divisions between the two nations, but to the similarities between them.

Beach towels

The beach towel motif was derived from the popular cultural myth growing out of package holiday experiences, that the Germans rise early in order to place beach towels on deck chairs and sun loungers, thus reserving them before the English can get there. Obviously, in referring to this as a myth, I do not mean to suggest that it does not happen. Rather, I am drawing attention to the way in which it has become an ideological element.[54] 'Ever wondered where Hans from Hamburg goes for his hols? No, of course you haven't, because there's his towel on the sunbed by your hotel pool' (*Daily Mirror* 13/7/02).

Since the growth of mass package tourism in the 1970s, the Germans and the English have been the most numerous European tourists, while Spain is the most popular destination. In 1991 34.9 per cent of foreign tourists to Spain came from Germany and 25.6 per cent from England, a total of 60.5 per cent from the two countries.[55] Inevitably then, the English and the Germans come into proximity with all the attendant possibilities for cultural differences becoming sources of antagonism. In fact there seems very little evidence for serious antagonisms – there has not, for instance, been a moral panic over English vs German holiday violence. The greater friction seems to take place in the interface between yobbish English laddism and affronted local sensibilities.

However, the joke about the Germans having their towels down early to reserve sun loungers has become a routinised element in the lexicon of national stereotypes. When the Germans qualified for the World Cup final in June 2002, the ITV commentary said that 'the Germans have got their towels down for the Final already'. In September 2001, one story headed HANS OFF MY TOWEL – I'M SITTING THERE featured English football fans using 'German tourist tactics' – placing beach towels to reserve seats in a pub with a big screen for the match (*The Sun* 1/9/01). The paper made a lot of references to the jokey spirit of this – *The Sun* seemed intent on avoiding the sort of charges of xenophobic nationalism levelled at the *Daily Mirror* in 1996 after its 'Achtung Fritz' headline. It is worth noting that Benny Hill and Mr Bean, both with a working-class following, are hugely popular in Germany and this may well provide clues to the disconcerting sense of an underlying male working-class commonality between two nations who have fought two wars in the last century.

The beach towel mythology is rooted in a whole set of assumptions:

- that certain deckchairs and sun loungers are the most desirable;
- that it is unfair to get up early to reserve them with a towel;
- that it should not be expected that the English get up early as well;
- that this instance of German efficiency is not a good thing – it offends against the notion of holiday as free-wheeling and it offends against the notion of fair play.

Leisure is supposed to be different from work, a break from routine, planning and regimentation. It is supposed to be a more spontaneous practice. So the idea of thinking ahead somehow breaks this convention – it marks an unwarranted importation of rational planning into the unstructured hedonism of 'holiday'. Fair play is a significant element of the English self-image. We are, at least in our own popular imagination, the nation that invented fair play, and have a sense of justice. The ethos of team sport, in the reformed public schools of the mid nineteenth century, emphasised sport as a means of instilling a moral education. Concepts of fair play, gentlemanly conduct, respect for the officials and the rules, accepting defeat with grace and victory with modesty, became part of an informal but well-established set of conventions. The phrase 'it's just not cricket' denotes the existence of a set of conventions of how to play, which are quite distinct from the laws of a sport. Early booking of a sun lounger breaks no rules, but is somehow seen as a transgression of convention.

Of course, what really offends the English sensibility here, it seems to me, is that reserving a lounger with a beach towel falls exactly into that most ambiguous of cultural territory, 'manners'. There is certainly no law or regulation forbidding it, it is not immoral behaviour, it is not cheating. Indeed it is a rational and sensible act. Yet it somehow transgresses an English social code – 'it's just not done'. It is a typically strange result of the complex ways in which cultural codes and class interact that a set of social manners that are a very distinct product of the genteel bourgeoisie should also appear to have pertinence in explaining cultural tensions around the far more working-class form of Spanish package holidays. It is perfectly possible to get up even earlier than the Germans to reserve loungers, but somehow more satisfying to have a signifier around which a communal recognition can develop. In short, maybe we like it that the Germans reserve the loungers before we wake because it functions to confirm the veracity of our stereotypes, and that is worth being a few feet further from the pool any day.

An interesting feature of English sporting discourse in the post-war era is the way in which efficiency is converted into unfairness. Efficiency and rational and scientific preparation are symptoms of 'taking it all too seriously'. In the post-war era it became clear that we could no longer compete on the world stage with the USA and USSR, and often other nations too (cf. the Hungary defeat[56]), and so took to regarding the USA as over-resourced and too serious. An interesting instance can be seen in the representation of the USA team, in *Chariots of Fire*, equipped with a large number of coaches and trainers. In similar vein, the USSR, in Western representation, is often depicted as over-regimented and too serious: note the images of the Soviet Union's disciplined, regimented but heartless environment in the film *Rocky IV*.

During the last World Cup, once England were eliminated, it was suggested in the press that the majority of the English public would prefer Germany not to win, and would be favouring Brazil. Some columnists seized on this as an example of an outdated prejudice that should be attacked. An article appeared in the *Evening Standard* headed WE SHOULD SUPPORT GERMANY ON SUNDAY. This article, by novelist Philip Kerr, aimed to make a case for backing Germany rather than Brazil (*Evening Standard* 28/6/02). The case was not particularly strong. The main reasons offered for not backing Brazil were – that they are a bunch of cheats and fakers (sole evidence offered was Rivaldo's faking an injured face when the ball hit his thigh); that Brazil was not safe (high crime rate in Rio); and that the country for many years harboured Europe's fugitives and war criminals (many of whom came from Germany of course). By contrast, the main reasons for supporting Germany were that it is safe and polite, that they are very like us; that we drink their beer, eat their sausages and buy their products (BMW, VW, Mercedes, Bosch, Siemens, Neff, AEG and Krups); they love our Royal Family (who as Kerr acknowledges are largely German); they employ our leading architects; and Hitler was Austrian rather than German anyway. It is a somewhat facile line of argument that shows no understanding of the reasons intrinsic to football history and aesthetics for an English preference for Brazil. However, it is interesting that the case for supporting Germany rests heavily on cultural proximity.

A more substantial argument was offered by Gary Yonge in *The Guardian* (28/6/02). He argued that 'voicing anti-German sentiments may be the last "acceptable" prejudice'. He pointed out that otherwise liberal types will use terms like Huns, Boche and Krauts. Yonge dismissed the idea that this was all related to the war, and said that the only other explanation was football. Yonge links this to a general British view that 'our best days are behind us' and during our best days 'foreigners knew their place', and asserts: 'What this antagonism truly reveals is an ingrained insecurity regarding Germany's post-war ascent which has coincided with Britain's post-colonial decline.' Yonge argues that on the one hand the seriousness of this should not be exaggerated – this is not a form of systematic discrimination, it is prejudice against an equally powerful nation, not racism against an historically oppressed people. On the other hand, no prejudice is tolerable and 'open the door to one form of xenophobia and you will soon find yourself well and truly swamped'.

The resentment of, and hostility towards, Germany in the 2002 World Cup was, it seems to me, more grounded in the football sensibility than broadsheet columnists like Gary Yonge acknowledged. There is a frustration amongst English football fans, expressed neatly in Gary Lineker's definition of football as a game played for 90 minutes between two teams of eleven men and at the end the Germans win. This frustration was heightened by the general judgement that the 2002 German side was fairly third rate (after all England beat them 5–1!) and yet they, unlike us, had reached the final and might win it yet again. Their opponents, Brazil, by contrast, had been praised to the skies for their flowing, attacking football. No huge surprise, then, that the English public expressed their preference for a Brazilian victory. This does not seem to me to be prima facie evidence of a disturbing anti-German-ness.

The intense rivalry between England and Germany seems to me to be a recognition of masculine cultural similarities – the beach towel joke itself marks a convergence of interests – we both go for Mediterranean holidays because we don't have beaches with hot sun. We prefer beer to wine. We are both north European countries, who take sport seriously (unlike the dilettante French), who believe that we play in a physical north European way, rather than a 'cheating'

Latin way. The angst is that, too often, in our cultural imaginings, and in reality, they win. There is in turn, as Yonge asserts, a post-imperial angst underpinning the complex meanings of German efficiency. We won the war, but they had the economic miracle. There is an uncomprehending jealousy underlying our stereotyped views about efficiency.[57]

So where does 'efficiency' come from, more broadly? Certainly, in the light of post-war reconstruction – in the contrast between Germany, who, with the benefit of a fresh start, new investment and sunlight industry, soared forwards, whereas England, with loss of empire, heavy historical investment in old industries that were declining, and insufficient investment in research and development, failed to capitalise on their lead in early developments in electronics, and failed to respond to new markets. In addition, our press barons have never been slow to lash the English working class with guilt – supposedly everyone else works harder, takes less time off sick and has less strikes, and our unions do more to obstruct progress. In fact, of course, the English work longer hours than do most other Europeans. However, the myth of German efficiency became a powerful prop in this broader discourse of working-class fecklessness. This discourse has continuities with contrasts made in the 1930s between fit German youth and sallow English unemployed men. These contrasts in the press of foreign efficiency with supposed English laziness are an instance of a fairly clear relation between economic interest and ideological construction. More recently, Wembley Stadium has become a signifier of a supposed national malaise – the supposed inability to organise. The national humiliation of our inability to replace Wembley successfully was contrasted with the Millennium Stadium in Wales, the Stade de France, the Italia 90 stadia, the Sydney Olympic stadium, and the futuristic stadia constructed for World Cup 2002 in Japan and South Korea.

Don't mention the war ...

BUT: the beach towel is also about ownership and territory – it is part of the set of artefacts that are used to colonise and demarcate territory on beaches and around pools. Note the ways in which the English (and others) use beach towels, beach mats, windbreaks and buckets and spades to establish their personal space, and protect it from incursion by others. Even when there is no wind, mats go down, and windbreaks surround them, like miniature walls, separating us from our neighbours. So, while I would not want to push this too far, the notion of the Germans getting an early start and invading and colonising with their beach towels might also appear to be dealing with the repressed of the war, and the joke marks a return of the repressed.[58] The notion that the Second World War is a deeply sensitive area between the British and the Germans, that cannot be spoken about, is still a significant factor in social interaction, even amongst those too young to have fought in the war – the unspoken question always being, 'What did your father do?' This power of the repressed provides the central joke in the episode of BBC comedy series *Fawlty Towers* in which hotel owner, Basil Fawlty, put on edge by the presence of German guests, warns all the staff not to mention the war but then, compulsively, cannot stop mentioning it himself. So the circulation of jokes that are about the ability of Germans to make an early start on seizing territory are, speculatively, also an instance of the return of the repressed.

Brass bands

Brass bands, or more exactly in this instance 'oompah bands', became part of the cultural battleground in the build-up to the key World Cup qualifying game. The scene was set by the construction in the press of the hotel the English team were staying in as a mistake on the part of the English Football Association (FA). Opposite a *bierkeller* in the centre of town, it supposedly exposed the team to noise and was therefore an instance of English inefficiency. Indeed some papers went further and suggested this was a plot by the Germans:

> England have been tricked into staying next to a rowdy beer hall before their World Cup clash with Germany. The five star Munich hotel was suggested by German FA chiefs. But it is just five yards from the notorious Hofbrauhaus where boozers swig lager and sing along to oompah bands into the early hours.
>
> (*The Sun* 29/8/01)

The Sun said that the *bierkeller* could hold 10,500 drinkers and sells 7,500 litres of beer a day. It also revealed that 'it is also a Nazi shrine. 78 years ago, Adolf Hitler launched an abortive coup from the hall' (*The Sun* 29/8/01). In fact, it was later suggested, much of these accusations of inefficiency and duplicity were spurious. The hotel, the Mandarin Orient, had perfectly good sound-proofing and double glazing, and good security, and had been thoroughly checked out by the FA. Notwithstanding, ideas that the Germans would organise loud oompah bands to disturb the sleep of our boys gained currency. A *Sun* headline proclaimed:

> STICK IT UP YER OOMPAH
> WE TEST OUT GERMANY'S WORLD CUP WEAPONRY
> An oompah band who belt out drinking songs next to England's Munich hotel warned Becks and co. yesterday 'don't forget your earplugs' …
>
> The resident band at the huge hall – where 3,000 revellers sing along to booming oompah music – plan to greet England with an ear-splitting version of Roll out the Barrel.
>
> (*The Sun* 30/8/01)

The Sun evoked images of *lederhosen*-clad horn players, and a rousing Bavarian welcome, in the bar in which 'Boozy Germans in traditional leather shorts and feathered hats slapped their thighs and laughed uproariously' (*The Sun* 30/8/01) and announced that you could 'Hear the band for yourself by dialling our rousing oompah hotline' (*The Sun* 30/8/01). In mode, then, these representations foregrounded jovial figures of fun, rather than the efficient but sinister. In retaliation, *The Sun* sent its own oompah band to lead a raid on the more secluded German hotel:

THE OOMPAH BAND STRIKES BACK
SUN PAGE 3 BAND BLOWS GERMANY'S PLAYERS OUT OF BED
The Sun's Page 3 oompah band flew to Munich yesterday to give dastardly Germans a taste of their own medicine. Maria, Nikkala and Joanne took an array of horns to blow them out of bed on the eve of the vital World Cup soccer clash. The trio were joined by *Sun* Cleavage Girl Danielle for an Up Your Brass dawn chorus – to avenge a German oompah band playing at full volume next to England's hotel.

(*The Sun* 31/8/01)

In the build-up to any major event there is a period when journalists and resources have been allocated, the public interest engaged and yet there is a dearth of material to report (hence the increasingly desperate tone of the reporters' questioning, as in the cliché 'what's the mood in the camp today?'). So this *Sun* escapade provided a front page story that kept the game in the news, whilst involving the paper and enabling sexual titillation of Page 3 girls in mock Bavarian serving wench costumes:

HERR WE BLOW
HERR WE BLOW
SUN BEAUTIES LET RIP
They think it's all blow-ver – and it will be once our pretty patriots give Germany's soccer aces an early morning ear bashing.
   Rudi Voller's men were getting a rude awakening today from Page 3 girls Maria, Nikkala and Joanne.

(*The Sun* 31/8/01)

It was not a total revelation to discover that the girls were not real musicians, that the instruments were hired and that tapes of brass band music were used. As the narrative developed, *The Sun* cast itself in the role of avenger, striking back against Germanic duplicity:

We planned our revenge raid after learning that England's heroes are staying at a Munich hotel that is next door to the riotous Hofbrauhaus – where 3000 boozers sing and swig lager into the early hours.
   The huge hall's resident oompah band has REFUSED to keep the noise down as they blast out tunes like Roll out the Barrel.
   Pundits fear that David Beckham and his boys could be kept awake long into the night – leading to tired legs and minds when they face Germany in tomorrow's vital World Cup qualifier at Munich's Olympic Stadium.

Of course a consignment of earplugs might have been more use to the team, but not nearly as photogenic. The story also constituted part of the process of inter-pellation, hailing readers to a national identity in which 'we' all get behind 'our' boys:

> Stunning Maria, 26, from Guildford, Surrey, tried out the giant sousaphone yesterday and said 'It's a fantastic idea – we will really be turning the tables on the Germans. I'm gonna give it all I've got – for the sake of our boys, we are going to make the Germans feel they have been hit by a bolt of lightning.'
> (*The Sun* 31/8/01)

The story also seemed to be spawning a lucrative sideline – *The Sun* announced that 'by popular demand we are continuing our oompah band hotline' (31/8/01). There is an old adage in popular journalism to the effect that if there is no news then create some, and by Saturday *The Sun* was striving to put itself in the fore-front of events:

> GERMANS GET THE OOMP
> THEY NICK OUR PAGE 3 BAND
> *The Sun*'s oompah band blasted the German soccer team out of bed yester-day – then got arrested. Operation Vakey Vakey was in full flow until a spoilsport hotel boss called cops … *Sun* girl Lorna Carmichael, who led the raid before today's World Cup qualifier, insisted, 'I was only obeying orders.'
> (*The Sun* 1/9/01)

It is notable that war references like 'only obeying orders' constantly find their way into the coverage, and the hotel manager is evoked as a token of the success of *The Sun*'s provocative act:

> HANS OFF OUR GIRLS
> GERMAN COPS SWOOP ON PAGE 3 BUS AFTER SUN DAWN HORN RAID
> Goggle eyed cops had their Hans full yesterday after *The Sun*'s oompah band blew into Germany.
>   When the girls ran out of puff, they were backed by an ear-splitting blast of recorded music from the bus's 400 watt speakers. The din brought the flus-tered hotel manager dashing out with his hands over his ears shouting, 'What is going on – you are waking up the players.'
> (*The Sun* 1/9/01)

However, it is here that the story departs somewhat from one aspect of the English stereotype of the Germans – their supposed lack of a sense of humour. The hote-lier may have been a humourless 'spoilsport', but everyone else is portrayed as seeing the funny side. German team manager Rudi Voller was quoted as saying: 'I think one or two of the players were woken up but it didn't do any harm. It was an original idea and brought a smile to our faces.' The German police 'burst out laughing when they arrived at the hotel to find the girls playing their hearts out for our boys … one officer at the scene said "this had to be the funniest emergency call ever. We think your band is great fun"' (*The Sun* 1/9/01). German diplomat Dr Wolf Kischiat praised *The Sun*'s raid. He said, 'It's a wonderful funny way to focus attention on the game' (*The Sun* 1/9/01).

Here we have another signifier that both divides and unites – a war in which the key symbol, the oompah band, has resonances in the national stereotypes of both Englishness and German-ness. In England a brass band sig-nifies a down-to-earth – of the people, salt of the earth – organised collectivity. It connotes that space where organised labour and organised religion meet. The brass band culture is that of the respectable working class, of self-improve-ment, of rational recreation.[59] But also, since *Brassed Off*, it has become associated with the anger of workers from the old heavy industries whose organised labour power, culture and way of life was destroyed by the Thatcher-led Conservative government.

The oompah band has a less clear image – it is a signifier whose signified has a less clear identity in England. Of course, recycled by *The Sun*, and in the context of postmodern tabloid jollity, it all becomes something else again. From the per-spective of England, bands in Germany might connote oompah music, *lederhosen*, *bierkellers*, steins of ale, sausages, but does it have any political dimen-sion – good German/bad German? Is it German jollity as opposed to German efficiency or German fascism? There is here an ambiguity but also a form of pub-lic entertainment with a recognisable familiarity.

What does this apparent similarity speak to us about? In both cultures the brass band signifies a degree of collectivity and pleasure, although in England it is also about a degree of serious worthiness; Victorian bandstands, town squares, and situations with a degree of pomposity, rather than fairgrounds and beer gar-dens. English brass bands aspire to seriousness in their repertoire – hymns and serious music – whereas German oompah bands are rather more steeped in rous-ing popular songs like the 'Beer Barrel Polka'. When the English have a good old knees-up it is not to a brass band, but to a honky tonk piano. Yet both the brass band and the oompah band are forms of that self-improving work that Stebbins has dubbed 'serious leisure'; playing in an instrumental ensemble requires work, practice and commitment, but bestows reward in the form of acquired skill that wins popular acknowledgement (Stebbins 1992a, 1992b). The brass band may be more respectable (Victorian rational recreation and the bandstand in the park) while the oompah band is more rough (raucous hedonism and the beer garden) but the oompah band may have a greater cultural proximity to working-class masculine Englishness than, for example, the accordion player and the chanteuse, still staple elements of French casual popular music.[60]

Undoubtedly, Maguire is right to identify an anti-European discourse in the press. *The Sun* is explicitly anti-Euro and, despite Blair's somewhat desperate attempts to placate and woo Murdoch by liberalising the rules of media ownership, is likely to be in the forefront of a strident anti-Euro campaign. The relation between individual examples such as England vs Germany and a more generalised anti-European discourse in the British Press are apparent. A story in *The Sun* used a graphic device to link the two. The headline proclaimed:

WE SAY NEIN TO STEINS
GERMAN ALE SALES SLUMP AS PUNTERS GO FOR PINTS

This was accompanied by an illustration of two glasses of ale labelled:

'Winner ... English Pint'
'Loser ... German Stein'

However, there are three elements that, in my view, make these images of German-ness more complex and contradictory: our ambiguous relation to 'efficiency', a sense of similarity invested in playful banter, and the relation of the war, jokes and the unconscious. Our relation to efficiency is ambiguous in that it is clearly a desirable characteristic, one that representation suggests we have not got, but could do with, and one that we half admire and half resent the Germans for having. This is an ambiguity which is the condensing point for all those complex forms of reconfiguring a post-imperial Britain. The oompah band joke works because of a degree of cultural similarity between German and English working-class masculinity – indeed it implicitly celebrates that proximity. In other words it is about similarity as well as difference. Humour plays a role in tabloid journalism, but in the case of England and Germany, these jokes very often have a manifest or latent relation to the history of European conflict. These jokes are precisely a means of dealing with the repressed and therefore a way of handling the war, which cannot yet be comfortably spoken about. Indeed our mutual complicity in the oompah jokes may well be an unconscious way of acknowledging that the channels are open, the cultures have a proximity. One day the repressed material of the war that lies between Englishness and German-ness will have to be dispensed with. Until then it will keep resurfacing in the form of tabloid humour. National identities are not cast into stone and the popular media are one of the sites on which contestation and transformation takes place, however slow and ponderous the pace may seem.

In recent years, the construction of national sporting contestation as the pinnacle of the sporting landscape has been weakened. The symbolic value and economic power of major sport stars, in their commodified form, constitutes a challenge to the primacy of nation vs nation sport. Global mobility of both performers and audiences, global circulation of images, and the commodification of images of young sexualised bodies have combined to produce a more individualised and sexualised cultural landscape.

Celebrity culture, masculinity and sexuality

> In the future everyone will be famous for fifteen minutes.
>
> Andy Warhol

> I want it all, I want it now.
>
> Freddy Mercury, *Queen*

> I want to Live Forever.
> Fame costs ... and this is where you start paying.
>
> both from *Fame*

> An educated man is a fool to be always thinking of enlarging his biceps ... try as you will you can never grow to be as strong as a first-class bull.
>
> The Roman philosopher, Seneca, quoted in Gummere 1922: 75–6

> You are the weakest link, goodbye!
>
> Anne Robinson, *The Weakest Link*, BBC

Among striking features of the celebrity culture, to which the quotations above relate, are intense individualism, narcissism, obsessiveness, expendability, and the tendency for aspiration to outstrip performance. The image of sport stars such as Rodman, Beckham or Tyson starts to eclipse their performative practices. The visual appearance of sport performers has come to constitute a significant factor in the marketing and promotional strategies of sporting organisations.

Ronaldinho seems to have a lot going for him. Voted the World Footballer of the Year in 2005, he is probably one of the world's highest paid footballers. Barcelona shirts and Brazil shirts are hot items that sell around the world – those with Ronaldinho's name are likely to sell particularly well. He stands at the intersecting point of marketing strategies for Barcelona, Brazil and their various sponsors and kit providers. The only flaw is that he is not as good looking as Beckham. Indeed, although he has an extraordinary on-pitch grace and speed, off it he is tall, somewhat gawky and slightly goofy in appearance. Not, then, the marketing dream product. That this is even a factor illustrates how much football has changed in the last few decades. Footballers such as Wayne Rooney, Ronaldo and Ronaldinho may be brilliant performers of the game, but none are likely to match Beckham's earning power from advertising.

Beckham, of course, also benefited from the crossover marketing effect of marrying another celebrity, pop singer Victoria Adams, Posh Spice from the *Spice Girls*. He was also lucky to become a football star just as the game became more glamorous in the wake of the establishment of the Premier League. The recently deceased George Best was unquestionably more talented and arguably even better looking. But he played out his career when wages were still relatively low, and fringe earnings had yet to outstrip on-pitch earnings. Best did, early on in his career, advertise pork sausages in Northern Ireland, but any subsequent chances of significant earnings from advertising and promotion were effectively sabotaged by Best's highly public and long-lasting love affair with the bottle.

Along with commercialisation and commodification, spectacularisation and globalisation, the emergence of a celebrity-centred culture has become a prominent feature of modern sport. Celebrities as social actors help to market the shows, the magazines and the newspapers in which they appear. They are also, themselves, marketable commodities, and the most commercially successful celebrities have transformed themselves into brands, as did Michael Jordan or try to, as has David Beckham. There is nothing totally new in this process – tennis players Fred Perry and René Lacoste both did it, giving their names to highly successful and now long established brands of clothing. Arnold Palmer and Jack Nicklaus did it to great effect as part of Mark McCormack's sports marketing empire. Indeed the most commercially successful celebrities now are those that manage not only the commodification of the self, but also the branding of the self. However, the expanded range of media, advertising and promotion, the globalised scale of media circulation, and the intensely rapid speed of media distribution have produced a transformed economic and cultural landscape around celebrity-dom. Celebrity-focused stories are temporarily able to suck all media focus inwards, in a process I have elsewhere called vortextuality (see Whannel 2002: 206–7).

It is a cliché to say so, but a significant proportion of the population of the world live in a media-saturated society. In public retailing spaces CDs, DVDs, posters, magazines, newspapers, are prominent. Cityscapes are dominated by advertising. Multiplex cinemas offer multiple choice, albeit within a limited range. In the home, digitalisation and media technology bring multi-channel television and the Internet. It is not a matter of choosing to consume media images, but of the virtual impossibility, at least in urban landscapes, of avoiding them. Newspapers and magazines are readily accessible to non-purchasers. Headlines, and stories, can be read at a distance, pictures seen on news-stands. Trains and buses are littered with discarded newspapers, and old magazines can be read at doctors, dentists, hairdressers, and waiting areas generally. Image-laden junk mail is stuffed through your letter box every morning.

In 1970 there were just 245 million television households in the world; by 1985 573 million, by 1992 725 million and by 2003 probably over 1,500 million. Video rental has grown massively. In 1986 there were 19 Blockbuster shops worldwide, in 1990 there were 1,500, and in 2000 there were 6,800. The new media technologies spread into the market with increasing speed. It took radio 40 years to reach 50 million US users; personal computers reached 50 million in 15 years; and the Internet managed it in just four years (Giddens 2002). Nor are these developments simply the preserve of the developed Western world. China is the second largest market for consumer electronics, after the USA, and has the world's largest manufacturing base for such products.[61]

In *Cultures of Consumption*, Frank Mort (1996) suggests that the growth of spectacular consumption has been characterised by an over-production of signs and images; a simulated rendering of reality, and the representation of history as nostalgic retrospective. In the process, human geographies and spatial organisation of urban landscapes have been transformed; we have seen the spectacular environments of redeveloped city centres, and localised milieus of shopping malls and retail parks. The dramatic growth of sportswear as fashion, spearheaded by the rise of the trainer, and the intense style wars between Adidas, Nike, Reebok and Puma, occupy a central visible role in mass retailing. 'Sportswear' became a stylistic concept. In the men's store of the Paris department store Printemps, male styles are now classified as 'town-wear', 'urban-wear' and 'sportswear'.

The coverage of sport in the media has grown considerably in volume over the last 20 years. The amount of sport on television has increased considerably both on existing channels and more dramatically with the introduction of dedicated sport channels on cable and satellite. The most dramatic area of growth has been the establishment of dedicated subscription channels, such as ESPN in the USA and Sky Sports in the UK. The revenue from these channels has greatly enhanced the financial power of their owners to outbid terrestrial channels for the rights to major sporting events. In the UK in 1980 there were over 1,800 hours of television sport on terrestrial broadcast channels, but by 1999 there were 3,940. This figure was dwarfed by the satellite and cable channels who brought the total to nearer 30,000 hours – 80 hours a day. The growth in scope, scale and speed of circulation of the media, the increased volume of sport coverage, the emergence of a celebrity culture, together have enhanced the visibility and marketability of major sport stars.

In the decade preceding my writing *Blowing the Whistle*, the rise of feminism challenged the easy, comfortable separation of domesticity and gender relations from public politics with the slogan, 'the personal is political'. A quarter of a century on, there appears to have been a peculiar reversal in which now politics is the personal – indeed everything is 'the personal'. The popular media place more focus on the individual style, habits, attitudes and behaviour of elite star individuals than they do on major and significant political issues. The contestation of political parties has become focused even more than before on the image of leaders, and dependent on the presentation skills of spin doctors and image consultants. The categories of politics and show business have become rather blurred as politics appears to foreground style over substance.[62]

The nature of news itself has changed. Information circulates more rapidly, and new technologies such as the Internet and the mobile phone shorten feedback loops. The gatekeeping and agenda-setting power of media institutions is disrupted. Newspapers have been transformed by the tabloid revolution, computer-based layout and the blurring of the division between the public and private. Sensation, scandal and gossip and a public fascination with the private life of celebrities feed off each other. The distinction between information and entertainment has been eroded. Where Hollywood generated a star system, the more intimate, domestic and face-centred medium of television developed a personality system (see Langer 1981). The culture of celebrity combined with the technology of surveillance has enabled the tabloid press to become the new village stocks in which sport stars like Paul Gascoigne and Dennis Rodman might periodically be displayed. The intensity of focus that I term vortextuality – the phenomenon whereby whole areas of the media become temporarily drawn into one central story – grows out of the growth in the range of media outlets, and media content; and the vastly increased speed of circulation of information.

The fax, email, mobile phones and the Internet enable contact with news organisations on a 24/7 basis. Up till the 1970s, public responses to events emerged mainly through letters. Stories built and developed at a relatively slow pace as public reactions emerged. Even official responses could be relatively slow. The development of the radio phone-in was the first significant popular form to enable a much greater crystallisation of public response to events and contribution to discussion. The growth of regular news slots on radio, conventionally every 15 minutes, produced a pressure on the pace of official response to events. Rolling news requires rolling response. The public relations industry grew in response, providing routinised channels of access, along with new management. The craft of spin began to refine its techniques.

Mobile phones took instant access into the great outdoors. It was not necessary to be at home or at work to respond and contribute, and texting meant it was not necessary to get through to the recipient to offer instant communication. The Internet expanded the range of all this technologised instantaneity onto a global scale. The cumulative effect of all these developments was to make it much more likely that dramatic stories, whether momentous or ultimately trivial, could rapidly take over and dominate the news agenda. Indeed the sheer speed of these processes meant news events acquired a momentum beyond the ability of the actors involved to easily control. It is no accident that the 1990s became the decade of spin. During major news stories, whether momentous or trivial, in moments of vortextual intensity, columnists and commentators are drawn in, as if by a vortex, and even those with no abiding interest in sport are impelled to comment. Cartoons, radio phone-ins, celebrity columnists, news magazines, cultural commentators and letter pages are all drawn into the central topic (Whannel 2002). The death of Princess Diana, the marriage of David Beckham and Victoria Adams (Posh Spice), the trial of OJ and the verdict announcement in the Michael Jackson trial can all be considered as examples of this process.

So top sport stars can provide unrivalled media focus and thus unique marketing opportunities. In 2000, Tiger Woods signed a marketing contract with Nike worth over $100 million (Jackson, Andrews and Scherer 2005: 9). In the 2005 Masters Golf Tournament, Tiger Woods hit a key putt, in which the ball approached the hole, slowing down and pausing tantalisingly on the edge for a few seconds, before dropping into the hole. The element that turned this moment of drama into a marketing miracle was that, in that second, the Nike swoosh on the ball rolled into view. The marketing team at Nike headquarters in Beaverton, Oregon, must have prayed in thanksgiving for a merchandising miracle, and contemplated that their investment was well judged. Sport stars, though, are also high risk. Defeat, scandal, misbehaviour and use of performance enhancing or recreational drugs can all tarnish the name of associated products. The safe, predictable and stable figures, such as Tiger Woods or Gary Lineker, are always likely to be more favoured choices of advertisers than the risky, edgy and unpredictable. Paul Gascoigne, Dennis Rodman and Wayne Rooney will always prompt careful and cautious thought by those with products to promote and images to protect.

If social life is saturated by media and social practices transformed by the dominance of brand and image, then what has been the impact of the rise of media sport? Arguably, the rise to centrality of media sport has both precipitated and at the same time masked clear divisions. Elite televised sport has become a totally different and distinct set of social, cultural and economic practices. The economic scale of televised sport separates it from other modes of sporting practice. Those sports that have little or no appeal on television carry on, and in many cases thrive, and bring great pleasure to participants and spectators, but for the vast majority of the public they could be invisible. There is also a greater divide than ever between the modes of participation and of spectatorship.

The activities that attract most heavy participation – walking, swimming, jogging and gym-based weight training and exercise – are not really spectator activities. Of the major spectacular media sports – football, tennis, athletics, golf, motor racing, American Football, basketball – football, tennis, golf and basketball do have significant, if small, participation rates. However, the forms and styles of participation are far removed from the professionalised and commodified world of elite sport. Potential talent is spotted at a young age and hot-housed. The dominance of media in providing images of sport has also masked the decline of collective and communal team-based sports and the rise of individual sporting practices, such as gym-based exercise, lifestyle sport, adventure sport and extreme sport.

So there are a number of very distinct forms of sporting practice. However, the drive of capital to commercialise and commodify has helped provide greater promotion for those informal and alternative sport practices which are equipment-intensive; those in which technology and equipment play a significant role, in which there is a fetishisation of sports gear, identity and the importance of the look. The branding and marketing of youthful bodies and youthful sexuality has become a central element of the marketing of sportswear as lifestyle.

The rise of sport during the twentieth century was part of high modernity, and the new configuration of sporting cultures is in part related to the impact of postmodern cultural elements. An intertextual self-referentiality, and a convergence of new technologies, has interesting impacts here. During the 1996 European Championships a colleague told me that his two sons had little interest in watching the matches, but would set their video games to play simulated and interactive matches between the same teams as featured in the 'real' games. It is notable that, with technological advances, computer football games mimic television's framing, angles, styles of cutting and modes of commentary. The rising crane shot looking through the goal net now used in both live action and on video games has come to look eerily unreal on television as it makes the live coverage look like a video game. Betting shop habitués will also be well aware that computer-fabricated horse races can now be used to fill the gaps between real racing. Large stadia are dominated by giant screens that provide a far clearer view than can be seen from distant seats, and the absence of action replay in some stadia seems to diminish the experience, to make it less 'real' than watching on television. No wonder then the enormous growth of public consumption of sport in bars; the ever greater focus on major events, and relative declining cultural fascination with minor spectator events, at the phenomenon of post-fandom (cf. Giulianotti 1999; Brick 2000, 2001a, 2001b).

Many of the manifestations of male involvement in sport – gambling, using betting shops, spread betting, the poker boom, watching football in bars, going on elaborate group trips to remote destinations, wearing fancy dress and other carnivalesque accessories – seem to displace sport itself. There has been a shift of emphasis onto the fan experience; the experience of consumption, and away from the centrality of the performative event, even though this is what provides a *raison d'être* for all the rest. Several things could be going on here – new laddishness, post-fandom, postmodern cultural sensibilities, a retreat from linear intensity of involvement with the sporting narrative, towards a reinvention of communal homosociality. However we try and conceptualise it, at its heart is heterosexual masculinity, working through a new repertoire of cultural practices which seek to demarcate, through space and ritual, a distinctive, defensive yet celebratory mode of being male.

Sport is still the pre-eminent social practice that divides the genders. Men who don't like sport, and women who do, are still, in a range of ways, marked as aberrant. It still confers and confirms heterosexual masculinity. Of all body cultures, it is the one in which sexuality is most firmly repressed. The public cultural institutions of sport have recognised racism, at least as an issue, are often equivocal about sexism, but have the greatest difficulties in even acknowledging gay and lesbian existences. Feminists writing on sport rightly identified that there was nothing arbitrary or natural about sport's discriminatory culture, argued that women could and should be able to engage in all sporting activities, and fought to bring those opportunities about. The range and extent of opportunities available to women in sport are greatly enhanced since the 1960s. However, attitudes to sport have not changed as dramatically. Far more women than men express an indifference to, or hostility to, sport. Indeed, for some, the cultures of sport are seen as constituting an alien and exclusionary freemasonry in which males bond around the competitive performance of physical prowess, and the exchange of sporting cultural capital. In short, while some women campaign for a transformation of the institutions of sport, others are simply disinterested in or opposed to sport per se. Many men, too, are indifferent or hostile to sport. But whereas amongst women disinterest in sport is a shared assumption, for men it is more likely to be a slightly isolating experience. I wrote about this in 1983, and it is interesting that so little has changed.

Immense faith appears to be placed in the ability of sport to generate positive role models for young people. These hopes appear to be constantly frustrated. Every time a sport star misbehaves the popular press is filled with articles, columns and letters that bemoan the poor example being set for the young, and the need for sport stars to act as role models. In actual fact the concept of role model should really be limited to those who have regular close and interactive experiential contact with children, such as parents, teachers, relatives and friends. To apply it to pop stars and sport stars is nonsense. That a perceived need for role models persistently re-emerges does, though, suggest a social unease about the young and about masculinity (see Whannel 2002). The reason that such hopes for the setting of positive examples are invested especially strongly in sport is because sport is, among other things, a machine for the production of masculinity (see Whannel 1999). Playing, watching and absorbing the cultural values of sport is an induction into the dominant values of masculinity – being tough and assertive while sticking to the rules, being physical without manifestly implying a sexual dimension, not crying except in moments of euphoric victory, standing up for oneself, whilst not engaging in brutal retaliation. As a set of cultural institutions, sport has also been a means of forging the homosocial contact, in the clubs, bars, organisations and playing fields that began life as exclusively male and in many cases still are. From an early age, boys have a tendency to hoard facts, and sport is a rich source of facts. Sports chatter is a mode of male exchange, part banter, part anecdote and part competitive performance of fact retrieval. Sporting facts provide an alternative form of cultural capital that can be spent to acquire acceptance in the society of sporting chaps.

Sport and its modes of representation also constitute a mode of policing masculinity, monitoring its boundaries and punishing those who transgress. As a social practice it is about the technologies of the self and the disciplining of the body. Undisciplined transgressions in pursuit of pleasure, such as drunken-ness, are punished by tabloid exposure – the modern version of the village stocks. Limits are placed on the unprincipled pursuit of success, such as the apparatus of drug testing and the punishments for the use of performance-enhancing drugs. However, the strongest sanctions are the unwritten, unspoken and unacknowledged ones associated with gay sex. There are now gay sportsmen, gay teams, and an established gay Olympics. There were 15,000 participants at the 1998 Amsterdam Gay Games (Pronger 2000: 223). But very few elite sports performers in major sports have felt able to come out as gay; indeed, the suggestion of gayness, almost invariably couched as if it were the worst imaginable slur, is taken within macho sport cultures as a deadly insult. According to Bryan Pronger, in North America during the last 20 years fewer than two dozen high performance athletes have declared their homosexuality publicly and only a few of those, such as Martina Navratilova and Greg Louganis, had significant public profiles. Pronger says that most studies of lesbians and gays in sport document the fearful extent of homophobia in sport (Pronger 2000: 224). So if sport cultures are machines for producing heterosexual masculinity, they are machines that tend to turn out a warped, fearful, repressed and homophobic masculinity. Pronger argues that men's sport is particularly homophobic because of the omnipresence of implicit homoeroticism in a cultural practice that is supposed to build heterosexuality – homophobia helps to prevent what is implicit from becoming explicit (Pronger 2000: 236). This, in turn, reflects back on sport as a practice of the body that cannot admit and thus represses sexuality, and where repression is routine, systematic and long-established, the repressed matter has a habit of breaking through in the form of a variety of morbid symptoms. From the anorexic bodies of jockeys, cyclists and marathon runners, to the grotesque muscle-bound hulks of weight training and bodybuilding, the signs are abundant that this social practice is not, in the end, about being healthy, feeling fit and looking attractive.

If gym cultures have a tendency to produce obsessive modes of behaviour, so do fan cultures, and the obsessiveness of football supporting was well captured in Nick Hornby's autobiographical *Fever Pitch* (1992), which was well reviewed, became a best-seller, and generated a film version, followed more recently by an American film version, in which football becomes baseball. It was, arguably, the first book on sport to attract significant attention from women critics and women readers, who generally admired, or at least responded to, the candid depiction of a somewhat dysfunctional and obsessive masculinity. As such it promised to bridge the divide sketched out earlier in this chapter.

The book emerged in the context of transformation of British football; indeed played a part in that transformation. After the Hillsborough stadium disaster of 1989 and the subsequent Taylor Report of 1990, investment in new and transformed stadia, the establishment of the Premier League, and the television deal with Sky had transformed both the image and the finances of the sport. The gradual decline of hooliganism, and the impact of Italia 90, brought growing crowds and an interest from new sectors of society. The launch of the Apple Macintosh in the mid 1980s and the subsequent development of page layout programs had initiated a revolution in desktop publishing that gave birth to a generation of football fanzines. These were of varying quality but provided a basis for an ongoing reflection by fans on the nature of the game.

The book should also be seen in the context of the rise of new lad culture, as marked by magazines such as *Loaded* and *FHM*, and television programmes such as *Fantasy League Football*, *They Think It's All Over* and *Never Mind the Buzzcocks*. The launch and runaway success of *Loaded* in 1994 transformed the field of men's magazines. All titles re-targeted themselves down-market, and soft-core pornographic imagery re-entered the mainstream of front covers. *Loaded* increased its circulation by 85 per cent during 1996, but the revamped *FHM*'s circulation went up 271 per cent to achieve monthly sales of 365,000. By 1997 it sometimes sold over half a million, giving it an estimated readership of over two million. This compared to a circulation of less than 50,000 in 1994, when it was acquired by EMAP and re-designed. EMAP spotted the middle ground between the laddishness of *Loaded* and the aspirational advertising-driven content of GQ (*The Guardian* 17/2/97). The successful launch of *Men's Health* in the mid 1990s offered a more middle-class aspirational discourse of body maintenance, but also contributed to the growing cultural centrality of sport, and increasing body-image awareness amongst men.

Hornby's first reactions, on being taken to football for the first time by his father, foreground a particular type of masculinity:

> I remember the overwhelming maleness of it all – cigar and pipe smoke, foul
> language (words I had heard before, but not from adults, not at that volume)
> – and only years later did it occur to me that this was bound to have an effect
> on a boy who lived with his mother and his sister.
>
> (Hornby 1992: 19)

My own first experiences of watching football from the age of eight were not so
dissimilar. I too remember the overwhelming maleness of it, and the ways in
which this combined with the separateness of the inside of football grounds.
Surrounded by walls, with giant inward-looking stands, they were literally worlds
apart, separate from all the concerns, excitements, tensions and disappointments
of the outside world. They had their own concerns, excitements, tensions and
disappointments, but they were of a different, a separate, order.

As a young boy, Hornby soon came to understand the value of a knowledge of
the esoteric details of sporting cultures, and the ways in which it functions as a
form of alternative masculine cultural capital. Boys acquire a detailed knowledge
of facts and information about football (as embodied in the world of *Match* and
Shoot). Possession of this cultural capital confers status, marks distinctions, and
can be stored away, used to advantage and used as a means to exclude unwanted
outsiders (i.e. girls, and 'wimpish' boys who don't like sport). Hornby comments
that 'transferring to secondary school was rendered unimaginably easy … as long
as you knew the name of the Burnley manager, nobody much cared that you were
an eleven-year-old dressed as a six-year-old' (Hornby 1992: 21). One marked feature of new lad culture was its self-knowing recalcitrance, expressed in the *Loaded*
masthead 'for men who should know better'. In describing his experiences as a
teacher, Hornby reveals this combination of self-reflexiveness and resistance:

> and yes, I am aware of the downside of this wonderful facility that men have:
> they become repressed, they fail in their relations with women, their con-
> versation is trivial and boorish, they find themselves unable to express their
> emotional needs, they cannot relate to their children, and they die lonely
> and miserable. But, you know, what the hell? If you can walk into a school
> full of eight hundred boys, most of them older, all of them bigger, without
> feeling intimidated, simply because you have a spare Jimmy Husband in your
> blazer pocket, then it seems like a trade-off worth making.
>
> (Hornby 1992: 23)[63]

In the hands of a writer of Hornby's talent, the irony produces a chuckle. It is
though, I think, this same mannered use of irony, this parading of a self-knowledge that 'I should know better', that is precisely what is most provocatively
irritating about new lad culture with its attempt to have it both ways on sexism
and sexist images. Thus in these wonderful postmodern times is self-knowledge
separated from self-improvement. The performance of the working-class masculinity of British football produces tensions for the middle-class Hornby who
lives in fear of 'getting rumbled' (p.50) and worries that in, venturing onto

Arsenal's North Bank, he will be spotted as a suburban interloper, with people chanting 'Hornby is a wanker', or 'we all hate Swots' (Hornby 1992: 74). His period as a student at Cambridge is characterised as an unease with the upper-middle-class milieu and the grasping at football as a protective bulwark. Indeed he catches very well the way that football as a way of life can also be a substitute for a life. Arsenal's FA Cup win in 1979, instead of bringing joy and fulfilment, poses a crisis, with Hornby

> facing up to the fact that on the afternoon of 12th May I had achieved most of what I ever wanted to achieve in my life and that I had no idea what to do with the rest of it. I was twenty-two and the future suddenly looked blank and scary.
>
> (Hornby 1992: 116)

The crisis exposes the ways in which the masculinity he inhabits is distinctly dysfunctional:

> For the whole season I did nothing else apart from go to the pub, work (in a garage outside Cambridge, because I could think of nothing better to do), hang out with my girlfriend whose course lasted a year longer than mine, and wait for Saturdays and Wednesdays.
>
> (Hornby 1992: 117)

Masculinity, of course, only makes sense in relation to femininity, and Hornby's own enrapture with the 'overwhelming maleness' of football contrasts with the reaction of the first girlfriend he takes to Highbury, who 'shakes with laughter at the sight of a row of mis-shapen male bottoms as everyone stood up to cheer the goal' (Hornby 1992: 101). It is one of the distinctive features of the book that, unlike most books on sport, it does bring masculinity into an awkward and negotiated encounter with its feminine other. I suppose it could be suggested that Ian Botham's *Don't Tell Kath* performs a not dissimilar task, but without ever threatening to become literature. Hornby's work identifies the obsessive nature of masculine enthusiasms, whether sporting or musical:

> I have met women who have loved football and go to watch a number of games a season, but I have not yet met one who would make that Wednesday night trip to Plymouth. And I have met women who love music and can tell their Mavis Staples from their Shirley Browns, but I have never met a woman with a huge and ever expanding and neurotically alphabeticised record collection.
>
> (Hornby 1992: 103)

In Hornby's novel *High Fidelity*, the central character, Rob, refers to his 'relentless triviality' (Hornby 1995: 78). Rob is absorbed by list rankings and tabulations, and is obsessive about details – it is a form of defending the castle of masculinity –

with its neat, dry, sterile taxonomical separation of the world into its constituent elements – against an incursion of the feminine – with all its complex interrelated and overlapping emotions that wash across categories blurring the demarcated lines of division. It is this same empiricist masculine impulse to reduce the world to quantifiable and categorisable units that Jean-Marie Brohm (1978) identifies in *Sport: A Prison of Measured Time*. Brohm portrays sport as the organised tabulation of human performance in which athletic performance is subjected to a Taylorisation of the body with the aim of producing maximum productivity.

However, in part as a result of the commercialisation and commodification of sport, there is another contradictory process taking place in which the objectification, sexualisation and display of bodies has moved to the fore. The sexualisation and objectification of female bodies in sport has been a well established process (see Hargreaves 1994). The swimsuit issue of *Sports Illustrated* has been singled out as a particularly striking instance. The growth in the volume of advertising, the extension of advertising to many new forms and sites, allied to the celebrity culture, has given top female stars a far greater visibility, enhancing their value for marketing and promotion. Appearance and style are important to this process. Women's sport has always had a tendency to be caught by this process. The governing body of women's golf has an obsession with selling itself through sexuality. The Ladies PGA, with the involvement of promotional advisors, have devised guidelines which include:

> Performance: If you play better, you'll be more marketable.
> Appearance: Great athletes have physical or personal appeal.
> Passion: Great athletes play as if they love the game.
> Approachability: None of the other three matters if you lack this.

Golfer Natalie Gulbis appears in *FHM*, on websites, in calendars in sexualised poses, but the big difference from the 1980s and the controversy over Jan Stephenson's calendar is that it does not seem to have upset anyone in the game, in fact most people seem to be all for it according to *The Guardian* (*Guardian* 30/7/05 Sport section, p.2).

During the 1990s the sexualisation of sporting bodies spread also to the male body. The marketing of male sport stars has now become a more narcissistic process in which grooming and posing have come to the fore. Yet, as I have argued, of all body cultures, sport is the one that most represses sexuality. On the one hand it is a performative practice which places fit, healthy and muscular bodies on display. On the other, the discourses of sport are constructed so as to deny and disavow the inherent and visible sexuality. So there is invariably a tension at work between the erotic potential of the performance and the enervating properties of the commentary. Note the distinction between weight lifting which displaces its narcissistic self-absorption onto measured performance, and bodybuilding, which, in acknowledging the body as spectacle, admits sexuality, thus marginalising it as 'sport'. Think for example of the unacknowledged but implicit scopophilic dimension of gymnastics – with pre-pubescent girls gazed at and assessed by middle-aged and often male judges. The cultures of sport cannot readily admit sexuality; indeed the eruption of sexuality into the sporting context threatens to disrupt and destabilise the spectacle.

The sexualisation and objectification of male bodies is a distinctly racialised process. Ben Carrington analyses the ways that, in recent years, black male bodies have become increasingly objectified and sexualised, in a 'spectacle of hyper-blackness' in which colonial discourses about the racial other are projected forwards into the post-colonial present (Carrington 2002: 2). He suggests that 'historical colonial fantasies about excesses of black sexuality continue to exercise a hegemonic role in the representation of blackness' but highlights here a contradictory process. On the one hand ideologies of race served to dehumanise and animalise black bodies, but they also 'became the subject of a romanticised Occidental idealism, being seen as reflecting a pure state of abandonment, against the unnatural technocratic developments of a newly emerging industrial modernity' (Carrington 2002: 8). Fanon identified the black athlete as a figure that served as the repository of white fears. Colonial discourse had to dismantle this potential power and render black masculinity subordinate. Thus, as Carrington outlines, the black sporting body is now 'sexualised and transformed into an object of desire and envy' (Carrington 2002: 19). The symbolic erasure of blackness has been replaced by the 'commodification of blackness' (Carrington 2002: 35). These processes tend to accentuate the tensions and contradictions between the implicit sexuality of athletic bodies and the repressing discourses of sporting cultures.

7 Globalisation
The global and the local

In place of the old local and national seclusion and self-sufficiency, we have inter-course in every direction, universal inter-dependence of nations. And as in material so in intellectual production.

Karl Marx[64]

There is nothing new about global trade, upon which imperialism was based, and many of the forces and relations suggested by the word 'globalisation' have been around for a long time. However, four significant developments have contributed to the identification of globalisation as a process. First, major corporations have moved from being multinational to transnational, and as such have moved beyond the point at which they can be easily controlled by individual nation states. Second, deregulation has fostered a much greater international division of labour in which production can more readily be relocated wherever wage rates are low, legal protection for workers is minimal, and unions are weak or, even better, illegal. Third, a postmodern consumer culture has produced a market for branded goods that tend to have a high profit margin. Fourth, an unprecedented global mobility of people during the twentieth century has had an impact on the reconstruction of markets around the cultures that have emerged from diasporas and hybridities.

In the years since the publication of *Blowing the Whistle*, the concept of glob-alisation and its impact has become a key issue in social analysis, raising a number of questions. How significant are globalising processes given that, as some argue, economies are still largely rooted in, and managed by, nation states? When is the key period of emergence of a globalised order? Robertson (1992) suggests the late nineteenth century as the take-off point, whilst others put it at varying points, some as recently as the 1990s. What forms of local response are there to globalising processes and what is the relation of local and global, which some argue have produced a new cultural form, 'glocalisation'?

Historian Eric Hobsbawm describes the post-Second World War Western world as characterised by a consensus that the aim of rising production, growing foreign trade, full employment, industrialisation and modernisation could be achieved by systematic government control and the management of mixed economies, and by co-operating with organised labour movements, so long as they were not communist. There was a growing internationalisation. Between 1965 and 1990 the percentage of exported goods doubled. However, Hobsbawm argues, the world economy remained international rather than transnational until an increasingly transnational economy began to emerge, from the 1960s. This new transnational world economy had 'no specifiable territorial base or limits, which determined, or rather sets limits to, what even the economies of very large and powerful states can do'. This new transnationalisation involved the emergence of transnational firms, a new international division of labour, and the growing significance of offshore finance. USA, Hobsbawm suggests, was the first country to experience the effects of these large sums of unattached capital that circulated the globe looking for quick profits, but by the early 1990s even joint action by leading central banks proved impotent. There was a growing tendency for enterprises to free themselves from the controls of the traditional nation state. The volume of manufacturing in the developing world rose dramatically from the 1980s, producing a new international division of labour (Hobsbawm 1994: 273–7). Anthony Giddens warns against exaggerating corporate power, or underestimating the continuing power of the nation state, but nevertheless expresses the impact of globalisation in stark terms when he points out that

> In the new global electronic economy, fund managers, banks, corporations, as well as millions of individual investors, can transfer vast amounts of capital from one side of the world to another at the click of a mouse. As they do so, they can destabilise what might have seemed rock-solid economies – as happened in the events in Asia.
>
> (Giddens 2002: 9)

It is clear that globalising processes have been underway, that their impact has been dramatic, and that while they have had transformative effects, most notably in Southeast Asia, they have not led to a weakening of the established centres of corporate power, or any transfer of wealth from rich to poor – in fact the reverse appears to be the case. This is not to say that the various impacts of globalising processes do not have contradictory effects. The rise of globalising processes and weakening powers of nation states has stimulated the growth of strong local and regional identities. The growing significance of the 'hollowed out' corporation, of franchising, and of subcontracting, has given rise to a new stronger entrepreneurial class in countries in the developing world, producing new localised forms of circulation of capital, that in turn produce new localised modes of consumption.

Arguably sport has been an important element in globalising processes since the late nineteenth century. Many of the first international modes of organisation, such as the IOC, the IAAF, FIFA and the ILTF, were sporting bodies. Alan Bairner (2001) reviews the problems posed by theories of globalisation. He cites

Holton as arguing (in *Globalisation and the Nation State*, 1998) that the key idea of globalisation is the single interdependent world and suggests that, while some regard globalisation as positive and some negative, both interpretations see it as inevitable and all consuming. Bairner suggests that the forces of globalisation also produce reactions and resiliences. He suggests utilising a single key dichotomy, Appadurai's (1990) concept of a tension between cultural homogenisation and heterogenisation. Bairner warns that the tendency to equate globalisation with the triumphant march of world capitalism, and indeed with the hegemonic domination of American cultural forms, takes an over-homogenous view of America, and discounts the patterns of overt resistance to Americanisation especially in Islamic countries.

Joseph Maguire (1999) acknowledges the profound changes of globalisation, and that this does to some degree displace the nation as a unit of analysis, but argues that globalisation cannot be regarded as simply a path to homogenisation. He emphasises the tendency towards diminishing contrasts and increasing varieties. Maguire, drawing on Pieterse (1997), suggests a multidimensional and open-ended process, geographically wide and historically deep, which emphasises the flows between West and non-West, the creolisation of cultural forms, and hybridisation of cultural identities. Paradoxically, in such processes, social practices such as sport become more marginal and more central in one and the same move. In terms of the great dynamic forces shaping the world, such as the dynamic tensions between local and global; the search for authenticity in the context of postmodern culture; the contradictions of a world based on growth and consumption situated on a planet with finite and diminishing resources; the scientific and technological capacity for destruction seemingly outstripping the moral and political authority to control it, sport, like many other social practices, does indeed seem small, epiphenomenal and marginal.

And yet in a world dominated by and in many ways defined by media imagery, it is in no small part sport that drives television – it is one of the primary forms pushing the commodification of television – it sells dishes, it sells subscriptions, and it is, apart from movies, the only viable pay-per-view form of television. In a world in which the power and authority of the United Nations has been considerably reduced, the major events of sport (the Olympic Games, the World Cup) constitute instances of the very limited number of institutions through which we define ourselves as a global collectivity. In a consumer culture in which, despite apparent endless variety and innovation, there is also a perceptible uniformity and predictability about commodities, sport offers intensity, excitement and unpredictability. Even though frequently derided for being over-competitive, and rife with cheating, drug abuse and gamesmanship, it is arguably one of the least destructive forms of contestation we have. So one cannot really examine globalising processes without taking sport into account. In terms of the global and the local, sport is one of the most visible and prominent commodity forms in which these tensions are played out. Shirts and hats proclaiming Manchester United, Brazil, New York Yankees and Beckham are seen around the world, whilst the intensity of anger amongst Manchester United fans around the takeover of

Manchester United by Malcolm Glazer provided a graphic and theatrical playing out of local–global tensions.

For Western scholars writing in the late twentieth century it takes a considerable effort of intellectual repositioning to reverse the picture, and to look at it from the other side. Globalisation is only a currently vogueish label for a set of processes that have a long history. Imperial adventures, colonial invasion, the slave trade, the ordering and regulation of world trade, and the migration of people all look very different as processes when viewed from the position of the colonised. Theories of postmodern culture can seem a very metropolitan and Western phenomenon, which portray a mediascape constructed in the image factories of the (Western) culture industries. Yet the smug assumptions of the Western metropolitan intellectual are frequently misplaced. Anthony D. King (1991) argues that the image of modern Western metropolitan cities as being in the vanguard of multicultural diversity and postmodernism does not hold up – at the turn of the century the great colonial port cities – Singapore, Hong Kong, Calcutta and Rio – were far more diverse and indeed were more accurate precursors of the twenty-first century than the great Western cities such as London and Paris. Globalisation *now* cannot really be understood without a consideration of colonialism *then*. Culture is being made and remade by processes that constantly link past and present, core and periphery, margin and centre in ways that re-juxtapose, reconfigure and hybridise these terms. Complex cultural trajectories intertwine. Scottish engineers, Spanish and Italian immigrants and Argentinian masculinity produced a particular context for football during the early part of the century, and 70 years later, in the 1980s and 90s, Argentinian footballer Diego Maradona cuts a swathe through Spain and Italy before the road to Coke-fuelled celebritydom, physical collapse, rehabilitation in Cuba and resurrection back home as a television star.

The popular image of the English, through their Empire, spreading sport around the world, is an over-simplification – it is more complex. Indigenous modes of play have been coming into contact with forms of culture brought by invading empires since the Romans. The imperial colonising forces of Holland, France, Spain and England have all had an impact on this process. The codification and reification of team games framed by muscular Christianity was the distinctive English contribution. The public school ethos fed into the work of muscular Christians (priests and missionaries, civil servants and diplomats, and army officers), all of whom fed English sports to the British Empire. Football, though, tended to spread via engineers and traders and became most strongly established outside the British Empire. Arguably, this process involved not so much imposition of games as of rules, governance and authority. Here, though, France played at least as significant a role, being to the fore in the establishment of the IOC and FIFA, among other key bodies. From the perspective of the colonised countries, the very dominance by a foreign power meant that, on the symbolic terrain of sport, playing the colonial masters at their old game and beating them became a politically charged ritual.

In the television era, of course, such rituals become symbolic events of considerable cultural visibility. The spread of jet travel from the 1960s made international sporting competition much more practical – boosting European football competition, for example. Major sport events offer an ideal commodity for international television. Television has high first copy costs, but very low replication costs. Having made a programme, the costs of extending it to further audiences around the globe are, by comparison, minimal. This has two main effects. First, there is a strong impulse to export television programmes where possible, as any extra overseas sales provides extra revenues at minimal cost. Second, because the consequent extra costs are small, the price to the purchaser can be relatively elastic, reducing according to the financial scale of the market. This applies to popular American television successes, from *I Love Lucy* to *Dallas*, that have been resold around the world over the years. Sport as a television commodity has an additional advantage – for the most part, it crosses language and cultural barriers relatively easily. Where sports are already understood, followed and consumed in many countries, all that is necessary is the dubbing on of a new commentary (in the case of live broadcasts, local language commentaries are provided either at origin or locally). So a major international sport event provides an ideal marketing medium for a corporation wishing to market globally. It used to be the case that relatively few corporations did market globally, and even now the sports market tends to be dominated by familiar names – Coca-Cola, McDonald's. However, digitalisation now allows for the superimposition of localised advertising on globally transmitted live events, giving advertising space sellers the best of both worlds – global and local advertising. The concept of virtual advertising was basically designed for sport (Jackson, Andrews and Scherer 2005: 5). The global distribution of the star teams and individuals who to a large degree are still based in the so-called 'developed' world has in turn been a major factor in the growth of the merchandising markets that have boosted the finances of the New York Yankees, Real Madrid, Manchester United and the other giants of corporatised sport.

This picture is complicated by the fact that sport does also have resistances to globalisation – by no means can all sports be readily exported. Football, motor racing, athletics, golf and tennis are amongst the most readily exportable; although 'soccer' still struggles to make significant inroads in the USA. American basketball has managed to build a global following, thanks largely to the marketing efforts of Nike around the iconic figure of Michael Jordan (see Andrews 2001). Attempts to popularise American Football and baseball outside the USA have had more limited success. Such diverse sports as Australian Rules Football, Sumo and handball have tended to remain as novelty events outside their established territories. Rugby union, despite vigorous development strategies, remains largely rooted in the white Commonwealth countries; whilst outside the old English empire, cricket is barely heard of, far less understood. The diversity of sports, and their cultural embeddedness, might reasonably be seen as a strength rather than a weakness, and only the perverse distortions of international marketing have managed to present this resistance to importation as a problem that must be overcome by more energetic promotion. Miller *et al.* (2001: 10) emphasise the continued dominant position of what they call the US–Western Europe–Japan triad in the economics of sport, pointing out that the three areas are responsible for well over 90 per cent of the money paid for Olympic television rights in 2000. They argue 'that the nation-state has lost its potency and relevance, but instead assert that in a globalising context, analysis must both encompass and transcend individual nation-states' (Miller *et al.* 2001: 22).

Global sport offers great opportunities for global marketing and the advertising strategies of large corporations are increasingly equipped to exploit this opportunity. The ten largest advertising agencies now have offices in more than 50 different countries with the largest global firm, McCann Erickson, having over 200 offices in 130 countries (Jackson, Andrews and Scherer 2005: 4). Branding is not new. In the 1950s, advertisers understood that they were selling image as well as product.[65] But growing sophistication of advertising and promotion, and heightened understanding of the market and patterns of consumption, together contributed to the tendency, identified by Baudrillard, for symbolic value to become the dominant characteristic of the commodity. At the same time, a number of key structural changes were altering the way that many big corporations functioned. The growth of a globalised post-Fordist mode of production gave rise to what has been called the 'hollowed out' corporation – based on a reduced manufacturing workforce, extensive subcontracting, casualisation of production, and a franchising of retailing. This, as Naomi Klein has pointed out, left corporations free to focus on production of image and identity, as embodied in logos and brands (Klein 1999). Klein refers to the 'seemingly innocuous' idea developed by management theorists in the mid 1980s: that corporations should produce brands rather than products. Traditional corporations came to be seen as too large. The new corporations were based more on brand, image and design; examples include Nike, Microsoft, Tommy Hilfiger, and Intel. Trade liberalisation and labour law reform made it easier to outsource production.

Secondary marketing (spin-off products) became another means by which the commercial potential of brands could be exploited. Brand and image enhanced the value of secondary merchandising, especially to children. According to Alissa Quart, marketing to children took off in the 1980s in the wake of two important events. The first was the release and success of *Jaws* in 1975 and *Star Wars* in 1977 – revealing huge merchandising potential. A contributing factor was the failure of the Federal Trade Commission to impose regulations regarding restrictions on child-oriented advertising – Congress vetoed the proposal. Quart also notes the enormous marketing success of the television series *Teenage Mutant Ninja Turtles* in the 1980s (Quart 2003). Klein points out that the companies that exited the early 1990s slump running were the ones that opted for marketing over cheapness – Nike, Apple, Body Shop, Calvin Klein, Disney, Levis and Starbucks. For these companies the ostensible product was mere filler for the real production – the brand. Some companies, of course, had always understood that they were selling brands – Coke, Pepsi, McDonald's, Burger King, and Disney. In the late 1980s and early 1990s Gap, IKEA, Body Shop and Starbucks were spreading like wildfire. 'Brands not products' became the rallying cry for a marketing renaissance led by a new breed of companies that saw themselves as meaning brokers instead of product producers (Klein 1999).

Since 1990, many corporations have been attempting to free themselves from manufacturing to focus on design and promotion. Klein points out that anyone can manufacture a product to order, and such tasks can be farmed out to contractors and subcontractors whose only concern is filling the order on time and under budget, ideally in the developing world, where labour is cheap, laws lax, and tax breaks available (Klein 1999). According to the 2005 *Fortune* Global Forum the sports industry has become a major factor in wealth generation in China, which is now the world's largest producer and exporter of footwear. Shoes are the number one export commodity in Chinese light industry. In 2004 China exported 6 billion pairs of shoes which earned 156.2 billion dollars in foreign currency.[66] Ironically, in 2005 a film was released in China about a football team, Africa United, composed mainly of Africans and playing in a Beijing local amateur league. It is called *African Boots in Beijing*.[67] The Chinese Government has established a baseball league, and has signed a contract with American Major League Baseball (MLB) to help develop China's baseball league through player and coach exchanges.[68] Basketball, though, has been the real growth sport – note the success of the enormous Chinese basketball player Yao Ming in the USA. His success has helped basketball rival football in popularity in China.

Klein identifies the growing importance of the logo. Until the early 1970s, logos on clothes were generally hidden from view. In the late 1970s the country club wear of the 1950s became mass style. Ralph Lauren's polo horseman and Izod Lacoste's alligator escaped from the golf course and scurried into the streets. By the mid 1980s Lacoste and Ralph Lauren were joined by Calvin Klein, Esprit and, in Canada, Roots. The logo itself was growing in size, especially in the case of Tommy Hilfiger (Klein 1999). Manchester United, Real Madrid, the New York Yankees, the National Basketball Association (NBA), the MLB and the National Football League (NFL) have all been working hard, with varying degrees of success, to promote and develop their brands. The logo, Klein argues, becomes central. It is part of a shift from an image into a lived reality. The effect is to marginalise the hosting culture and foreground the brand as the star (Klein 1999). One impact of the permeation of globalising processes by branded commodities is a heightened reconfiguring of identities. Giddens suggests that

> In more traditional situations, a sense of self is sustained largely through the stability of the social positions of individuals in the community. Where tradition lapses, and lifestyle choice prevails, the self isn't exempt. Self identity has to be created, and recreated on a more active basis than before.
>
> (Giddens 2002: 47)

Branded clothes constitute primary materials utilised in order to express self-identity, but identities are also remade in the context of histories, traditions and movements. The processes of diaspora, migration and hybridity are not new; on the contrary, they have marked the process of human interaction, exchange and

Figure 7.1 'Welcome Real Madrid to Hotel Kunlun'.

Figure 7.2 Raul poster.

Figure 7.3 Chinese man wearing Beckham shirt. The Real Madrid 'galacticos' marketed their brand in China in July 2005 with some success, but then failed to win trophies in 2005–06, suggesting that globetrotting may not be the best form of pre-season training. Manchester United were also in China and other Asian countries during July 2005.

contestation since the beginnings of trade. However, the shrinking of the globe by technology, the ease and speed of travel, the instantaneity of electronic communication, the perfect replication of digitalisation, and the nature of access to the 'back catalogues' of cultural production have bestowed a greater complexity. I want to explore this with two meta-narratives. The second features the development of a nation; the first is the story of a man of remarkable skill and meagre self-discipline.

Argentina, Europe and Maradona

When Diego Maradona arrived in Europe it was as a tough, short but stocky man with an uncanny ability to move, swerve and control a football. But when Argentina beat England in the 1986 World Cup, Maradona's 'hand of God' goal elevated him to the mythic level. It was a goal that crystallised so much in the complex history of relations between the two countries, both footballing and non-footballing. It was a goal of immense cheek, a cheat that succeeded against the odds, with only the referee not noticing. So it was a triumph for the *pibe*, the street urchin, that Maradona, in style, background and personal appearance, epitomised. It was, for Argentinians, a joyous revenge for the perceived injustice of the sending-off of their captain Rattin in the 1966 World Cup, in yet another quarter final game against England. Indeed it was taken as a blow against the hypocrisy of the English citadel of 'fair play'; the 1966 World Cup was widely perceived in Argentina as rigged to ensure the smooth progress of England towards the final, and the resentment at the defeat in the Malvinas War was still very fresh. It was, to put it mildly, a goal with history.

Argentina has a more distinctively European dimension to its culture than most South American countries. Between 1870 and 1914 around six million Europeans arrived in Argentina, by which time around one-third of the Argentinian population were foreign born, the majority being Italians (39.4 per cent) and Spaniards (35.2 per cent) (Archetti 1999: 1). Just as Argentina is the most European-oriented of Latin American countries, so Buenos Aires is the most Europe-oriented of its cities. Grant Farred points to the racial underpinning of this when he suggests that 'with its historic attachment to Europe, Argentina conceives of itself as white because it is high cultured, literate and racially distinct from its Latin neighbours' (Farred 2004: 53). To this day, there is a tendency for Argentina to look disparagingly on its neighbours. Farred recounts that, in football commentary, 'Argentine commentators, with no fear of censorship or approbation, from their networks, or their viewers, refer to the Brazilian players as "macacos", monkeys' (Farred 2004: 54).

However, Buenos Aires was not simply Paris in South America, but was the site of interacting cultural currents. Anthony King (1991) has argued that it was not the established metropolitan centres of Europe, but the great port cities of Asia and Latin America, that most embodied a cosmopolitan, multicultural, hybridised set of cultural exchanges. Cities such as Singapore, Calcutta, Rio de Janeiro and Buenos Aires are more precise precursors of the present-day urban landscape than Paris or London. In present-day Argentinian culture, football, polo and the tango are all significant elements. Football and polo are sports codified by the British, and exported to Argentina, while the tango is an Argentinian cultural product exported to the world. Cultural practices, Archetti argues, become de-territorialised (Archetti 1999: xvi). One of the world's largest cities, characterised by its key and dominant position as entry and exit point for Argentina, Buenos Aires grew rapidly from the 1890s, when advances in refrigeration techniques enabled a lucrative export trade in beef. The culture of its citizens, the *porteños*, has been described as combining a European focus, a dynamic creative energy and a melancholic nostalgia.

Eduardo Archetti cites J. Clifford's description of Buenos Aires as a 'truly global space of cultural connections and dissolutions'.[69] Archetti suggests that

> The Argentinian elite imagined that Paris was the only city comparable to Buenos Aires. Paris had achieved, at the end of the nineteenth century, the title of the world's capital of elegance, sophistication and pleasure. But Paris was more: it was a scientific centre, a place for technical innovations, an international milieu, where ideological debates flourished and artistic fashions were shaped. Paris was perceived as the core of modernity. It was also the city where the hitherto most successful World Exhibition was held in 1900, attracting more than 50 million visitors. But above all Paris promised entertainment and enjoyment, with its cafés and restaurants, its theatres, vaudevilles and cabarets, its department stores and colourful local fairs and markets. Paris functioned, in what was the world of the travellers at that time, as a fabric of fantasies and illusions. Buenos Aires operated in the same way in Argentina and later, once its prestige was consolidated, in South America. For the South Americans fun and elegance were not enough: the fact that Buenos Aires was seen as a typical European (and white) city was crucial in their positive image.
>
> (Archetti 1999: 4)

Grant Farred wrote that

> Argentina, in Latin folklore, is the South America country where the inhabitants speak Spanish but think in Italian, and identify with Europe. Buenos Aires is less, as popular parlance would have it, the Paris of Latin America than it, subliminally, imagines itself as being psychically at one with the capitals of Europe. Its residents, especially the 'portenos', live imaginatively in Paris, if only at a geographical remove.
>
> (Farred 2004: 52)

Karush says that during the 1920s a distinctive, new urban culture developed in Buenos Aires growing out of the city's new, outlying barrios where manual workers lived side by side with skilled workers and members of the middle class. The strong economy enabled social mobility, and the new barrio culture revealed a less militant attitude on the part of *porteño* workers, reflected in a decline in union membership. The dominance of Buenos Aires and the emergence of popular mass media meant that this city-based culture became a dominant element in national identity. The 1920s witnessed 'the commodification and massification of tango and football, two popular cultural practices that were now transformed into quintessential representations of *Argentinidad*' (Karush 2003).

But within this Latin city with European imaginings there was also a macho tradition – the meeting ground of Latin masculinity and the toughness and rugged values that grow out of physical labour whether in docks, factories or on the land. There were tough areas in which working-class masculinity performed itself in the social rituals of the café bar and the football ground. The area of La Boca (literally the mouth, referring to the river mouth on which it sits, where the *Riachuelo* joins the far larger river *Plata*) is invariably described in guide books as 'colourful' partly because of a small area of wooden houses that are painted in bright, contrasting primary colours, supposedly with the ends of paint pots used to paint boats in the nearby docks. The main street of Caminito has become gentrified, with art galleries, street markets and café bars with tango displays, but the rest of the area, littered with the remnants of decaying industry, decrepit car body-shops and tumbledown housing, is poor and rough.

In the middle of this dockside desolation rises a massive stadium, exactly as similar stadia loomed above the working-class districts of Liverpool, Glasgow, Birmingham and Manchester. The ground is the home of Boca Juniors, founded in 1905, and known by such nicknames as 'los bosteros' – the manure collectors. In just four years in the first decade of this century five major football clubs had been formed – River Plate (1901), Racing Club (1903), Boca Juniors, Independiente, and San Lorenzo (all 1905). Boca Juniors' ground was in the Genovese barrio in the docklands area. The choice of name, though, involved identification with place rather than ethnicity. 'Boca' referred to the mouth of the river, while Juniors suggested that they considered themselves to be children of that place, rather than immigrants. Boca Juniors, though, did develop a close association with the roots of their local community (Duke and Crolley 2002: 97).

Their ground is known as La Bombonera (the chocolate box) after the distinctive upright appearance of the box-laden main stand. Here Maradona became, and remained, a hero. In 2004, the mere sight of his distinctive and now portly silhouette, framed against the setting sun through the glass walls of the main stand, was enough to bring an entire crowd to its feet, cheering and chanting his name. Maradona was born in 1960. He played his first match in the Argentine top division with Argentinos Juniors when he was still 15, and played for the Argentina national team at 16. His early popularity was exploited by the military for propaganda purposes, and after 1978 a huge pressure developed to prevent top stars, and especially Maradona, from leaving the country (Burns 2002: 60–3). In 1981 he joined Boca Juniors, who won the Argentine championship in his first season with them. Although he was there for less than two seasons, according to Burns

Figure 7.4 La Bombonera, Buenos Aires, where Diego Maradona is still a local hero. To the left of the picture can be seen the distinctive executive boxes, one of which Maradona still uses. The glass back wall means that when he arrives the crowd, recognising his distinctive shape in silhouette, erupt in celebratory clamour.

in the Maradona family there was never any question that Boca was the natural place to be. In the team, Maradona returned to his maternal roots. And each time he walked by the huge mural that covers one of the galleries leading to the changing rooms, he thought of his father too. For there depicted were the port workers, lugging their cargo, just as Chitoro had done so many years ago.

(Burns 2002: 76)

In 1982 he went to Barcelona, and then to Napoli in 1984, but first came the World Cup, played as the Argentinian attempt to reclaim the Malvinas collapsed in abject defeat and the subsequent collapse of the military regime (Burns 2002: 94). For the Argentine players, used to the propaganda of the Argentine Military Government, access to the coverage in the Spanish press revealed a very different picture of the war, that, according to Burns, helped to demoralise the team. Maradona returned to start with Barcelona after the 1982 World Cup; Burns writes that the Barcelona stadium and surrounding complex, 'in a modern suburb of Barcelona, reduced La Bombonera ... to the memory of a rather squalid backyard' (Burns 2002: 99).

Barcelona did win the Cup in 1983, but while Maradona was with them, the greater prizes of League and European success eluded them. More serious was a cultural clash between the flamboyant and indulgent lifestyle of Maradona and his entourage and the more sophisticated and sober-minded gentlemen who ran Barcelona, which led to a breakdown in relations, and the departure of Maradona to Napoli. Burns writes that

> Naples has lived much of its history amidst subjugation and disaster, its rebellious leanings suppressed by a richer, more powerful North, and its closeness to death was symbolised by the volcano of Vesuvius and the remains of the last great earthquake.
>
> (Burns 2002: 126)

Maradona's entourage soon appeared to establish relationships with the Camorra, the local mafia, who were able to benefit from local merchandising of Maradona-branded goods (Burns 2002: 134). With his fame reaching its peak, and having attained celebrity status, Maradona, like many other celebrities, became a media soap opera character. He was granted an audience with the Pope, and made an ambassador for UNICEF. He broke up with long-time girl-friend Claudia and had an affair with Cristiana, whom Burns says is possibly the only woman he really loved. She became pregnant, he dumped her, and later in 1986 Claudia returned, and Cristiana's baby was born. There was a five-year legal struggle before Maradona had to acknowledge paternity. In 1986 came the World Cup victory, preceded by the notorious 'hand of God' goal and the second, brilliant, individual goal against England. In 1986–7, thanks to Maradona, Napoli won the championship for the first time in their history. Napoli narrowly failed to retain the championship in 1987–8 but did win the UEFA Cup. Claudia bore him two daughters and they were married in 1989. Napoli won a second title in 1989–90, but only after being awarded two compensation points as a result of a match in which their goalkeeper was struck by a missile.

In 1990 Argentina again reached the final of the World Cup, but the following year Maradona was banned from football for 15 months after a positive drug test. Meanwhile Napoli's growing disillusion with his lifestyle led to his exposure as a user of prostitutes and cocaine, and a positive drug test after a game. Refusing to return to Napoli, he returned to Argentina where he was caught with cocaine and forced into rehabilitation and psychoanalytic counselling. He was banned from football for 15 months, and then joined the Spanish club Sevilla, like Napoli, a club struggling against northern dominance. Burns writes that

> During the year, Seville as a city has attracted international interest thanks to the staging there of the Expo Fair. It is no longer Spain's provincial backwa-ter. It has built a new international airport, a network of motorways and a 'bullet' train link with Madrid. To have Maradona is to carry on where Expo ends, bringing in its wake some lucrative broadcasting and sponsorship deals.
>
> (Burns 2002: 207)

But once again it ends in tears, after Maradona's indiscipline and brothel visits alienate the club. He remained at Sevilla for just one year before returning to Argentina to play for Newell's Old Boys, the name alone redolent of colonial legacy. He returned to the international stage to lead the national team in the 1994 World Cup only to receive a second ban for drug use. In 1995 he returned to Boca Juniors, until in 1997 a third, and questionable, drug test led to his retirement at age the of 37.

The facts of Maradona's career, though, are insufficient to record everything that was exciting, dramatic, scary, everything that enabled Maradona to attract the love of a nation and the attention of a world. They miss everything that made him a hero, a fool, an icon and a villain. To understand these things we need history and we need politics because these are the things that shape us just as we shape, under definite limits, them. Our own understandings of Diego Maradona are formed by our own places in a history and a politics, just as he and his actions were similarly shaped. The relation between England and Argentina is complex, marked by affections and antagonisms, both deep-rooted. Although the English were not the colonial power, an English elite exerted a powerful influence on the Argentina of the late nineteenth century. The trade connections were strong and significant. The 1966 World Cup marked difference and antagonism: England's manager Alf Ramsey dubbing the Argentine players 'animals'; the Argentinians regarding the English as part of a European conspiracy to do them down. The exhilarating football that Argentinians could produce came to England in the 1980s, in the shape of Osvaldo Ardiles and Ricky Villa, signed by Tottenham. The popularity of Ardiles with the English public even survived the Malvinas War. Indeed neither the war nor the 'hand of God' appears to have resulted in a long-lasting enmity. It is notable that while English football culture has neither forgotten nor forgiven the 'hand of God' episode, neither has it forgotten or ceased to admire Maradona's second goal in the same match, which has, in England, regularly been voted the best goal of all time. There is a strange sense of respect for a challenging adversary in football. It is as if, as with Germany, there is a working-class male sensibility that recognises its like – we are like the Germans and Argentines, and not really like the French or Italians. More recently two highly dramatic football matches between the two countries have continued the fractured narrative. In 1998 a close, dramatic and exciting encounter was won by Argentina in penalties, with a sent-off David Beckham taking the blame. In 2002, England finally managed another victory, only to fail against Brazil in the quarter-final.

Maradona has spent much of the last seven years attempting to recover from addiction, and massive weight gain. He spent much time in Cuba, where he has forged a friendship with Fidel Castro, never a man to underestimate the power of image and symbol. As this book was being written, a new Maradona, looking slim and clear-eyed, has suddenly bounced back into public life in Buenos Aires with a television show, featuring an interview with Castro as one of the first items. More dramatically he has become a declared supporter of anti-imperialist struggle, leading a demonstration against President Bush and attempts to impose a neoliberal free trade structure on South America. So the young hero returns home, returns to his roots, reconnects with the popular classes and the historic struggle of Latin America. It would, of course, be dangerous to over-romanticise this – Maradona is in no sense a programmatic political activist. When Maradona put in a rally appearance to support the left-wing Venezuelan leader, Hugo Chavez, the Mexican president Vicente Fox commented acidly that 'He has a good foot for kicking, but he doesn't have a good brain for talking' (*The Guardian* 10/11/05).

This, though, would be to underestimate Maradona: it is the case that his expressed sympathies have consistently been with underdogs, despite his cocaine-fuelled egocentric lifestyle, and dubious associates whilst in Italy. Although more by accident than design, it is striking that at every stage of his club career he has been involved with clubs struggling for ascendancy against a more powerful and dominant elite: Boca Juniors against the more middle-class River Plate; the Catalan Barcelona against the nationalist Real Madrid; the southern peasants of Napoli against the sophisticated and arrogant northerners of Milan; and the southern upstarts of Sevilla against the more established north-ern sides in Madrid and Barcelona. The lesson here is that, where stars are involved, politics is not the personal, but the symbolic. Maradona remains a hero, a focal point and a rallying point for many Argentinians – defining who they are, where they want to go, and what they are against.

The changing face of the Padang: Empire, Kuala Lumpur, and the Commonwealth Games

The forging of identities is one of the meeting grounds of individual and collec-tive, but it is also a process in which histories, routes, traditions come up against the dynamic processes of change, and one in which relations between dominant and subordinate groups are constantly reinscribed and renegotiated. The British imperial networks did play a significant role in spreading English ideas of sport to the Empire countries. Decolonisation prompts reconstruction of the cultural map, including the place of sport, its rituals, practices and sacred spaces.

Malaysia stands in the middle of a network of trade routes linking China, Southeast Asia, India and Europe. It has always been an ethnically mixed area. The Orang Asli, who probably came from China and Tibet, have been there for thousands of years. The Malays have been there almost as long. Chinese and Indian influences spread along trade links established 2000 years ago. Hinduism and Bhuddism left their marks, before Islam took over as the dominant religious influence in the thirteenth century. European colonists arrived in the sixteenth century – the Portuguese, being defeated by the Dutch, who in turn yielded to the British, who established bases in Penang, Malacca and Singapore and pur-sued a strategy of political unification.

The British colonial strategy in this period was to establish a 'Resident', a British official who was notionally there to advise the local government, and to ensure that the cost of what was in effect British control was met through local taxation.[70] The British established and nurtured a hierarchical racially based structure in which white men from Britain and the old white empire countries were in the top positions, clerical positions were filled by Eurasians, the police by Indians and Malayans.[71] The dominant wisdom, with the British Resident Frank Swettenham as its leading guru, was that only the English and perhaps the Chinese had what was required to succeed in Malasia's modern economy.[72] As the system later developed the Chinese increasingly emerged as the dominant economic force, but the British ensured that the Malays would become the dominant political power. As well as the rubber plantations, the economic base of Malaysia was partly based on opium, with the various provincial governments profiting from taxation and licensing of the trade. During the first third of the twentieth-century, around one quarter of government revenue came from the trade.[73]

The capital, Kuala Lumpur, is the largest city in Malaysia with a population of just under two million. It is sited at the point where the Gombak and Klang rivers join, and was originally a trading centre for tin mining. During the nineteenth century a period of civil war developed between rival princes and rivals for leadership of the Chinese community. After peace was restored, the town grew rapidly to assume the status of a capital. When the British colonial officials moved inland from Klang, their fears of a hostile reception from the Chinese led them to build an official quarter on raised ground across the river from the 'native town' to the east (Gullick 1994: 10). It is clear from pictures that even in 1880 Kuala Lumpur was still a relatively undeveloped and rudimentary town, a fact which makes the lavish scale of the new Government Offices built in this period even more astounding.

In an 1895 map of Kuala Lumpur, subsequently redrawn but undated, the Padang is shown as the 'Parade Ground', and is very centrally placed at the heart of the city. It has the Church of England church immediately to the north, the Government Offices immediately to the east, the station to the south, and surrounding it in the west, two barracks, the armoury, the government printing office and the General Hospital (Gullick 1994). In another book on Kuala Lumpur, the first image is an aerial shot of the Royal Selangor Club and the Padang almost dead centre (Chay, undated). So all the key institutions of colonial power, army, church, bureaucracy, media, sport and medicine, were grouped closely together. The Resident, Frank Swettenham, had the residency built on even higher ground to the north. He was apparently fond of demonstrating, to his guests at afternoon tea, the howitzer gun placed on his lawn, by lobbing shells into the jungle, offering a clear implicit warning of the power behind the urbanity (Gullick 1994: 10). Gullick writes that

> For the European community, the Police Parade Ground (Merdeka Square) was the centre of social life. Here in the course of the 1890s, were built the Selangor Club, St Mary's Church, the Chartered Bank Building, and the new government offices. It was no longer just a police parade ground. Under the influence of enthusiastic sportsmen it became a playing field for cricket and other team games and was made into a level sward and called 'the Padang'.
>
> (Gullick 1994)

Figure 7.5 The Padang and the Selangor Club, Malaysia, where the British Empire still echoes in post-colonial rituals. The parade ground of the forces upholding the Empire is now overseen by a new post-colonial elite, in which the Chinese and Indian Malays play a significant role. Yet the club retains much of the atmosphere and ritual of its colonial origins.

Cricket was a social event, in which men proved they were the right sort for administrative responsibilities. The Padang was too small for first class cricket, and the sport never became especially popular outside the British community. Football and rugby were also played on the Padang. The Padang today remains a focus of Kuala Lumpur's celebratory events, especially on Independence Day, August 31st. On the western side of the Padang stands the Royal Selangor Club, a key institution of British colonial rule in the late nineteenth century, and still a meeting ground for Malaysia's new administrative and cultural elite.[74] Its striking mock Tudor design emphasises its iconic home county character.[75] Chay says that the club 'was a favourite social meeting place of British residents during the colonial times and as such it became a symbol of British colonial era' (Chay, undated: 99).

Originally women were not admitted, although it is unclear when this restriction was dropped.[76] Indeed the Long Bar still does not admit women, except on New Year's Eve. The extent to which the club was largely whites only is unclear. Gullick refers to an Indian businessman, Thambusamy Pilla, who supposedly 'knew everybody and was known to everybody' who was a leading light at the Selangor Club (Gullick 1994: 37). Other accounts refer to it as 'whites only'. Even if welcome, the Islamic Malays may well not have relished the 'stengah' and gin and tonic ambience.[77] Gullick says that in the 1890s it was a mixed club but that senior members of the European Community were not keen about associating even with 'lesser European mortals whom they met in their working lives'. In 1890 a group of them formed the more exclusive Lake Club, with rates of subscription set to discourage applications from less well-paid colleagues (Gullick 1994: 38–9). It is surprisingly difficult to find information about such social institutions in secondary literature.[78]

The club today is still rooted partly in English sporting practices. It runs teams in cricket, rugby, football and many other sports. It has bars that feature darts and snooker, as well as a ballroom and a disco. There is a golf club, and a satellite club just outside the centre, with a larger sports field. Chinese and Indian Malays are actively involved as club officers and members. To sit in the long bar, as I was able to do in 2005, drinking whisky, and gazing out at the setting sun reflected in the windows of the colonial era government buildings, in the company of men of Indian and Chinese origin, was to be confronted with both continuity and change in a very immediate, material and tangible form. Cultural influences are rarely a simple one-way process. In 1938, a group of Englishmen and Australians who frequented the club decided to deal with their hangovers by running. This led to the establishment of a club, the Hash House Harriers. In 1969 a second substantial branch was established in Singapore; there were around 50 groups in the mid 1970s, and the club has since spread around the world, with branches in around 160 countries.[79] It is a distinctly male middle-class professional movement with its members consisting of bankers, accountants, engineers, businessmen, lawyers, and civil servants. The founding branch of the Hash House Harriers now has its own dedicated room at the Royal Selangor Club. The old imperial links are reforged in a new form, and residual practices of Edwardian male clubbiness are reshaped in the decolonised context.

The Malaysian Federation became independent in 1957. For independence celebrations, a large stadium, Stadium Merdeka (Independence Stadium), was built. On the Padang, the union jack was lowered and the Malaysian flag raised. During the late 1980s and early 1990s under the impact of the Asian economic boom and the rise of the so-called 'tiger economies', Kuala Lumpur grew rapidly and saw significant development, symbolised by the Petronas Towers, the tallest building in the world, when built. Despite significant public investment in transport, the infrastructure at first struggled to cope with the rapid pace of growth. This reinvention of Malaysia as a tiger economy with Kuala Lumpur at its heart, and concepts such as the multimedia super corridor, was given an ideological buttressing with the opening of a Museum of National History, which presents the British as originally there just for trade but finding themselves interfering in local politics, although according to Hooker, it is implied that the unstable forms of governance were a contributory cause (Hooker 2003: 6). However, the strategy of pinning the local currency to the dollar backfired with the collapse of the Thai Baht and the collapse of the asset price bubble 'encouraged by financial liberalization' (Jomo 1998). In a period of recovery and reconstruction, the Malaysian government utilised the Commonwealth Games as a global media spectacle, both to gain international publicity and as an opportunity to celebrate its multicultural national identity and thus 'market' Malaysia as a model modern Muslim society (Van der Westhuizen 2004).

The original idea for a multi-sport event linking Empire countries has its origins in Imperial power and racism. John Astley Cooper began proposing a Pan Britannic Festival in print in 1891. This idea was overtaken by the modern Olympic Games, first held in 1896, but it laid the seeds of the idea that resurfaced as the Empire Games. Cooper's idea combined

> several important aspects of life – culture, industry and athletics – in a grandiose festival celebrating the British race. The concept implied, but did not explicitly state, that the race was superior; Cooper asked if Britons were ready to undertake 'actions for the benefit of mankind which may make the name of England to be sung for all time as an example to races yet to come'.
>
> (Moore 1987: 146)

It is clear, according to Moore, that Cooper's idea was intended to include 'only adult males from the so called white Dominions – Australia, New Zealand, Canada and South Africa – as well as those subjects eligible in Great Britain' (Moore 1987: 148). The Empire Games were first staged in 1930 in Hamilton, Ontario, at a moment when the relationship between the UK and the old 'white' Empire countries was being reshaped. Phillips quotes Holt as saying that 'the loosening bonds of Empire came at the same time as new economic pressures were being placed upon the relationships between the Dominions and Britain' (Holt in Phillips 2000: 5).

The very title of the event, unlike that of the World Cup or the Olympic Games, has had to keep changing to match contemporary political realities. Until 1950 it was the British Empire Games, after which it became the British Empire and Commonwealth Games. In 1970 the embarrassment of 'Empire' was dropped, and the Games became the British Commonwealth Games. Four years later, in a symbolic de-territorialisation, 'British' was dropped and the event became the 'Commonwealth Games'. This shedding of imperial nomenclature enabled the Games to be re-branded as 'the Friendly Games' after the success of Edinburgh 1970, which at a budget of £616,000 were also the Bargain Games. The 1982 Games in Brisbane cost £15 million. Edinburgh 1986 proved that even if the athletes were no longer amateur the organisers could be. They (Edinburgh 86) sold worldwide rights to the BBC for £500,000 (see Bateman and Douglas 1986: 16). Had they kept the world rights and just sold the British rights, or done a deal for profit sharing with the BBC, things might have been rather different. As it was, the year leading up to the Games saw organisers struggling to avoid a funding shortfall and a looming deficit. Robert Maxwell's Mirror Group stepped in, and attempted to maximise the positive publicity to be garnered for 'saving the Games'.

Struggling with the impact of a boycott over apartheid, though, the Games were ultimately only able to cover their deficit thanks to a large donation from a mystery benefactor, arranged by Robert Maxwell, who turned out to be a right-wing Japanese businessman (Bateman and Douglas 1986).

Undeterred by the fiascos of the past, cities around the world have grown ever more enthusiastic about the supposed benefits of mega events. In their efforts to promote tourism and trade, cities are 'going global' on the basis of integrating economic and cultural activity as an urban regeneration strategy, frequently involving the staging of major events (Yeoh 2005). The increasingly common attempts to bid to stage major events is linked to both the perceived expansion of 'marketing power', and to the legitimisation and celebration of conceptions of national identity (Black and Van der Westhuizen 2004). So bidding to stage major international events covered by television is both an economic and an ideological project. The staging of the event raises visibility, and is intended to attract trade, inward investment and tourism. To do so it is necessary to promote an image. The Malaysian staging of the Commonwealth Games embraced both of these intentions. The images of Kuala Lumpur were re-imagined and promoted as young, dynamic, modern and unified (Silk 2002: 775–94). In a different version of the country, emphasis might be placed on the ways in which Malays, Chinese and Indians exist alongside each other, in a society in which structured inequalities persist. Amongst Indian and Chinese origin Malaysians that I talked to one could often sense a repressed anger that preferment for public posts was underpinned by systematic discrimination. The compact between major political organisations to attempt to avoid political division along ethnic lines has not solved a problem but put an ill-fitting lid on it. This does not make Kuala Lumpur or Malaysia as a whole atypical of course; most societies of the world have similar problems. Its rhetoric of national unity is entirely in keeping with the discourse of major event staging, and is one more indicator of the ways in which the world is now written by image consultants. The 1998 Commonwealth Games held in Kuala Lumpur, partly in the Bukit Jalil National Stadium, between 16 and 21 September, were only one element in a more comprehensive strategy of economic and ideological reconstruction. The main stadium, holding 100,000 and costing around £330 million, was built as part of a longer-term strategy towards the mounting of an Olympic bid. Phillips asserts that

> The gregarious and wildly enthusiastic citizens of Kuala Lumpur in 1998 provided a first infusion of Asian culture for the Games even though their political masters were working to another agenda entirely and had really built their monumentally breathtaking sporting complexes in the interests of the longer-term grandiose scheme of hosting an eventual Olympic Games sometime in the 21st Century.
>
> (Phillips 2000: 3)

It is interesting that the more the Commonwealth Games has sought to decouple itself from the Empire and the centrality of Britain, the more the British have developed a tendency to dismiss it as a second-class event. The recent Games in Melbourne were presented with somewhat lukewarm enthusiasm by the BBC, and the Queen's Christmas Message in 1998 and 1999 made no reference to the Commonwealth Games. Of course, the Games are arguably lower in the sporting hierarchy and in the level of local public excitement than, for example, the Asian Games. In a visit to Kuala Lumpur in 2005 I did not encounter any noticeable enthusiasm to discuss the Games amongst the local residents with whom I raised the topic. The Olympic Games, on the other hand, is a major prize in the battle to promote a city and a country, and the bidding race has become the catalyst for extensive speculative investment around the world.

To end the chapter, in 2001 a great story went around the world on the Web. It is a story that illustrates how individuals armed with basic technology can unsettle giant corporations. If laughing at powerful figures and institutions robs them of some of their power, then we could benefit from more symbolic guerilla activity like this. Nike had begun allowing people to personalise their shoes by submitting a word or phrase which they will stitch onto your shoes, under the swoosh. So Jonah Peretti filled out the form and sent them $50 to stitch 'sweatshop' onto his shoes. Strangely, Nike seemed uncomfortable with the idea, but appeared to have problems spelling out just why they were so sensitive. A computer reply cancelling the order prompted Peretti to write:

> Greetings,
> My order was canceled but my personal NIKE iD does not violate any of the criteria outlined in your message. The Personal iD on my custom ZOOM XC USA running shoes was the word 'sweatshop.' Sweatshop is not:
> 1) another party's trademark,
> 2) the name of an athlete,
> 3) blank,
> or
> 4) profanity.
> I choose the iD because I wanted to remember the toil and labor of the children that made my shoes. Could you please ship them to me immediately.
> Thanks and Happy New Year.

Nike replied that the order was cancelled 'because the iD you have chosen contains "inappropriate slang"'. Peretti disagreed, citing *Webster's Dictionary*, and helpfully pointed out to Nike that

> 'sweatshop' is in fact part of standard English, and not slang. The word means: 'a shop or factory in which workers are employed for long hours at low wages and under unhealthy conditions' and its origin dates from 1892. So my personal iD does meet the criteria detailed in your first email.

Now, beginning to sound somewhat rattled, Nike suggested the word was inappropriate and that they did not want it on their product. Jonah Peretti took this blow well, courteously replying,

Thank you for the time and energy you have spent on my request. I have decided to order the shoes with a different iD, but I would like to make one small request. Could you please send me a color snapshot of the ten-year-old Indonesian girl who makes my shoes?

He received no reply.

8 Back to politics

Nothing is more difficult than the art of manoeuvre. What is difficult about manoeuvre is to make the devious route the most direct and to turn misfortune to advantage.

Sun Tzu, *The Art of War*, p.102

Fidel Castro was a clean-shaven civil liberties attorney in a gray suit in downtown Havana until he couldn't stand it anymore. The established order builds the incubator for its overthrow.

American comedian Mort Sahl (1976: 5)

Young people are no longer interested in politics, it is argued. They are seen as disinterested, as not following politics, as not seeing the point of voting. Electoral and party politics have become seen as irrelevant; a cosmetic contest between politicians and their spin doctors in which there are few meaningful differences between the candidates. Whereas in the past, the young have been moved by great issues – civil rights, poverty in the developing world, nuclear disarmament, women's rights, peace – today's young have a narrower and more individualised focus – concerned with career opportunities, consumption identity and style and value for money. Clearly, though, it is more complicated. There has been an apparent decline in involvement in electoral politics in many Western countries, as measured by turnout; but in the last 30 years, large popular movements demanding greater democracy have emerged and become powerful. Solidarity in Poland, popular movements in Hungary, the German Democratic Republic and other eastern communist states, contributed to the dramatic collapse of the Soviet Union and its sphere of influence. De-investment in South Africa, prompted by public pressure, helped bring about the end of the apartheid system. A process, admittedly uneven, driven by popular enthusiasm, of re-democratisation in Latin America, has instigated a transition from the era dominated by military dictatorships. In Islamic countries as different as Iran and Algeria fundamentalism has been challenged by a more reformist and democratically oriented sensibility. In all these instances, young people have been active and to the fore.

An apparent disaffection from electoral politics has to be set against the significant appeal of issue politics – millions around the world marched in protest against the invasion of Iraq; cancellation of developing-world debt became a major campaign focus; and forms of ecological protest and anti-capitalist protest succeed in mobilising significant numbers. The representation of young people as complacent consumers is not an adequate conceptualisation. In *Runaway World*, Giddens suggests that the battleground of the twenty-first century will be between cosmopolitanism and fundamentalism (Giddens 2002: 4–5). This of course represents an interesting re-inflection here of the more common construction of an opposition between a modernising West and a tradition-rooted Islam. Tariq Ali, in *The Clash of Fundamentalisms* (2002), reminds us that fundamentalism has been just as important and just as dangerous a social force in the USA as it has in the Middle East.

Television and the Internet have transformed the nature of the political process, elevating the image and the spectacular gesture, and displacing both the linear political discourse of the prepared speech, and the imposing yet dull mass protest march. Single dramatic moments, such as the fall of the Berlin Wall, come to have great resonance, as Giddens points out:

> A small group of us got down there very quickly. Ladders were being put up against it, and we started to climb up. But we were pushed back again by television crews who had just arrived on the scene. They had to go up first, they said, so that they could film us scaling the ladders and arriving at the top. They even persuaded some people to go back down and climb twice more, to make sure they had good television footage. Thus is history made in the closing years of the twentieth century. Television not only gets there first, but also stages the spectacle.
>
> Anthony Giddens, reflecting on the opening of the
> Berlin Wall, on 9 November 1989 (Giddens 2002: 67–8)

Of course, nowadays television companies would also draw on pictures transmitted from mobile phones, eyewitness reports phoned in, and text, email and Internet blogged responses. All of which goes to illustrate the ways in which the possibilities of political action need to adjust to the transformative impact of cultural and technological change.[80]

In the midst of turbulent risk-laden times, with a rapid pace of change, surely Marxism is now irrelevant? Why cling on to socialism? To take the first of these questions, the case against the continuing relevance of Marx is strong. Eastern communism collapsed and deservedly so; the USSR and the other Eastern bloc countries came to be governed by elitist cliques of men, and they were largely men who no longer had vision.[81] Their techniques of control and surveillance produced societies characterised by secrecy and paranoia. Deprived of both freedoms and material luxuries, their citizens could all too readily regard freedom and materialism as linked. The Soviet Union was undermined by a ruinous arms race with the USA which it could not win; but the regimes of eastern communism fell because they lost legitimacy with their citizens. In Gramsci's terms they could no longer sustain a hegemony, an ability to lead, and force alone was insufficient to retain control. Marx's analysis undoubtedly underestimated the resilience of capitalism and its ability to regenerate itself. He did not foresee the enormous growth of a relatively affluent class of middle-class functionaries, a large-scale service sector and a greatly expanded state. The historical process has not thus far followed a Marxist model, and there are very few signs that it is likely to do so in the foreseeable future. Indeed the most advanced capitalist countries – the UK, the USA, Germany and Japan – have generally been the most stable whilst revolutions have happened predominately in relatively pre-industrial contexts – Russia, China, Cuba and Iran.

However, the failures of communist states, and the weaknesses in Marx's schematic historicist and teleological account of the road to socialism, should not be allowed to obscure the continued pertinence of his forensic dissection of the mechanisms of capitalist exploitation. The fundamental principles and processes – expropriation of surplus value for example – are still relatively unchanged. The need for capital to reproduce itself, and the consequent need to penetrate new areas, underpins changes in the sphere of cultural life and especially sport. The tendency of the rate of profit to decline and consequent need to introduce greater efficiencies and new cost-effective means of exploiting the workforce underpins most of the developments that go under the name of Thatcherism, such as casualisation of the workforce, privatisation of parts of the state, and legal restrictions on trade unions. Despite the evocation of concepts such as the 'Information Society', most of the information that circulates, whether on the Internet or elsewhere, concerns goods and services that can be consumed at a price. Despite the concept of 'post-Fordism' many of these goods are still produced in factories – it is just that they are out of the sight of (and out of the mind of) Western analysts, in the Enterprise Zones of Southeast Asia. Despite the concept of the post-industrial society, the consumer boom is all about commodities that have to be produced, transported and retailed.

To support all this, there is an ever-growing gap between an affluent consuming West, which now extends to affluent strata around the world, and a new impoverished international proletariat. No one reading the account of the production of goods for companies such as Nike in Naomi Klein's *No Logo* (1999) could be in any doubt that the industrial system of exploitation is alive and flourishing. It is just that, now, such production is increasingly hidden behind layers of brokers, agents and subcontractors, so that it becomes harder for major international corporations to be held responsible. For some, influenced by Lyotard's *The Postmodern Condition* (1984), Marxism was just another grand narrative that could now be safely consigned to the dustbin of history, along with Freud, Darwin and the Enlightenment project.[82] But it is not really the case that there are no grand narratives any more – ecology is one, and religion, in the form of the two warring fundamentalisms, Christianity and Islam, which stand as additional examples. Socialism is still of thundering relevance, if only because we need a route out of the way in which a globalised society, driven by corporate power and individual consumption, is hastening down the road to destruction. After decades of public awareness that the gap between the rich and poor needs to be narrower, it has steadily become wider. In 1989 the poorest 20 per cent of the world had 2.3 per cent of global income, but by 1998 this had dropped to 1.4 per cent (Giddens 2002). It may have become rather fashionable in the affluent West to deride socialism as yesterday's political philosophy, but this would not be a dominant view in Latin America. In recent years, many South American countries have been able to end dominance by military rule, and have managed to restore democratic rule. In country after country, voters have then opted for left of centre government, and in many cases leaders, such as Hugo Chavez of Venezuela, have an explicitly socialist programme.

Which brings me to the second question, why cling on to socialism? Well, the first and most obvious answer must be that far from bringing freedom, and affluence to all, the various 'democracies' of capitalism have neither reduced exploitation, nor been able to narrow the gulf between rich and poor; indeed the gap has continued to grow wider. Nor have they, as yet, made any meaningful impact upon the problem of global warming. Democracy has been unable to curb the excesses and corrupt practices of powerful corporations and individuals and the crimes of the powerful go without punishment. I am for a free and genuinely democratic society, and by that I include freedom from exploitation. It is not apparent that neoliberal economics, privatisation, the reduction of state legislation governing corporate activities contributes to this goal. Indeed the most powerful capitalist nation in the world has a substantial percentage of its citizens living in poverty, many needing two or even three jobs just to survive, a growing gulf between rich and poor, a private health service that is cripplingly expensive, a public health service of shameful inadequacy, a political system dominated by ruthless powerful corporate interests, and an electoral system that, on the basis of the last two Presidential elections, really requires UN observers. I am for forms of governance that curb the power of the rich, that redistribute wealth, and that ensure that key services such as health and education are developed for the benefit of society as a whole, and not distorted by the ability of rich people to buy privilege. When we need a doctor, a hospital, a bus, a school or a university we are *not* customers choosing to consume, we are people who need a service. If health, fitness and sport are public goods, a properly run society should not allow sport centres to be colonised by the private sector and transformed into expensive bastions for the narcissistic cultivation of fit bodies.

So what has changed in the politics of sport since the publication of *Blowing the Whistle* in 1983? It is important not to underestimate the achievements of political struggle in the sporting context. The original cover of *Blowing the Whistle* referred to apartheid in South Africa, and the era of rebel tours. The apartheid regime has gone, and the sport boycott was a significant part of the ideological and cultural battle that preceded its demise. The sport boycott was a constant visible signal to the world that the apartheid regime was unacceptable, and it was a great achievement for that struggle that a major governing body such as the IOC expelled South Africa from its ranks. The advances made by women in sport, in numbers participating, standards reached and, more importantly, in confronting sexist and patriarchal restrictions, have been extraordinary (see Hargreaves 2000). When *Blowing the Whistle* was written women were still barred from several athletic events. The Olympic Games did not allow women to run further than 800 metres until 1972. The first women's 3000 metres, 400 metres hurdles and marathon were in 1984. Women were barred from the pole vault and throwing the hammer until 2000. Now sporting involvement and achievement by women is far more routinised and accepted than ever before. Of course there are still many institutions that still discriminate, both formally and informally, but even these places are on the defensive.

Racism in football crowds is still a problem, but now it is an issue, a matter of public concern and a site of struggle. There are well-established campaigns. *Let's Kick Racism Out of Football* was established in 1993. It works throughout the football, educational and community sectors to challenge racism and work for positive change. The campaign is supported and funded by the game's governing bodies, including the Professional Footballers Association (PFA), the FA Premier League, the Football Foundation and the Football Association. *Kick It Out* plays a leading role in the *Football Against Racism in Europe* (FARE) network and has been cited as an example of good practice by the European governing body UEFA, the world governing body FIFA, the Council of Europe, the European Commission, European parliamentarians and the British Council. FARE also seeks to combat racism in football. It aims to combine the resources of anti-racist football organisations throughout Europe.[83] *Football Unites, Racism Divides* was formed in 1995 by a group of Sheffield United fans who were concerned about a number of incidents of racist abuse both in and around the stadium.[84] *Libero* was formed in 1996 as a football supporters network with a left libertarian perspective and a journal called *Offence*. The organisation grew out of objections to the 'Sunday School mentality', with 'as many rules for watching the game as for playing it' and to the 'gentrification' of football. *Hit Racism for Six* was founded in 1995, in the wake of an article in *Wisden Cricket Monthly* which argued that black people should not be chosen to play for England. Under pressure, the editor subsequently admitted publication of the article was an 'error of judgement' and offered 'unreserved apologies'.[85] *Hit Racism for Six* has held public meetings, published a pamphlet, issued a regular newsletter, and lobbied the cricket authorities to adopt positive measures to deal with the problem of racism in the game.[86] In 2005 conferences with involvement of government figures were staged on *Sport and Race in British Society: Key Issues and Challenges for the 21st Century* and on *The Future for Asians in British Football*.

The developments in the area of homophobia have been less impressive. Gay and lesbian visibility in sport has been heightened by the steadily growing profile of the Gay Games, but this is still portrayed in the media more as a freak show than a sporting event. For a man in any field coming out as gay can be an intimidating and fear-laden process, but in most spheres of cultural life – music, theatre, dance, film – it is at least a viable option. Not so in sport, where the prevalent climate of homophobia is still so entrenched that very few elite sport performers are known and acknowledged to be gay.

Corruption within the Olympic movement has been exposed and IOC members and other sport officials forced to resign. It is unlikely that this could have happened without a combination of whistle-blowers prepared to leak key documents, and political activists and investigative journalists asking awkward questions and being persistent. The most dogged and prominent, Andrew Jennings, has produced two trenchant attacks on the International Olympic Committee and leading figures within it. Co-authored with Vyv Simson, *The Lords of the Rings* (1992) caused consternation amongst the IOC hierarchy, who have spent a lifetime being treated with obsequious deference. Undeterred by lawsuits and the threat of being banned from Switzerland for life (!), Jennings went on to publish *The New Lords of the Rings* in 1996.[87] Helen Lenskyj argued, in *Inside the Olympic Industry* (2000), that, in many bids, the misleading structure of budgeting tends to prevent proper community accountability. Rigid deadlines are used to force through infrastructural projects without democratic accountability, whilst non-Olympic priorities are neglected. She argues that local citizens are disenfranchised, whilst also being subjected to extra taxation, and that the pressures of civic boosting result in massive local pressure not to criticise or oppose Olympic bids. However, she also believes that community campaigning has forced the IOC to take more account of environmental issues, and that, despite IOC attempts at news management, the global media played a key role in putting Olympic controversy on the public agenda and forcing IOC action (Lenskyj 2000). However, it has to be acknowledged that the engagement with these issues has been patchy. The successful London bid conducted an impressively managed media campaign in which negative coverage of the bid was minimised. It benefited, though, from a general climate of goodwill, and a lack of coherent organised oppositional groups asking tough questions about budgeting, project management, potential escalation of costs and burdens on London's ratepayers. World football has not escaped scrutiny either, with a number of accounts drawing attention to questionable business practices, financial probity and the tactics used by countries seeking to stage major events. In particular, John Sugden and Alan Tomlinson have drawn on interview, observation, archive research and some of the resources of investigative journalism to produce, across several publications, a rich picture of the ways in which FIFA, UEFA and the other players in the world football business operate.[88]

Supporters fight back?

The perceived threat to the relationship between fans and their clubs posed by the growing involvement of international capitalist organisations in football ownership has produced lively and combative campaigns, demanding that boards should include supporters' representatives. In the UK, the concept of clubs owned by their supporters has gone from a utopian pipe-dream to reality, and is becoming a common strategy at the lower and more impoverished ends of the game.[89] During the 1980s, the availability of cheap computer-based desktop publishing gave impetus to amateur publishing, and in British football a vibrant culture of fanzines, the best of which, *When Saturday Comes*, became a nationally distributed and professionally produced magazine.[90] The development was part of a new self-conscious model of fandom, which sought to combat the problems of football from within the terrace subculture. In the wake of a series of highly pub-licised episodes of crowd disorder, a tragic fire in a stand at Bradford, and government proposals for a football supporter's ID card, a group of fans formed the Football Supporters' Association (FSA), offering a more radical and strident alternative to the rather staid National Federation of Supporters' Clubs (NFSC). In the wake of the Hillsborough stadium tragedy, the voice of the fans found new shape, focus and unity, speaking out against all-seated stadia, the power of BSkyB to dictate match scheduling, and the rapidly rising prices.[91] Goldberg and Wagg saw political scope in these developments, suggesting that there was a role for an independent Pan-European supporters' organisation that might organise con-sumer boycotts against major corporations. They proposed that UEFA adopt a European supporters' charter which could require clubs to accept supporters' rep-resentation on boards. They suggested that even though the influence of transnational media corporations was increasingly determining the shape of foot-ball, a growing fan activism would provide a base for expressions of resistance (Goldberg and Wagg 1991: 252).

A coalition of supporters' organisations was formed in England in 1999 to try and create a unified campaigning body and a Supporters Charter was established. Its demands were:

- independent regulation of football;
- the redistribution of wealth, including TV income, within football;
- controls over the type of people who are allowed to own football clubs;
- controls over the activities of plcs running football clubs;
- ticket prices to be pegged at levels which keep the game accessible to all fans;
- the democratisation of football to give supporters a voice.

The Charter was presented to the government's Football Task Force in August 1999.[92] The Trust principle emerged during the 1990s as a potential solution to the financial problems of clubs in lower divisions, and as a response to demands for supporter representation on boards, and has received a degree of central gov-ernment support since Labour came to power in 1997. Supporters Direct, a government initiative, aims to help people 'who wish to play a responsible part in the life of the football club they support' and offers support, advice and informa-tion to groups of football supporters. It exists to 'promote and support the concept of democratic supporter ownership and representation through mutual, not-for-profit structures'. To this end it encourages the formation of Supporters' Trusts, their democratic representation on Football Club Boards, and their own-ership of shares in clubs. There are now over 100 such trusts, 61 of which hold shares, and 39 of which have board representatives. Four Football League clubs and eight non-league clubs are now owned or controlled by their supporters.[93] In 2002, the Football Supporters' Association and the National Federation of

Figure 8.1 'If teams could transfer fans, what would you be worth?' As Rogan Taylor has often said, 'the fans are the real sponsor'. Sponsors have become highly visible at sporting events, but without the supporters there would be no event. When in 2002 Wimbledon FC was granted permission to relocate to Milton Keynes, its supporters, recognising their own worth, and discovering their ability to fight back, launched their own club, AFC Wimbledon, now well established and successful.

Football Supporters' Clubs merged to form the Football Supporters' Federation. The new organisation campaigns on such issues as franchising, safe standing at football, fair treatment for away fans and also provides 'Fans' Embassies' at international tournaments for England supporters. It currently represents over 130,000 fans.[94]

Also in 2002, the FA granted permission for Wimbledon FC to relocate to Milton Keynes, 70 miles from its home in South London. Initially devastated, a group of supporters reacted by rejecting the move and creating their own club, AFC Wimbledon. The new club, backed by the Wimbledon Independent Supporters' Association (WISA) and the Dons Trust, got off to a flying start. In just six weeks they obtained a ground, and played their first friendly in front of a crowd of over 4,500. They won promotion from the Combined Counties League at their second attempt, and joined the Isthmian League in 2004, which Wimbledon FC had been in 40 years earlier. The Dons Trust is a not-for-profit organisation that owns AFC Wimbledon and is guardian of its operating principles.[95]

A contrasting example emerged during the attempted and ultimately successful take-over bid for Manchester United mounted by American businessman Malcolm Glazer. Manchester United, far from being a club in financial trouble, were one of the world's most financially successful sporting organisations. The acquisition of the club by an American with no apparent previous knowledge of or involvement in football, and the subsequent massive debt burden the club acquired as a result, inflamed many fans, who staged large-scale and angry protests. One group of fans, some of whom had previously also opposed a takeover bid by Rupert Murdoch, were so disillusioned that, emulating Wimbledon fans, who were generous with their advice, they formed their own club. FC United of Manchester is owned and democratically run by its members.[96]

It has been argued that the politics of these developments are rooted in a romanticised and idealised version of the relation between supporter and club. After all, the Glazer takeover of Manchester United is, arguably, merely one more instance of an affluent businessman, with no previous record as a fan of the club, or of the sport, buying a football club. No change there, then, except that he is from the USA, which tends to mobilise a stereotype of 'overpaid and over here' to add to the 'ignorant of football' theme. Some suggest that the actions of the fans who have 'walked away' from their clubs have a juvenile and self-flagellatory character – that they involve punishing the love object, the football club.[97] However, an alternative view is that here are two groups of people who decided that they had had enough, and that they were going to do something about it, and then they did something about it. This is the basic condition for effective political action, and in the relative absence of other examples of effective supporter action, the formation of these two clubs is certainly worthy of attention. More broadly, the football trust movement is clearly producing a new organisational form at lower levels of the game that might yet provide a model for alternative structures at the top. It is worth remembering that one of the world's greatest clubs, Barcelona, is owned by its members, and cannot be subject to take-over by corporate interests.

The international context

Houlihan argues that until the late 1950s or early 1960s, sport was of only marginal interest to most governments (Houlihan 1997: 61). It would be wrong, though, to ignore the establishment, in the three decades following the end of the Second World War, of the National Recreation Centres and the work of the Central Council for Physical Recreation (CCPR) – independent, but prompted by official concerns. Sport policy never exists in a vacuum, and as Houlihan and White (2002: 2) argue, it must be seen as 'occupying policy space in the interstices of other services such as education, health, foreign policy, social services and sport itself'. The long-standing policy principle of Sport for All has been made subordinate to the goal of fostering a small elite (Houlihan and White 2002). Houlihan and White also draw attention to the 'marginalisation of local government and heavy emphasis on a relatively narrow range of traditional sports within schools' (Houlihan and White 2002: 66–7). The high profile of elite sport in the media has led governments to drift away from a broad-based sport policy, towards the channelling of resources to the elite level.

The modes of struggle and contestation I have outlined above are the more visible, dramatic, exciting and publicised events. As John Horne (2006) points out, in *Sport in Consumer Culture*, sport has tended to be a forum for reformist politics rather than cultural revolution. It is important to acknowledge the long, painstaking reformist work being done by people in international organisations, such as UNESCO. One of the first significant developments in international organisation was the founding of the International Council of Sport Science and Physical Education (ICSSPE) in Paris in 1958 to serve as an international umbrella organisation concerned with the promotion and dissemination of results and findings in the field of sport science.[98] The International Charter of Physical Education and Sport declared in 1978 that the practice of physical education and sport was a fundamental right for all.[99] UNESCO began to include physical education in its policy formations, recognising that achieving the objectives of Education for All requires 'keeping a healthy mind in a healthy body from early childhood'. Teaching of PE at primary level was seen as a necessity for physical, intellectual and moral education and initiation into citizenship.[100] Strengthening human resources in physical education was marked as a priority for several developing countries.[101] In 1999, UNESCO staged a World Conference on Education and Sport for a Culture of Peace.[102]

In 1999, MINEPS III adopted a worldwide survey from ICSSPE which identified the alarming situation of PE teaching and the marked decrease of practising sport and physical activities.[103] The MINEPS IV Agenda dealt with the work of three commissions on doping, development of PE and sport, and sport and women. Delegates at MINEPS IV in 2004 were reminded that the International Charter of Physical Education and Sport says 'physical education and sport form an essential element of lifelong education in the overall education system' and 'every overall education system must assign the requisite place and importance to physical education and sport in order to establish a balance and strengthen links between physical activities and other components of education'. They were also aware of the gradual deterioration of the general status of physical education and adverse trends engendered by budget cuts in PE and sport programmes.[104] Abstract aspiration and the provision of concrete resources appeared to be on divergent paths. Needs were identified for a policy of renewal; to give physical education proper disciplinary status; to mobilise resources; to develop a coherent mechanism for consultation; and to encourage or establish sport specialisations in the curriculum.[105] There is plenty of goodwill around, together with the mushrooming of organisational forms that bedevils sport organisation. The European Non-Governmental Sports Organisation (ENGSO) aims to promote the unity of sport from children and youth sports to elite sports.[106] The more bodies there are the more elaborate the apparatus of liaison, consultation and debate has to become. Meanwhile, the situation of physical education in the developing world does not seem to be improving.

The second-class status of physical education has long been a problem, exacerbated by the narrow and old-fashioned approaches that have characterised the field, and the tendency of governments to impose sport policies aimed mainly at creating an elite group of national champions.[107] In numerous developing countries, notably in French speaking areas, training structures do not have university institution status. To help training structures in these countries, UNESCO has initiated a project for creating a Masters degree in PES in Africa.[108] The case for physical education has been strengthened by research: 'Several studies have shown that increasing the time students spend at physical education instead of more "intellectual" disciplines results in an improvement, not a decline, of their learning performance. Children who do five hours of physical activity a week have significantly better results than those who have only 40 minutes of physical activity per week.'[109]

It is interesting that the Graecian concept of healthy mind and healthy body is still constantly invoked. A UNESCO *Brochure on the International Year for Sport and Physical Education 2005* carries the strapline 'A healthy mind, a healthy body, that helps in life'. The concept of harmony and balance derived from Greek philosophy, the development of mind and body in harmony to cultivate the soul, and it has constantly reappeared in different forms, most notably during the Italian Renaissance and in the Victorian English Public Schools, as the foundation of muscular Christianity. *Mens sana in corpora sano*, a healthy mind in a healthy body, the notion of development of mind and body, was a key element in the early formation of the sporting discourses of modern sport. Birley refers to it as a Graeco-Roman ideal (Birley 1993: 11). It comes from Juvenal, a Roman satirical poet who lived from 60–140 AD, and who said that one should 'pray for a healthy mind in a healthy body'. Typically, though, in the Western tradition, the two have become separated, and the cultivation of the body takes place in an intellectual vacuum, whilst the intellectual world is still thought, stereotypically, to disdain exercise.

Clearly physical well-being is important for all. According to Education for All (EFA) the minimum requirements for quality in physical education and sport cannot be met in an environment of reduced curriculum time, inadequate and insufficient teacher-training programmes and low status and self-esteem within education systems overall. International statistical information suggests that there is a global crisis of physical education, characterised by reduction of course time devoted to physical education and sport in educational programmes, human resource constraints, material and financial limitations, and a failure to apply the statutory recommendations for physical education and sport. According to the WHO, the repercussions of physical inactivity on health include obesity – and diabetes, cancer, cardio-vascular ailments, dental disorders, osteoporosis and bone fractures. Imbalances in nutrient intake and physical inactivity are the main sources of chronic diseases.[110]

According to an ICSSPE report, neglecting physical education is more expensive for the public health system than investing in the teaching of physical education.[111] In 92 per cent of the 126 countries sampled, physical education is legally required but few countries actually implement their statutory requirements. Studies have shown that when more physical activity is included, marks for school work or general tests never go down; on the contrary, many pupils improve their marks and their ability to acquire intellectual knowledge. A comparison of children aged between 6 and 12 who exercise for five hours a week with children of the same age who exercise for only 40 minutes showed that the intellectual performance of the children who exercise more is considerably better than that of the others.[112] According to Bruce Kidd, a 25 per cent increase in participation in a physical activity (on the basis of 33 per cent of the population taking part in regular physical exercise) would reduce public health costs by $778 million (reference year 1995) and would result in a productivity gain of 1–3 per cent, in other words $2 to $5 for each dollar invested. The direct cost of encouraging more physical exercise would amount to no more than $191 million.[113]

In 1979 an international programme for women and sport was proposed, as part of the United Nations Convention on the Elimination of All Forms of Discrimination Against Women (1979). A strategy developed on the basis that contributions to the development of a culture of equality between men and women were consistent with the practice of sport recognised as a human right. The strategy developed around a number of initiatives, such as the adoption of legislative and regulatory measures to ensure at the national level the promotion of physical activities and sport by girls and women; the development of co-operation ties between PE and sport and other sectors such as health; the promotion and presence of women in positions of responsibility in sport administration; and the conduct of studies to evaluate and assess developments.[114] In the European Parliament in 2003, a resolution noted that 29.5 per cent of men in Europe but only 16 per cent of women declared that they practised a physical or sporting activity regularly, and called for the effective implementation of equal access policies.[115]

Given the commonality of intention the variations in spending commitments are fascinating. In 2003 Norway spent 12 times as much per head of the population on sport as did England; Italy spent nine times as much, Germany seven and France five times as much. England did, however, spend four times as much as Spain.[116] 2005 was the International Year for Sport and Physical Education, and there were plans for poster campaigns, another media activity to ensure the broadest possible impact on the public at large. Of course, the effectivity of initiatives always needs to be tested. How many readers of this book were aware that 2005 was the International Year for Sport and Physical Education, for example? An evaluation report of the International Year was due to be produced for the United Nations General Assembly in 2006.

It is widely accepted that although drug testing has been carried out on a systematic basis since the 1960s, it has not succeeded in clamping down on the use of performance-enhancing drugs. In Olympic Games between 1968 and 1996 there have been an average of 1,629 tests, with an average of six positives, equivalent to 0.36 per cent or one in every 271 tests.[117] An optimist might conclude that the problem of drugs in sport has been exaggerated; a realist might suspect that the test process is imperfect – the effects of drugs can be covered up, that certain performers may be protected and even that positive results may not always be revealed. The lessons gradually learned from past experience are that testing needs to be genuinely random, to take place all year round, that sports-people need to be available to give tests at all times, and that testing bodies need to be totally independent from sport governing bodies and, as far as is possible, free of pressure from nations or governing bodies. This is easier to state than to achieve. The establishment of WADA in 2000 was seen as a big step forward. The Draft International Convention Against Doping in Sport was the first text on doping to be both universal and legally binding. The idea was launched dur-ing the ministerial round table at UNESCO in January 2003; the text was submitted to the 33rd session of UNESCO's General Conference in October 2005, with the intention that it be adopted before the 2006 Winter Olympics in Turin.[118] It remains to be seen how effective these new initiatives can be and there are those who advocate a strategy that would abandon testing and simply acknowledge that those who seek elite success may use all sorts of means. While a coherent case can be made in abstract philosophical terms this is a scenario of surrender. I would prefer that we continue to hope, optimistically and in some-what Manichean manner, that the good scientists will eventually catch up with the bad drug cheats.[119]

Meanwhile, the commodification of sport goes largely unconfronted. Health and fitness are, it would seem, perfectly valid goals for public policy. A fit and healthy population would appear to be a public good, although the consequent burden on pension provision of longer life spans is considerable. Nor is the apparent saving in health-care costs as much of a benefit as it would appear, as even the fittest and healthiest will eventually age, become ill and die, and not necessarily in a cheaper manner. Paradoxically it would make better economic sense, for society as a whole, if we died shortly after ceasing to be economically productive, a form of departure for which unhealthy lifestyles seem to equip us quite well. The real problem, though, is that in a mixed economy, with sub-stantial inequities of resources, health and fitness are not and have never been distributed equally: there are striking class differences in life expectancy. The new technologies of health and fitness centre on the gym, the health club and the fitness centre. They foreground equipment and consumption; and are advertised by young, trim bodies in chic, stylish leisure wear. This does not seem an open communal game that anyone can play, but is rather exclusive, competitive and elitist. The decline of school sport, the privatisation of sport centres, the economics of sport provision, and the tendency to prefer short bursts of indoor activity, all contributed to the rise of the fitness centre. Such centres are based around individualised and privatised exercise, marking a transition from sport as fun to sport as work. We have fostered a culture in which the gym is all about individual self-improvement, personal vanity, and above all work, routine and discipline. Ironically the modern gym looks more and more like a factory – an assembly line of the body utilising the gleaming technologies of the self. Most people who belong to gymnasia make only inter-mittent use of them, whilst others develop compulsive exercise patterns, and there is a tendency to socially pressure people into going to the gym as an obligation. There is a confusion of health with fitness, and tendency for pursuit of fitness to turn into body transformation of a radical kind that may be anti-thetical to fitness. The technologies of athletic excellence are widening the gulf between the 'normal' body and the athletic body. Genetic modification may ultimately take this process a lot further.

In the affluent West, there has been a substantial growth of anorexia and bulimia, dysfunctional behaviours that develop out of obsessions with youthful skinniness. The affluent yuppies of the 1980s had everything – the one thing they couldn't buy (yet) was eternal life, hence the components of fitness chic: 'I want to live forever' and 'Fame costs', 'this is where you start paying', and 'no pain no gain'. Paradoxically, while poverty is still rife and starvation common in much of Africa and Asia, obesity has become an endemic issue in the affluent West. No symbol better catches the paradoxes and ironies of gym culture and our attitudes to it than the much circulated picture of the Californian fitness centre that has an escalator to help its customers climb the six punishing steps to the entrance. Gym culture is highly segmented – far more affluent than poor people use gyms. A dramatic gap in health and fitness has opened up. An affluent middle-class culture has become concerned, if not obsessed, with healthy living – the low calorie, reduced fat, low sugar, organic vegetable mode of eating has become a lucrative element in food retailing. Meanwhile the huge growth of fast food, con-venience food, and snacking has had its impact primarily in working-class culture in which obesity has become a growing phenomenon. Any proposition about the declining significance of class as a category should be tested against the revealing health statistics.

The idea of sport used to be far more about fun, and collective fun, at that. Can we not work to get back to fun, to playfulness, to pleasure, to games playing? When leisure is transformed into work, as it is in gym culture, beware, something alarming is happening. There is enough joylessness in our working lives without importing it into leisure time. Lawrence commented on the importance of plea-sure in revolution; Reich analysed the sexual repressions that underlie authority. The situationists declared that beneath the pavement lay the beach. Adrian Mitchell wrote: 'I have read your manifesto very carefully but it says nothing about dancing.'

There's not much chuckling in the gym, not much joy, not much laughter. Instead, there is a heavily individualised, machine dominated, culture of work that is punishing to the point of masochistic. The machinery of the gymnasium – the exercise bikes, the weight machines, the jogging machines and the ski-jog equipment – has begun to resemble the technology of the sado-masochistic brothel – the rack, the wheel, the cross and the cage. The self-punishing labour of the transformation of the self is an aspect of the commodification of the body, in which bodies, separated from any holistic relation to the personality, become a form of cultural capital – a lean and sleek appearance becoming tradeable in the market for sexual partnership. The tyranny of appearance that has been a marked element in cultures of femininity has been extended to both sexes.

There are other cultural manifestations of sport that have reintegrated plea-sure – such as fun runs, charity walks, and even the London Marathon with its

Figure 8.2 Paris Plage (above)
Figure 8.3 Hôtel de Ville with sanded areas for volleyball (below)

Sport, pleasure and public provision: every summer the city of Paris closes a riverside road and transforms the area into a beach, complete with loungers, climbing walls, a pool, a library, cafés, and many other attractions. Beach volleyball is played in a giant sandpit outside the town hall. This re-inscription of sport as pleasure rather than work brings to mind the old situationist slogan 'Sous les pavés, la plage!' ('Beneath the pavement, the beach!'), although certainly leading situationist Guy Debord would have hoped for a rather more dramatic social transformation than volleyball outside the town hall. It does, however, represent a festive, pleasurable, accessible and free alternative to the overblown corporate spectacles of contemporary sporting mega events.

significant elements of the carnivalesque. The establishment in Paris each summer, by the socialist Mayor, of an area of beach life in Paris, dubbed Paris Plage, constitutes a successful instance of municipal intervention creating spaces of fun. A road alongside the Seine is closed every summer for a month from mid July, and transformed into a beach. Areas of sand, sunloungers, beach bars, beach volleyball, a swimming pool, circus entertainers, massage centres, a mountain climbing area, exercise sections, and even a library all contribute to a free and jolly atmosphere. The whole enterprise has a sense of fun, and also of course a distinct sense of camp. The designer drew upon images of French seaside holidays in the 1950s, and the beach hut designs are taken from Jacques Tati's *Monsieur Hulot's Holiday* (1953). It is hard to imagine a similar camp wit emerging from any British sport governing body. More broadly though, a camp sensibility is rarely admitted into the well policed and doggedly heterosexual masculinity that pervades sport. Sport has little sense of irony or pastiche. It takes itself all too seriously. Twenty to thirty years ago, it seemed important to insist that sport had its own politics, and that situated and embedded local struggles within the practices of sport were important. Today, it seems to me that the reverse is the case. There is a need to re-connect, to link up struggles within sport to the broader picture, to re-place the politics of sport within a broader politics – conceptualised in terms of battles against the economic and cultural impact of globalising processes, in terms of environmental issues, and in terms of the exploitations inherent in the culture industries.

My early experiences of sport were rooted in the huge and exciting appeal of uncertainties, unpredictabilities, and moments of *jouissance*; in the very distinct local embeddedness of its various rituals. Yet bit by bit the chaotic, informal, carnivalesque intensity has become ordered, structured and regulated. The transition from participant spectatorship to customer, to consumer, eloquently sketched by Chas Critcher (1979), is one feature of this process. With the rise of television spectacle, globalisation, commodification and the rising power of advertising and sponsorship has come a commodifying of spectatorship itself. Watching a major sport event now feels like having a role as an extra in a blockbuster. I resent the objectifying of my experience.

Environmental issues and particularly climate change can only become more significant as the impact of climate change grows. Motor sport will come under more pressure as, even only symbolically, it signifies our selfish squandering of resources without regard to environmental impact. The establishment of golf courses catering to the elite has become an issue in many parts of the world. In areas of water shortage, golf courses stand out as grotesquely green in a parched brown landscape. The bids of cities competing to stage the Olympic Games have had to acknowledge the green agenda by completing environmental assessments, although the massive movement of competitors, media workers and spectators around the world is hardly 'green'.

Like many of my generation I have turned from a gauche angry young man to a grumpy old one. And nothing wrong with that, except that the phrase 'grumpy old man' is typically used to patronising and belittling effect. There are things that people ought to be angry about, and being critical is a first step to the fermenting of discontent, the desire for change and the imperative to action. Indeed, there is a value in critique itself; negation is an important part of the dialectic process; someone has to rage against the dying of the light. The problem, to leap backwards from Dylan Thomas to Matthew Arnold, is how to lay in a stock of light, to keep the candles of hope burning through the gloom of pessimism. It helps to take a realistic view of sport, and recognise that while it is of cultural and political importance, it is not in the end an all-encompassing practice. Despite the appearances of unified audiences and nations, a large proportion of the population remain indifferent to sport *even* at times of peak moments in peak events. Even in the case of the largest television audiences in the UK, around half the population was *not* watching. At other times, even football, by far the most popular regular television sport, usually only gets audiences of between five and seven million in the UK – around 10 per cent of the population.

Taking a view from outside, from the perspective of those disinterested, sport constitutes a profoundly odd phenomenon. The intense investment of emotion, time and money appears as a regressive and juvenile masculine obsession on a par with trainspotting. The obsessive pursuit of completeness, involving attending every match, collecting every programme, visiting every stadium, the intense emotional identification with the fate of teams who will probably never win anything significant, the unreasoned romanticism about the identification between fans and the object of their affections, the lack of any sense of proportion about sporting defeat, which blights the life of fans, the tendency to prioritise sport over work, family and friends, and the monoculture of the life of fans, who so often lack any other hinterland; all seem the mark of the incomplete and unsubstantial life. From within, of course, this obsessional life seems a rich and full roller coaster of emotions. Just as the stadium demarcates sport as separated from real life by a high wall, there is a profound gulf between the committed sports fan and the uninterested citizen. I hope this book will have done something to explain the former to the latter; I am less well equipped to explain the perspective of those disinterested in sport, which is a writing task for someone else.

Could we do without sport? Yes, probably. Exercise may be vital for health, but sport is not. But I am not sure a viable and healthy society can dispense with public and communal pleasures, in which case are there valid reasons for discriminating against sport as spectacle, as opposed to other forms of spectacle? There is much joy, excitement and communality to be had in a sports crowd. These are, or can be, people's festivals – and there is something worth recapturing from the grasp of corporate capitalism. This can probably only be achieved through a process by which the gaps and separations within 'sport' are addressed – the severing of spectator sport from participant sport, the separating of the elite level from the rest of sporting practices.

It is important to remember that just as all activities are contradictory, so all practices are, always, in the process of change. Sport is not a static object. 200 years ago the word meant, predominantly, hunting, shooting and fishing. Fifty years ago team sports, international competition and professionalism were prominent features. Twenty-five years ago, the era of television and sponsorship had been established. Today adventure sports and extreme sports are emergent forms. If there is a positive future it may be taking shape in Africa. The appalling apartheid regime is over; African poverty is on the agenda of global politics; some movement is occurring on debt relief, even if too often yoked to a neoliberal agenda for economic restructuring. African countries threw off the imperial yoke 30 years ago, only for fledgling democracies to give way to corruption and military dictatorships. The next decades may see the rise of new, more mature democratic structures. It appears likely that the staging of major sport events such as the Olympics and the World Cup in Africa may act as catalysts for broader social change. It may be the time for the extraordinary cultural resources and dynamic enthusiasms of the people of the various African countries to start shaping a new way forwards, and to find a path that avoids the various oppressions of Stalinist communism, religious fundamentalism and global capitalism. It won't be easy, but as singer Carl Perkins wrote, 'If it wasn't for the rocks in its bed, the stream would have no song.'

I want to conclude by offering the thoughts of three great political philosophers – Antonio Gramsci, Bertolt Brecht and Bill Shankly.[120] Antonio Gramsci recognised that critical analysis of capitalist society and the possibilities of socialist transformation could, in particular conjunctures, offer dispiriting results, but urged us to combine pessimism of the intellect with optimism of the will. Socialist analysis has in some circumstances been prone to a crippling religiosity – elevating the analyses of Marx and Lenin to the status of sacred texts. Yet it is hard to maintain a confident faith in the working class as the agent of social change. As the times transform, the analyses need to adjust. Bertolt Brecht warned against a nostalgic attachment to the certainties of the past when he urged us not to start from the good old days but from the bad new ones. And as for Shankly, he famously said that 'Football is not a matter of life and death – it's far more important than that'. There can be no more pithy reminder that we should never regard popular culture as epiphenomenal or marginal – it remains a central element in the political process. It constitutes a meeting ground between popular common sense and organised political discourse, and for that reason alone, it is vital that we continue subjecting it to analysis and critique.

Notes

1 It was widely rumoured that the security forces had turned the mobile network off. However, according to an article in *Strategic Insights*, senior police officers considered turning off the mobile phone network, in case it was being used to detonate bombs, but decided against it. (Terrorism: London Public Transport – July 2005, by Glen M. Segall, in *Strategic Insights*, Volume IV, Issue 8, August 2005. *Strategic Insights* is a monthly electronic journal produced by the Center for Contemporary Conflict at the Naval Postgraduate School in Monterey, California.)
2 For discussion of the ways in which Western clubs have benefited from the Asian market, see Manzenreiter, Wolfram and Horne, John (2004) *Football Goes East: The People's Game in China, Japan and Korea*, London: Routledge.
3 I was fortunate to see the presentations by the bidding cities at the 1986 IOC Congress, working at the time for Flashback on a television documentary about the Olympic Games. Chirac held the audience transfixed with a compelling evocation of the potential of a Paris Olympics. The Paris bid, for 1992, though, was weaker on technical details. Barcelona arguably had a superior bid, and, crucially, the support of the IOC President, Juan Antonio Samaranch. After building the Stade de France, and staging the 1998 World Cup, Paris was able to mount a much stronger bid for 2012.
4 Belinda Wheaton (2004: 11) offers an interesting definition of lifestyle sports, based on a set of nine characteristic features. This serves as an illustration that sport is not a fixed stable category; and that definitions are always contingent, drawing on specific characteristics that emerge out of specifiable histories and social contexts.
5 CCCS was the Centre for Contemporary Cultural Studies, based at the University of Birmingham, which had a huge influence on the subsequent development of cultural studies. The main work on sport produced there during the 1970s was Critcher, Charles (1971) Football and cultural values, in *Working Papers in Cultural Studies*, n2, Birmingham: CCCS; Clarke, John (1973) *Football Hooliganism and the Skinheads*, London: CCCS; Critcher, Charles (1975) *Football since the war*, CCCS stencilled Paper, Birmingham: CCCS; Peters, Roy (1976) *Television Coverage of Sport*, Birmingham: CCCS; Critcher, Charles (1979) Football since the war, in *Working Class Culture* (eds Clarke, Critcher and Johnson), London: Hutchinson.
6 In Ingham (ed.) 1978.
7 My father died in 1980 and my mother died in 1984, so I have been unable to confirm these details.
8 I am struck by the similarity of my description of football spectating and Dyer's outline of the utopian sensibility, which involves energy, abundance, communality, transparency, and intensity.
9 Le Carré, John (1986) *A Perfect Spy*, London: Hodder and Stoughton.
10 Rubin, Jerry (1970) *Do It*, New York: Simon and Schuster.
11 Interview with author, in television documentary series *The Games in Question* (1988), produced by Flashback for Channel 4, England.

12 See Gruneau, Richard (1989) Television, the Olympics and the question of ideology, and Whannel, Garry (1989) History is being made: television, sport and the selective tradition, both in *The Olympic Movement and the Mass Media* (eds Roger Jackson and Thomas McPhail), Calgary, Canada: Hurford; and also Segrave, Jeffrey O. and Chu, Donald (eds) (1988) *The Olympic Games in Transition*, Champaign, Illinois, USA: Human Kinetics Books.

13 Aris, Stephen (1990) *Sportsbiz: Inside the Sports Business*, London: Hutchinson; Wilson, Neil (1988) *The Sports Business*, London: Piatkus; and Whannel, Garry (1992) *Fields in Vision: Television Sport and Cultural Transformation*, London: Routledge.

14 *The Games in Question* (1988), op. cit.

15 *Washington Post*, 16/2/92.

16 SRI Research Center, 1984.

17 *Washington Post*, 29/3/91.

18 *Financial Times*, 2/8/90.

19 *Sponsorship: Its Role and Effects* (1988), Global Media Commission of the International Advertising Association.

20 Text of Coca-Cola advertisement, 1992.

21 *Washington Post*, 8/10/91.

22 Lord Killanin, then President of the International Olympic Committee, speech at the Moscow Olympics, 1980.

23 *Washington Post*, 29/3/91.

24 *Washington Post*, 16/2/92.

25 Brewer, J., Williams, C. and Patton, A. (1988) The influence of high carbo-hydrate diets on endurance running performance, in *European Journal of Applied Physiology*, 57: 698–706.

26 Text of Ricoh advertisement, 1992.

27 *The Guardian*, 9/3/92.

28 Authors note: In the event it was Diana Ross. She missed an empty net from 12 yards away, helping set the tone for some of the absurdities to follow.

29 *The Guardian*, 9/3/92.

30 Fletcher, Winston (1992) *From a Glittering Haze*, London: NTC.

31 *Financial Times*, 15/2/92.

32 Barthes distinguishes between the cosy and comfortable familiarity of *plaisir* and the more disruptive, engulfing experience of *jouissance* (Barthes 1975).

33 See Schofield 2006 for a fascinating insight into the world of the travelling fan, *There's Always One*, Diable Vert Publishing.

34 These issues should also direct attention towards the question of the consumer – who consumes sport in what circumstances? The corporate colonisation of major event sport has produced a far greater hierarchisation in which whole categories of people have little chance of attending major events, or are priced out, and instead choose between watching at home or in a bar. With more sport disappearing to pay per channel television, the bar is often the only option. Sport is driving us to drink, literally!

35 I return to these themes later in this chapter.

36 See O'Brien, Danny and Slack, Trevor (2004) Strategic responses to institutional pressures for commercialisation: a case study of an English Rugby Union club, in *The Commercialisation of Sport* (edited by Trevor Slack), Abingdon: Routledge.

37 See Smythe, Dallas (1977) Communications: blindspot of Western Marxism, in *Canadian Journal of Political and Social Theory*, 12 (3): 1–27; Murdock, Graham (1978) Blindspots about Western Marxism: a reply to Dallas Smythe, in *Canadian Journal of Political and Social Theory*, 2 (2): 109–19; Smythe, Dallas (1978) Rejoinder to Graham Murdock, in *Canadian Journal of Political and Social Theory*, 2 (2): 120–9; and Jhally, Sut (1982) Probing the blindspot: the audience commodity, in *Canadian Journal of Political and Social Theory*, 6 (1–2): 204–10.

38 See the work of Giulianotti, Bonney and Hepworth (1994) and Brick (2000, 2001a, 2001b, 2004).

39 The event and its context were the subject of a television programme on which I worked as a researcher. The programme *Take the Money and Run*, directed by the immensely talented documentary maker Michael Dibb, was part of a series, *Open The Box* (Beat/BFI 1984), produced by Michael Jackson and broadcast by Channel 4 in the UK.

40 It has to be said that my friend, fellow academic researcher on sport and commercialisation and Fulham fan David Andrews, was also at the game and has different recollections. It is also worth noting that as I was doing final revisions in March 2006, Fulham beat Chelsea 1–0. This was remarkable partly in being only Chelsea's third defeat of the season, but more so in that in the course of a local rivalry lasting 100 years, Fulham have rarely beaten Chelsea and the last time they did so was in 1979, a match that I was at. David has been good enough to allow me to use his own recollections. I think the differences between our respective accounts, partly overdetermined by the perspectives of our ages at the time (I am 11 years older), illustrate the interesting and complicated ways in which 'memory' involves the active re-narrativisation of the past.

Summarised, David wrote: 'I've thought about the Lincoln game overnight. As I said before, I do have a different experience from yours, and as much as I would like to think that I went on the pitch, I don't think I did. I believe we, myself and my Dad, experienced the whole thing from the "Andrews family position" at the top mid/left of the Hammersmith End. It really was a big moment as we hadn't won anything for years, and I think the crowd were suitably up for it. I don't remember the cheque, but perhaps I was too far away...

'...I have always felt that Fulham's commercialisation – even of the Al Fayed variety, and definitely in 1981 – was so half-hearted and low-key as to be almost quaint and unthreatening, almost endearing: from Fulham Flutter tickets, to the ridiculous scoreboards, and anonymous kit manufacturers. So, I don't think I even considered the significance of the cheque. My sense was that I was, at this stage, still overtaken with the euphoria of the moment.

'I think my uncritical romanticism lasted until last year when I went with my Dad to the home game against Birmingham. The tickets were ridiculously expensive, we couldn't "sit" anywhere near the Andrews spot, and had to endure seats by the corner flag, and pay huge parking in our Horder Road spot. The weather was freezing, the football dire, and the atmosphere non-existent. We lost 3–1 and we both came away having felt both cheated, and having a sense of loss for the experience that we used to have; our Fulham experience that had shaped my great grandfather's, my grandfather's, my father's, and my relationship with each other was replaced by a Cravenette-inducing sense of dismay and disappointment. Now it seems Fulham is best experienced via the television/web when I can superimpose my affective orientation *c*. 1981 onto the crass commercialism of the present; a willing suspension of cynicism if you like. So, I guess the Lincoln game plays a different role for me, it is part of the "memory work" I do to rescue a "noble" past from the ignobility of the present.'

Pursuing this further, I have found a photograph of the balcony of Craven Cottage in which at least eight players are visible celebrating, with no sign of the giant cheque. This would appear to undermine the validity of my own memory, yet not to invalidate it, as the moment of the fetishisation of the giant cheque may well have happened. The whole episode does, though, demonstrate the powerful and potentially self-delusional process of self-narrativisation.

41 As the book was being finished, the *Evening Standard* was reporting that the projected cost of the London Olympics could already have risen to as much as £10bn. There appeared to be deadlock between the Treasury, the Department of Culture, Media and Sport, and the Mayor of London as to where the extra funding will come from. A strong lobby was developing to defend the National Lottery Fund against

further appropriations to cover Olympic costs. Londoners will be hoping that the Mayor will be able to uphold his pledge not to allow any further increases in the extra sums already levied in local taxation, and will, I hope, be very angry if this pledge cannot be met.

42 'The architect Guillaume Tronchet, architecte en chef de gouverment, imagined "le plus beau stade du monde" – un edifice grandiose, conçu en béton armé revêtu sompteusement de formes magistrales' (Gravelaine 1997: 13).

43 See Musée d'art et d'histoire de Colombes, 1993.

44 'Autre innovation, la création d'un village intégré au complexe olympique. Cette idée de village lancée à Colombes sera l'amorce de réalisations plus importantes, construites en dur et utilisées les Jeux terminés à d'autres fins que les activités sportives' (Charpentier, Henri, and Euloge Boissonnade 1999: 118).

45 Gaston Benac, *L'Intransigeant*, 28/2/24, quoted in Charpentier, Henri, and Euloge Boissonnade (1999).

46 Musée d'art et d'histoire de Colombes (1993).

47 For discussion of the Dome and its (dis)contents, see McGuigan (2000) The disastrous dome: damned and doomed, McGuigan (2003) From associative to deep sponsorship at the Millennium Dome, McGuigan and Gilmore (2000) Figuring out the Dome, and Philips and Whannel (2000) Faith was made possible by generous donations...

48 *Beijing This Month*, July 2005.

49 I am grateful to Jim McKay, who circulated this item to fellow researchers.

50 I use 'England' deliberately here, rather than Great Britain, or the United Kingdom, or the British Isles. The nation state of which I am part presents unusual complexities at the level of name. Too many different names seem to have attached themselves to the object of description. There are other states of which this can be said to be the case – Holland, Netherlands, Dutch, Pays-Bas, Low Countries, for instance. Nations have changed their names as a result of revolution, decolonisation, merger or division (consider for example Russia/Soviet Union/Russian Federation, West/East Germany/Germany, Czechoslovakia/Czech Republic, etc.). Few countries, however, present quite so many ambiguities at the level of nomenclature. The official name of the state, the United Kingdom, is rarely used in everyday speech – few respond with 'United Kingdom' when asked where they come from. 'England', 'Britain' or 'Great Britain' might be given in response to this question. England is one component, albeit the dominant one, of the nation state, UK. The terms 'Britain' and 'Great Britain', exclude Northern Ireland. Other terms such as the 'British Isles' have also been in circulation. Clearly the subordinate Celtic nations of the UK have distinct national identities with distinct historical determinants, on which I have commented elsewhere (see Whannel 1995). Englishness is a distinct formation within the complex of English/British/Celtic identities, and in this chapter it is Englishness that I focus upon.

51 Note that Bergson has commented on the mechanised human as a figure of fun, arguing that humour emerges when people act in a mechanical way – see Mathewson 1920. This theme is explored in N. F. Simpson's play, *A Resounding Tinkle*.

52 It is worth noting, though, that the widespread adoption of the Flag of St George, in the context of the simultaneous staging of the 2002 World Cup, and the Royal Jubilee, was proclaimed by some as reclaiming this national symbol from the far right. I noticed many Black-British and Asian-British people displaying the Flag of St George, and with the 2006 World Cup still a fortnight away, this phenomenon has been even more striking. This serves to illustrate both the fluid nature of constructions of national identity, and the ways in which such images are always, at least potentially, a site of struggle and contestation over meaning.

53 The sheer unexpectedness of the 5–1 victory over Germany induced a degree of wallowing in national prowess, even amongst those who might normally be sceptical or

critical about chauvinism. The author recalls waiting for a lift at an academic conference, with a British scholar on his left and a German scholar on his right. The lift indicators showed that the first lift was on floor 1 and the second on floor 5, producing a display that showed 1–5. The Brit nudged the German to bring it to his attention. The interpellation of national identity moves in mysterious ways.

54 The concept of mythology as utilised here is derived, of course, from the work of Roland Barthes (see Barthes 1973).

55 OECD figures quoted in Barke, Towner and Newton (1996: 125).

56 England maintained a patrician disdain about the World Cup and the governing body, FIFA, for many years, seemingly because it was the French, rather than the English, who established them. So it came as a shock when, entering the World Cup for the first time in 1950, England were beaten by the USA. That result was dismissed as an aberration, but the real trauma came when Hungary came to Wembley in 1953 to beat England 6–3. It was the first time England had lost at home to any nation from outside the UK.

57 I am using the term 'we' here to characterise English positionalities I take to have a typicality about them. I am not trying to construct an all-embracing English unity, but rather pinpoint a structure of feeling that is distinctly English. The patriotic mode of address can be decoded in various ways, and many positioned by nationalist discourse will inhabit that position in ambiguous fashion. I am half Scots by parentage, my father was from a working-class family, but I grew up in the home counties and in London, in a far more middle-class setting. In the recent World Cup, I felt hailed by the English 'we', and wanted England to win, but with far less fervour than many of the other people in the bar I was in. By contrast, many of my own associates felt largely untouched by the event and by its accompanying orgy of patriotism.

58 I am drawing here upon the concept of the return of the repressed and on the analyses of humour offered by Freud (see Freud 1960).

59 Obviously this is an over-simplification and an image of the brass band that contributors to *Bands: The Brass Band Movement in the 19th and 20th Centuries* (Herbert 1991) would argue does not correspond to reality. But it is precisely image and cultural connotation that I am discussing here. Not all brass bands grew out of the milieu I describe, but enough of them did to establish a relation between cultural practice and social setting that justifies my description.

60 Indeed, although there is not space to develop the argument here, it can reasonably be suggested that while there is a level of affinity between English and German working-class masculinity, there is a greater degree of distance between English and French working-class masculinity. The stereotype view of the French, as not a nation passionate about football, less committed to beer and more to wine, more concerned with personal appearance and with sex and the quality of food, somehow implies a challenge to English laddish masculinity. Relations between the two cultures have a degree of mutual suspicion.

61 *China Pictorial*, July 2005, p.7.

62 For interesting discussion of the restyling of politics, see Corner and Pels (2003).

63 The phrase 'a spare Jimmy Husband' refers to a collectors card with a picture of footballer Jimmy Husband, who was fairly obscure even when *Fever Pitch* was written and now would largely be remembered only by old or terminally sad men.

64 *The Communist Manifesto*, originally published in 1848 (Marx and Engels 1968: 71).

65 See Vance Packard's *The Hidden Persuaders* (1957).

66 *China Pictorial*, July 2005, p.6.

67 *That's Beijing*, 16 July 2005, p.47.

68 *That's Beijing*, 16 July 2005, p.25.

69 Archetti, 1999: 3 quoting J. Clifford (1988: 4), *The Predicament of Culture*.

70 Sir Frank Swettenham, the first British Resident in Kuala Lumpur, quotes from a despatch from Lord Carnavon on 1 June 1876 which Swettenham says contains the most detailed instructions on the role of Residents ever laid down by the Colonial Office. The despatch defines the functions of the Resident as 'giving influential and responsible advice to the ruler, a position the duties of which are well understood in the East. The Residents are not to interfere more frequently or to greater extent than is necessary with the minor details of government; but their special objects should be, the maintenance of peace and law, the initiation of a sound system of taxation, with the consequent development of the resources of the country, and the supervision of the collection of the revenue, so as to ensure the receipt of funds necessary to carry out the principal engagements of the Government, and to pay for the cost of the British officers and whatever establishments may be necessary to support them' (Swettenham 1907: 217). Swettenham comments drily that 'For one white man to maintain the law – something unwritten and unknown – and preserve the peace in a foreign state of which he knew very little, initiate a sound system of taxation and get it observed, develop the resources of the country, supervise the collection of revenue so as to provide means to meet all the costs of administration and yet "not interfere more frequently or to greater extent than is necessary with the minor details of government" was surely an impossible task' (Swettenham 1907: 217).

71 Swettenham outlines the racial stratification of colonial employment: 'For several years it was understood that only the Residents were servants of the British Government; all subordinates were servants of the State which employed them...Still for posts of trust and responsibility it was necessary to have Englishmen while the clerical service was mainly recruited from Eurasians of the Straits or Ceylon, the rank and file of the police from India and Malay countries, and the railways post and telegraph offices from India and Ceylon. Subordinate posts requiring intelligence and financial skills in the holders were best filled by Chinese.' Swettenham helpfully adds a footnote to explain that, in this context, 'Englishman' includes Scotchmen (sic), Irishmen, Welshmen, Channel Islanders, Australians, New Zealanders, Canadians and other white British subjects! (Swettenham 1907: 247). Baker (1999: 142) comments on the contradictions of the Resident system, in which Britain attempted to rule through one remove – bestowing power back on local sultans, who would be supervised by the Resident. Hooker suggests that the Residents were trying to modernise and preserve at the same time (Hooker 2003). Baker suggests that Swettenham managed to manoeuvre well in this situation, keeping the support of the Sultans for a system that only appeared to give them power. In reality, Baker suggests, 'The British never intended to give any real power to the Malay rulers through the conferences or the federal council. Their plan was to create an efficient and effective government with the British in charge. Swettenham was appointed the first Resident General and proceeded to demonstrate how the power of a centralised bureaucracy could usurp local power' (Baker 1999: 148).

72 Baker (1999: 196)

73 'The Chinese community also provided the market for what would prove to be Malaya's most important source of government revenue. Throughout British Malaya in the first few decades of the twentieth century, much of the money needed to build roads and railways came from the sale of opium. The various governments of British Malaya made money from opium in two ways: through import duties on opium when it entered the country and through licences sold to those who in turn sold opium to the addicts, (Baker 1999: 184–5). Baker says that between 1900 and 1930 around a quarter of government revenue came from opium and that this enabled them to keep taxes on tin and rubber, dominated by British interests, low (Baker 1999: 185).

74 Note that Frank Swettenham doesn't mention the Selangor Club, although it must have been a significant location for the forging of links between the colonial administrators and the local Indian, Chinese and Malay elites. But one can exaggerate the extent to which the attempts to popularise British sports as a means of colonial integration were led from the top in a programmatic manner. In Swettenham's *Footprints in Malaya* (1942) a chapter entitled 'Sport in Malaya' is devoted almost entirely to his own shooting exploits.

75 The mock Tudor design of the Selangor Club was the work of Arthur Norman of the Public Works Department, who had qualified as an architect in Devon before coming to Selangor in 1883. He had previously worked around Plymouth on the restoration of genuine Tudor houses and Gothic country churches. The latter expertise helped him in designing St Mary's Church (Gullick 1994: 38).

76 Source: Royal Selangor Club website (http://www.rscweb.org.my/).

77 The first Saturday of the month is Planter's Day. They appear early in the morning, by every train and every road, to fetch the pay money for the estate labourers from the bank. The town awakes in agitation like a nest of white ants invaded by red ants. There is a new element in the air – gay, brutal, reckless. Voices are more resonant and rickshaws go faster. This access of fever lasts until midday. 'At the sound of a gun signal announcing the time at midday, the planters filed into their bar at the Club. ...to happily while the night away, downing quarts of "stengahs" namely whiskey soda. As the bar closed for the night, planters would stagger on to the Coliseum Hotel for nightcaps before turning in for the night. After the bouts of merrymaking, the planters would trickle back to their far off rubber estates, sometimes on bicycles, already making plans for the next Planter's Day (http://www.journeymalaysia.com/MHIS_klcolonial1.htm).

78 For example, in Yeoh 2003, *Contesting Space in Colonial Singapore*, in what otherwise is an interesting book, there is no reference in the Index to the Padang, to the Singapore Cricket Club, to the Singapore Recreation Club, to cricket or to sport. This seems a strange omission in a book with this title, about a city with a great big sacred sport space from the colonial era in the middle of downtown, just across from Raffles Hotel.

79 Sarajevo Hash House Harriers website: http://sarajevohash.com/history.htm

80 For very interesting discussions of the ways in which politics is being reshaped by a changing media, see Corner and Pels 2003.

81 The exception is Mikhail Gorbachev, General Secretary of the USSR Communist Party from 1985–1991, who began an ultimately futile attempt to transform the Soviet Union with glasnost (open-ness) and perestroika (reconstruction), and one of the more beguiling speculations of recent history is to ask what might have happened if the West had supported him rather than Boris Yeltsin.

82 It is interesting to compare evidence of Internet search interest in intellectual figures on the recently introduced Google Trends, which registers terms used for Google searches. Karl Marx, Charles Darwin and Sigmund Freud, in that order, all register significantly higher than postmodern theorists such as Baudrillard and Lyotard. This is not, of course, particularly firm evidence, but it does suggest that, even if grand narratives have collapsed, there is still a healthy degree of interest in them.

83 See http://www.kickitout.org, and http://www.farenet.org

84 http://www.furd.org/

85 For an analysis of the issue, see http://www.mikemarqusee.com, In search of the unequivocal Englishman.

86 See *Anyone for Cricket? Equal opportunities and changing cricket cultures in Essex and East London* produced by the CSDR in collaboration with the London Community Cricket Association and the Essex County Cricket Board.

87 See Simson and Jennings 1992, Jennings 1996.
88 See for example Sugden and Tomlinson 1994, 1998a, 1998b, 1999, 2002, 2003 and Yallop 1999.
89 See Brown, Adam (ed.) (1998) *Fanatics: Power, Identity and Fandom in Football*, London: E & FN Spon; Taylor, Rogan (1992) *Football and its Fans*, Leicester: Leicester University Press; Lightbown, Chris and Schwarz, Chris (1989) *Millwall in the Community*, London: Millwall FC; Williams, John and Wagg, Steve (1991) *British Football and Social Change*, Leicester: Leicester University Press.
90 See Shaw, Phil (comp.) (1989) *Whose Game is it Anyway?*, London: Argus. Phil Shaw's collection of fanzines from the period is now housed by the Chelsea School, University of Brighton, UK.
91 See the Football Governance Research Centre, Birkbeck, http://www.football-research.org, *Uniting the fans*, Alison Pilling.
92 The Football Governance Research Centre, Birkbeck, http://www.football-research.org, *Uniting the fans*, Alison Pilling.
93 SUPPORTERS DIRECT, http://www.supporters-direct.org, accessed November 2005.
94 Football Supporters Federation, http://fsf.org.uk/, accessed November 2005.
95 AFC WIMBLEDON, http://www.afcwimbledon.co.uk, accessed November 2005.
96 Football Club United of Manchester, http://www.fc-utd.co.uk, accessed November 2005.
97 See for example Carlton Brick (2001a, 2004) and Brick's forthcoming book, *Anyone But: Manchester United and the Fight for the Soul of Football* (Oxford: Berg).
98 www.icsspe.org
99 Article 1, International Charter of Physical Education and Sport, UNESCO, 1978.
100 UNESCO document on Education: Physical Education and Sport, http//portal.unesco. org/education
101 UNESCO document on Education: Physical Education and Sport, http//portal.unesco. org/education
102 UNESCO document on Education: Physical Education and Sport, http//portal.unesco. org/education
103 UNESCO document on Education: Physical Education and Sport, http//portal.unesco. org/education
104 Agenda of MINEPS IV. The International Conference of Ministers and Senior Officials Responsible for Sport and Physical Education, 2004, Greece, 6–8 December.
105 Source: Agenda of MINEPS IV. The International Conference of Ministers and Senior Officials Responsible for Sport and Physical Education, 2004, Greece, 6–8 December.
106 Source: Sports in Europe: Newsletter of the European Non-Governmental Sports Organisation, No 1/2005 (March 2005).
107 Source: UNESCO press release re MINEPS IV, 30/11/2004.
108 UNESCO document on Education: Physical Education and Sport, http//portal.unesco. org/education
109 Source: UNESCO press release re MINEPS IV, 30/11/2004.
110 WHO/FAO expert consultation on the prevention of chronic diseases, 2003.
111 K. Hardman, ICSSPE – World-Wide Audit Survey of the State and Status of Physical Education in Schools, 1999.
112 Brochure on the International Year for Sport and Physical Education 2005, Unit for Physical Education and Sport, UNESCO, France.
113 B. Kidd, World Summit on Physical Education (Berlin, 3–5 November 1999).
114 Source: Agenda of MINEPS IV. The International Conference of Ministers and Senior Officials Responsible for Sport and Physical Education 2004, Greece (6–8 December).
115 EUROPEAN PARLIAMENT RESOLUTION ON WOMEN AND SPORT 5/6/03 (European Parliament press release).
116 Source: CCPR/DCMS, quoted on RFU website, www.rfu.com

117 Figures derived from Charpentier and Boissonnade (1999: 848):

Les Disqualifications Pour Dopage aux Jeux Olympiques

	Tests	Positives	Per cent
1968	667	1	0.15
1972	2079	7	0.34
1976	1768	11	0.62
1980	1645	0	0.00
1984	1507	12	0.80
1988	1598	10	0.63
1992	1848	5	0.27
1996	1923	2	0.10

118 Source: UNESCO press release re MINEPS IV, 30/11/2004.
119 See McNamee and Parry (1998) and Houlihan (1999).
120 Bill Shankly was manager of English football team Liverpool between 1959 and 1974, and laid the foundations for their golden era during the 1970s and 1980s, which included four European Cup wins.

Bibliography

Ali, Tariq (2002) *The Clash of Fundamentalisms*, London: Verso.

Anderson, Benedict (1983) *Imagined Communities*, London: Verso.

Andrews, David (2001) Michael Jordan: corporate sport and postmodern celebrityhood, in *Sport Stars: The Cultural Politics of Sporting Celebrity*, David Andrews and Steve Jackson (eds), London: Routledge.

Appadurai, A. (1990) Disjuncture and difference in the global cultural economy, in *Theory, Culture and Society*, 7 (2–3): 295–310.

Archetti, Eduardo P. (1999) *Masculinities: Football, Polo and the Tango in Argentina*, Oxford: Berg.

Aris, Stephen (1990) *Sportsbiz: Inside the Sports Business*, London: Hutchinson.

Bairner, Alan (2001) *Sport, Nationalism and Globalization: European and North American Perspectives*, Albany, NY: State University of New York Press.

Baker, Jim (1999) *Crossroads: A Popular History of Malaysia and Singapore*, Singapore: Times Editions.

Bakhtin, M. (1968) *Rabelais and his World*, Cambridge, MA: MIT Press.

Barke, M., Towner, J. and Newton, M.T. (eds) (1996) *Tourism in Spain: Critical Issues*, Wallingford, Oxford: CAB International.

Barthes, Roland (1973) *Mythologies*, London: Paladin.

Barthes, Roland (1975) *The Pleasures of the Text*, London: Jonathan Cape.

Bateman, Derek and Douglas, Derek (1986) *Unfriendly Games: Boycotted and Broke*, Glasgow: Mainstream.

Baudrillard, Jean (1972) *Pour une Critique de l'Économie Politique du Signe*, Paris: Gallimard.

Beck-Burridge, Martin and Walton, Jeremy (2001) *Sports Sponsorship and Brand Development*, Basingstoke: Palgrave.

Birley, Derek (1993) *Sport and the Making of Britain*, Manchester: Manchester University Press.

Black, David and Van der Westhuizen, Janis (2004) The allure of global games for 'semi-peripheral' polities and spaces: a research agenda, in *Third World Quarterly*, 25 (7): 1195–214.

Botham, Ian (1994) *Don't Tell Kath*, London: Collins Willow.

Brewer, J., Williams, C. and Patton, A. (1988) The influence of high carbo-hydrate diets on endurance running performance, in *European Journal of Applied Physiology*, 57: 698–706.

Brick, C. (2000) Taking offence: modern moralities and the perception of the football fan, *Soccer and Society*, 1 (1) (Spring): 158–72.

Brick, C. (2001a) Can't live with them, can't live without them. Reflections on Manchester United, in *Fear and Loathing: Oppositional Cultures in World Football*, G. Armstrong and R. Giulianotti (eds), Oxford: Berg.

Brick, C. (2001b) Anti-consumption or 'new' consumption? Commodification, identity and 'new' football, in *Leisure: Culture, Consumption and Commodification*, J. Horne, (ed.), Eastbourne: *Leisure Studies Journal*, Berg, pp. 3–15.

Brick, C. (2004) Misers, merchandise and Manchester United: English football and the peculiar political economy of consumption, in *Manchester United: An Interdisciplinary Study*, David L. Andrews (ed.), London: Routledge.

Brohm, Jean-Marie (1978) *Sport: A Prison of Measured Time*, London: Ink Links.

Brown, Adam (ed.) (1998) *Fanatics: Power, Identity and Fandom in Football*, London: E & FN Spon.

Burns, Jimmy (2002) *Hand of God: The Life of Diego Maradona*, London: Bloomsbury.

Carrington, Ben (2002) 'Race', representation and the sporting body (*Critical Urban Studies* Occasional Paper), London: Centre for Urban and Community Research, Goldsmiths College.

Charpentier, Henri and Boissonnade, Euloge (1999) *La Grande Histoire des Jeux Olympiques*, Paris: Editions France-Empire.

Chay, Peter (undated) *Kuala Lumpur: Minarets of Old, Visions of New*, Foto Technik San bhd.

Clarke, John (1973) *Football Hooliganism and the Skinheads*, London: CCCS.

Clifford, James (1988) *The Predicament of Culture: Twentieth Century Ethnography, Literature and Art*, London: Harvard University Press.

Corner, John and Pels, Dick (eds) (2003) *Media and the Restyling of Politics: Consumerism, Celebrity and Cynicism*, London: Sage.

Critcher, Charles (1971) Football and cultural values, in *Working Papers in Cultural Studies*, n2, Birmingham: CCCS.

Critcher, Charles (1975) *Football since the war*, Birmingham: CCCS.

Critcher, Charles (1979) Football since the war, in *Working Class Culture*, J. Clarke, C. Critcher and R. Johnson (eds), London: Hutchinson.

Duke, Vic and Crolley, Liz (2002) Futbol, politicians and the people: populism, and politics in Argentina, in *Sport in Latin American Society: Past and Present*, J.A. Mangan and Lamartine DaCosta (eds), London: Frank Cass.

Easthope, Antony (1990) *What a Man's Gotta Do: The Masculine Myth in Popular Culture*, London: Unwin Hyman.

Farred, Grant (2004) Fiaca and Veron-ismo: race and silence in Argentine football, in *Leisure Studies*, London: Routledge.

Fletcher, Winston (1992) *From a Glittering Haze*, London: NTC.

Freud, Sigmund (1960) *Jokes and their Relation to the Unconscious*, London: RKP.

Galbraith, J.K. (1958) *The Affluent Society*, Boston: Houghton Mifflin.

Giddens, Anthony (1988) *The Third Way: The Renewal of Social Democracy*, Cambridge: Polity Press.

Giddens, Anthony (2002) *Runaway World: How Globalisation is Reshaping our Lives*, London: Profile.

Giulianotti, Richard (1999) *Football: A Sociology of the Global Game*, Oxford: Polity.

Giulianotti, Richard, Bonney, Norman and Hepworth, Mike (eds) (1994) *Football, Violence and Social Identity*, London: Routledge.

Goldberg, Adrian and Wagg, Stephen (1991) It's not a knock-out: English football and globalisation, in *British Football and Social Change: Getting into Europe*, Leicester: Leicester University Press.

Gravelaine, Frédérique de (1997) *Le Stade de France: au coeur de la ville pour le sport et le spectacle*, Paris: Le Monteur.

Gruneau, Richard (1989) Television, the Olympics and the question of ideology, in *The Olympic Movement and the Mass Media*, R. Jackson and T. McPhail (eds), Calgary, Canada: Hurford.

Gullick, J.M. (1994) *Old Kuala Lumpur*, Oxford: Oxford University Press.

Gummere, Richard Mott (1922) *Seneca the Philosopher and his Modern Message*, London: George Harrap.

Hall, Stuart, Critcher, Chas, Jefferson, Tony, Clarke, John and Roberts, Brian (1978) *Policing the Crisis*, London: Macmillan.

Hargreaves, Jennifer (1994) *Sporting Females*, London: Routledge.

Hargreaves, Jennifer (2000) *Heroines of Sport: The Politics of Difference and Identity*, London: Routledge.

Herbert, Trevor (ed.) (1991) *Bands: The Brass Band Movement in the 19th and 20th Centuries*, Milton Keynes: Open University Press.

Hobsbawm, Eric (1994) *Age of Extremes: The Short Twentieth Century*, London: Michael Joseph.

Hobsbawm, Eric and Ranger, Terence (eds) (1983) *The Invention of Tradition*, Cambridge: Cambridge University Press.

Holton, R.J. (1998) *Globalization and the Nation State*, Basingstoke: Macmillan.

Hooker, Virginia Matheson (2003) *A Short History of Malaysia*, Australia: Allen and Unwin.

Hornby, Nick (1992) *Fever Pitch*, London: Victor Gollancz.

Hornby, Nick (1995) *High Fidelity*, London: Victor Gollancz.

Horne, John (2006) *Sport in Consumer Culture*, London: Palgrave.

Houlihan, Barrie (1997) *Sport, Policy and Politics: A Comparative Analysis*, London: Routledge.

Houlihan, Barrie (1999) *Dying to Win: Doping in Sport and the Development of Anti-doping Policy*, Strasbourg: Council of Europe Publishing.

Houlihan, Barrie and White, Anita (2002) *The Politics of Sports Development: Development of Sport or Development through Sport*, London: Routledge.

Ingham, Roger (ed) (1978) *Football Hooliganism – The Wider Context*, London: Interaction Inprint.

Jackson, Steven and Andrews, David (2005) *Sport, Culture and Advertising: Identities, Commodities and the Politics of Representation*, London: Routledge.

Jackson, Steven J., Andrews, David L. and Scherer, Jay (2005) Introduction: the contemporary landscape of advertising, in *Sport, Culture and Advertising: Identities, Commodities and the Politics of Representation*, London: Routledge.

Jennings, Andrew (1996) *The New Lords of the Rings*, London: Pocket.

Jhally, Sut (1982) Probing the blindspot: the audience commodity, *Canadian Journal of Political and Social Theory*, 6 (1–2): 204–10.

Jomo, K.S. (1998) Malaysian debacle: whose fault? *Cambridge Journal of Economics*, 22 (6): 707–22.

Karush, Matthew B. (2003) National identity in the sports pages: football and the mass media in 1920s Buenos Aires, in *The Americas*, 60 (1), The Academy of American Franciscan History.

Kettenacker, Lothar (1997) *Germany Since 1945*, Oxford: Oxford University Press.

King, Anthony D. (ed.) (1991) *Culture, Globalization and the World-System*, Basingstoke: Macmillan.

Klein, Naomi (1999) *No Logo*, London: Flamingo.

Knightley, Phillip (1975) *The First Casualty*, London: Andre Deutsch.

Langer, John (1981) Television's personality system, in *Media, Culture and Society*, 3(4), London: Academic Press.

Le Carré, John (1977) *The Honourable Schoolboy*, London: Hodder and Stoughton.

Le Carré, John (1986) *A Perfect Spy*, London: Hodder and Stoughton.

Lenskyj, Helen Jefferson (2000) *Inside the Olympic Industry: Power, Politics and Activism*, New York: State University of New York Press.

Lightbown, Chris and Schwarz, Chris (1989) *Millwall in the Community*, London: Millwall FC.

Lyotard, J.-F. (1984) *The Postmodern Condition*, Manchester: Manchester University Press.

Maguire, Joseph (1999) *Global Sport: Identities, Societies, Civilisations*, Cambridge: Polity Press.

Maguire, Joseph and Poulton, Emma K. (1999) European identity politics in Euro 96: invented traditions and national habitus codes, in *International Review for the Sociology of Sport*, 34 (1): 17–29.

Maguire, Joseph, Poulton, Emma and Possamai, Catherine (1999a) The War of the Words? Identity politics in Anglo-German press coverage of Euro 96, *European Journal of Communication*, 14 (1): 61–89.

Maguire, Joseph, Poulton, Emma and Possamai, Catherine (1999b) Weltkrieg III? Media coverage of England versus Germany in Euro 96, *Journal of Sport and Social Issues*, 23 (4): 439–54.

Manzenreiter, Wolfram and Horne, John (2004) *Football Goes East: The People's Game in China, Japan and Korea*, London: Routledge.

Marx, Karl and Engels, Frederick (1968) Manifesto of the Communist Party, in *Karl Marx and Frederick Engels: Selected Works*, London: Lawrence and Wishart.

Mathewson, Louise (1920) Bergson's theory of the comic in the light of English comedy, in *Studies in Language, Literature and Criticism*, No. 5, Nebraska: University of Nebraska.

McGuigan, Jim (2000) The disastrous dome: damned and doomed, paper presented at *Third International Crossroads in Cultural Studies Conference*, University of Birmingham, 23 June 2000.

McGuigan, Jim (2007) From Associative to Deep Sponsorship at the Millennium Dome, in *Media in the Age of Marketization*, G. Murdock and J.Wasko (eds), New Jersey: Hampton Press.

McNamee, M.J. and Parry, S.J. (1998) *Ethics and Sport*, London: E & FN Spon.

Miller, Toby, Lawrence, Geoffrey, McKay, Jim and Rowe, David (2001) *Globalization and Sport*, London: Sage.

Moore, Katharine (1987) The Pan-Britannic festival: a tangible but forlorn expression of Imperialism, in *Pleasure, Profit, Proselytism*, J.A. Mangan (ed.), London: Frank Cass.

Mort, Frank (1996) *Cultures of Consumption: Commerce, Masculinities and Social Space*, London: Routledge.

Murdock, Graham (1978) Blindspots about Western Marxism: a reply to Dallas Smythe, *Canadian Journal of Political and Social Theory*, 2 (2): 109–19.

Musée d'art et d'histoire de Colombes (1993) *Les Yeux du Stade*, Paris: Musée d'art et d'histoire de Colombes.

O'Brien, Danny and Slack, Trevor (2004) Strategic responses to institutional pressures for commercialisation: a case study of an English Rugby Union club, in *The Commercialisation of Sport*, Trevor Slack (ed.), Abingdon: Routledge.

Packard, Vance (1957) *The Hidden Persuaders*, London: Longmans Green.

Packard, Vance (1960) *The Status Seekers: An Exploration of Class Behaviour in America*, London: Longmans.

Peters, Roy (1976) *Television Coverage of Sport*, Birmingham: CCCS.

Philips, Deborah and Whannel, Garry (2000) Faith was made possible by generous donations...Conceptualising 'Economy' and 'Culture' in the growth of commercial sponsorship, paper presented at *Third International Crossroads in Cultural Studies Conference*, University of Birmingham, 21–25 June 2000.

Phillips, Bob (2000) *Honour of Empire, Glory of Sport: The History of Athletics at the Commonwealth Games*, Manchester: Parrs Wood Press.

Pieterse, Jan Nederveen (1997) Multi-culturalism and museums: discourse about others in the age of globalisation, *Theory, Culture and Society*, 14 (3): 123–46.

Priestley, J.B. (1929) *The Good Companions*, London: Heinemann.

Pronger, Brian (2000) Homosexuality and sport: who's winning? *Masculinities, Gender Relations and Sport*, Jim McKay, Michael A. Messner and Don Sabo (eds), London: Sage.

Quart, Alissa (2003) *Branded: The Buying and Selling of Teenagers*, London: Arrow.

Rambert, Francis (1995) *D'un stade à deux: Histoire du project de Grand Stade Sarfati-Quillery*, Paris: Editions de Layeur.

Robertson, Roland (1992) *Globalization: Social Theory and Global Culture*, London: Sage.

Roche, Maurice (2000) *Mega-Events and Modernity: Olympics and Expos in the Growth of Global Culture*, London: Routledge.

Rubin, Jerry (1970) *Do It*, New York: Simon and Schuster.

Sahl, Mort (1976) *Heartland*, New York and London: Harcourt Brace Jovanovich.

Schofield, Shaun (2006) *There's Always One*, Dunstable: Diable Vert Publishing.

Segrave, Jeffrey O. and Chu, Donald (eds) (1988) *The Olympic Games in Transition*, Champaign, Illinois, USA: Human Kinetics Books.

Shaw, Phil (comp.) (1989) *Whose Game is it Anyway?*, London: Argus.

Silk, Michael (2002) 'Bangsa Malaysia': global sport, the city and the mediated refurbishment of local identities, *Media, Culture & Society*, 24 (6): 775–94.

Simson, Vyv and Jennings, Andrew (1992) *The Lords of the Rings: Power, Drugs and Money*, London: Simon and Schuster.

Smythe, Dallas (1977) Communications: blindspot of Western Marxism, *Canadian Journal of Political and Social Theory*, 12 (3): 1–27.

Smythe, Dallas (1978) Rejoinder to Graham Murdock, in *Canadian Journal of Political and Social Theory*, 2 (2): 120–9.

Spracklen, Karl (1995) Playing the ball or the uses of league: class, masculinity and rugby – a case study of Sudthorpe, in *Leisure Cultures: Values, Genders, Lifestyles*, Graham McFee, Wilf Murphy and Garry Whannel (eds), Eastbourne: LSA, pp. 105–20.

Spracklen, Karl (1996) 'When you're putting yer body on t'line fer beer tokens you've go'a wonder why': expressions of masculinity and identity in rugby communities, *Scottish Centre Research Papers in Sport Leisure and Society*, vol. 1, Edinburgh: Moray House Institute of Education.

Stebbins, Robert A. (1992a) *Amateurs, Professionals and Serious Leisure*, Montreal: McGill-Queens University Press.

Stebbins, Robert A. (1992b) Costs and rewards in barbershop singing, in *Leisure Studies*, 11 (2): 123–33.

Sugden, John and Tomlinson, Alan (1994) *Hosts and Champions: Soccer Cultures, National Identities and the World Cup in the USA*, Aldershot: Ashgate.

Sugden, John and Tomlinson, Alan (1998a) Power and resistance in the governance of world football: theorising FIFA's transnational impact, *Journal of Sport and Social Issues*, 22 (3): 299–316.

Sugden, John and Tomlinson, Alan (eds) (1998b) *FIFA and the Contest for World Football: Who Rules the People's Game?*, London: Polity.

Sugden, John and Tomlinson, Alan (1999) *Great Balls of Fire: How Big Money is Hijacking World Football*, Edinburgh and London: Mainstream.

Sugden, John and Tomlinson, Alan (2002) *Power Games: A Critical Sociology of Sport*, London: Routledge.

Sugden, John and Tomlinson, Alan (2003) *Badfellas: FIFA Family at War*, Edinburgh and London: Mainstream.

Swettenham, Frank (1907) *British Malaya*, London: Bodley Head.

Swettenham, Sir Frank (1942) *Footprints in Malaya*, London: Hutchinson.

Taylor, Rogan (1992) *Football and its Fans*, Leicester: Leicester University Press.

Tomlinson, Alan and Whannel, Garry (eds) (1984) *Five Ring Circus, Money Power and Politics at the Olympic Games*, London: Pluto.

Tomlinson, Alan, and Whannel, Garry (eds) (1986) *Off The Ball: the 1986 Football World Cup*, London: Pluto.

Tzu, Sun (1963) *The Art of War*, Oxford: Oxford University Press.

Van der Westhuizen, Jan (2004) Marketing Malaysia as a model modern Muslim state: the significance of the 16th Commonwealth Games, *Third World Quarterly*, 25 (7): 1277–91.

Veblen, T. (1912) *The Theory of the Leisure Class*, New York: Macmillan.

Waugh, Evelyn (1938) *Scoop*, Boston: Little, Brown.

Whannel, Garry (1983) *Blowing the Whistle: The Politics of Sport*, London: Pluto.

Whannel, Garry (1989) History is being made: television, sport and the selective tradition, in *The Olympic Movement and the Mass Media*, R. Jackson and T. McPhail (eds), Calgary, Canada: Hurford, 7.13–7.22.

Whannel, Garry (1992) *Fields in Vision: Television Sport and Cultural Transformation*, London: Routledge.

Whannel, Garry (1994a) Profiting by the presence of ideals: sponsorship and Olympism, in *International Olympic Academy: 32nd Session*, Olympia, Greece: International Olympic Academy.

Whannel, Garry (1994b) Sport and popular culture: the temporary triumph of process over product, *Innovations*, 6 (3): 341–50.

Whannel, Garry (1995) Sport, national identities and the case of Big Jack, *Critical Survey*, 7 (2): 158–64.

Whannel, Garry (1997) Individual stars and collective identities in media sport, in *Sport, Popular Culture and Identity*, Maurice Roche (ed.), Oxford: Meyer and Meyer, pp. 23–36.

Whannel, Garry (1999) From 'motionless bodies' to acting moral subjects: Tom Brown, a transformative romance for the production of manliness, in *Diegesis: Journal for the Association for Research in Popular Fictions*, no. 4, Liverpool: Association for Research in Popular Fictions.

Whannel, Garry (2002) *Media Sport Stars, Masculinities and Moralities*, London: Routledge.

Whannel, Paddy, Hodgdon, Dana and Purwin, Sig (1976) *The Book of Darts*, Chicago: Henry Regnery.

Wheaton, Belinda (ed.) (2004) Introduction: mapping the lifestyle sportscape, in *Lifestyle Sport: Consumption, Identity and Difference*, Belinda Wheaton (ed.), London: Routledge.

Whitson, David (1983) Pressures on regional games in a dominant metropolitan culture: the case of shinty, *Leisure Studies*, 2 (2): 138–53.

Williams, John and Wagg, Steve (1991) *British Football and Social Change*, Leicester: Leicester University Press.

Wilson, Neil (1988) *The Sports Business*, London: Piatkus.

Yallop, David (1999) *How They Stole The Game*, London: Poetic.

Yeoh, Brenda (2005) The global cultural city? Spatial imagineering and politics in the (multi) cultural marketplaces of South-east Asia, *Urban Studies*, 42 (5–6): 945–58.

Yeoh, Brenda S.A.(2003) *Contesting Space in Colonial Singapore*, Singapore: Singapore University Press.

Index

Routledge Sport

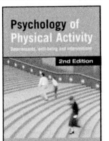